First Degree

Titles recently published under the SRHE/Open University Press imprint:

Michael Allen: *The Goals of Universities*
Christopher Ball and Heather Eggins: *Higher Education into the 1990s*
Tony Becher: *Academic Tribes and Territories*
William Birch: *The Challenge to Higher Education*
David Boud *et al.*: *Teaching in Laboratories*
Heather Eggins: *Restructuring Higher Education*
Colin Evans: *Language People*
Oliver Fulton: *Access and Institutional Change*
Derek Gardiner: *The Anatomy of Supervision*
Gunnar Handal and Per Lauvås: *Promoting Reflective Teaching*
Vivien Hodgson *et al.*: *Beyond Distance Teaching, Towards Open Learning*
Peter Linklater: *Education and the World of Work*
Graeme Moodie: *Standards and Criteria in Higher Education*
John Pratt and Suzanne Silverman: *Responding to Constraint*
John Radford and David Rose: *A Liberal Science*
Marjorie Reeves: *The Crisis in Higher Education*
John T. E. Richardson *et al.*: *Student Learning*
Derek Robbins: *The Rise of Independent Study*
Geoffrey Squires: *First Degree*
Gordon Taylor *et al.*: *Literacy by Degrees*
Kim Thomas: *Gender and Subject in Higher Education*
Malcolm Tight: *Academic Freedom and Responsibility*
Susan Warner Weil and Ian McGill: *Making Sense of Experiential Learning*
David Watson: *Managing the Modular Course*
Alan Woodley *et al.*: *Choosing to Learn*

First Degree

The undergraduate curriculum

Geoffrey Squires

The Society for Research into Higher Education
& Open University Press

Published by SRHE and
Open University Press
Celtic Court
22 Ballmoor
Buckingham MK18 1XW

and
1900 Frost Road, Suite 101
Bristol, PA 19007, USA

First Published 1990

British Library Cataloguing in Publication Data

Squires, Geoffrey, *1942–*

    First degree: the undergraduate curriculum.
    1. Great Britain. Higher education institutions.
    Curriculum. Development
    I. Title.   II. Society for Research into higher education
    378.41

    ISBN 0 335 09316 7
    ISBN 0 335 093159 (pbk)

Library of Congress catalog number is available

Squires, Geoffrey.
    First degree: the undergraduate curriculum/Geoffrey Squires*.*
       p.   cm.
    Includes bibliographical references.
    ISBN 0 335 09316 7   ISBN 0 335 09315 9 (pbk.)
    1. Universities and colleges – Great Britain – Curricula.
I. Society for Research into Higher Education.   II. Title.
LB2362.G7S67   1990
378.1'99'0941 – dc20   89–39045
                                         CIP

Typeset by Scarborough Typesetting Services
Printed in Great Britain by St Edmundsbury Press,
Bury St Edmunds, Suffolk

Contents

Preface

This is a book about what is taught to undergraduates during the three or four years that lead to their first degree in this country.

Although the first chapter is descriptive, the book does not pretend to constitute a survey of undergraduate courses; and although the final chapter discusses current policy, it is not primarily intended to be prescriptive. The main thrust of the book is analytic, and the three middle chapters explore what seem to me to be the three main frames of reference for thinking about the curriculum, about what to teach: the nature of knowledge, the culture or society of which higher education is a part, and the development of the individual student. The analysis does not give priority to any one of these frames of reference; that would involve a different essay.

I began work on the book, without knowing it, in 1972 when I joined a Nuffield Foundation research team which was exploring changes in curricula and teaching in higher education. Over the next four years, members of the team spent a week in every university and two-thirds of the polytechnics in the country, interviewing several thousand academics, administrators and students, some of whom were then brought together in meetings and conferences. The project resulted in over 20 reports or newsletters on a wide range of topics, many of them related to the curriculum. I thought, when I began writing this book, that much of that experience would now be out of date because of all that has happened since in higher education; now I am not so sure. Curricular change relates in a complex way to systemic or institutional change, and responds to a different drum, or rather set of drums, because the rhythms of change vary from subject to subject.

My involvement in the field continued after the Nuffield project, but more intermittently. I contributed to the SRHE/Leverhulme programme in the early 1980s, prepared several reports for the OECD, made a study of modular courses, was involved in a series of Anglo-Swedish conferences on professional education, and wrote sundry other papers. In addition, I did work on 16–19 and continuing education which I think is not irrelevant. This book is thus in part an attempt to draw together these various pieces of work over the years, but I also attempted to gather data specifically for it. I obtained 1981 and 1986 prospectuses from a large number of institutions, often with comments on the intervening changes, analysed degree course guides and reports produced by various professional bodies and subject associations, as well as making a general literature search. I also sent out sets of questions; details of which are given in Chapter 2, to a range of academics, some of whose responses are quoted in the text. (The mobility of labour knows no bounds: one 'nil' return informed me that he was no longer an academic but a traditional Chinese acupuncturist.) I would like to take this opportunity of thanking very sincerely all those administrators and academics who helped me at various stages in the study.

My thanks also go to others who gave me more specific assistance, in particular the Statistics Branch of the Department of Education and Science, the Northern Ireland Department of Education, the Universities Statistical Record, the Careers Research and Advisory Centre, Hobsons Press and Jennie Knight, and the Council for National Academic Awards. In a wide-ranging book such as this I have had to rely heavily on the expertise of others, and I am therefore especially grateful to the following colleagues who commented most helpfully on all or part of an earlier draft: Tony Becher, John Brennan, Keith Drake, Sinclair Goodlad, John Gubbay, George MacDonald-Ross, Robert Murray, David Raffe and John Richardson. The irresponsibility remains, of course, my own.

In the belief that what is taught and what ought to be taught are issues which should concern everyone in higher education, I have tried to write a book which would interest any academic, administrator or student, and not just those who specialize in the study of education. The problem, of course, is that one is then writing for a general audience of specialists. I have attempted therefore to keep the main text as clear and accessible as possible, and have used extensive notes at the ends of chapters to explore certain points in more detail and to make some connections with current policy. The breadth of the subject matter and the diversity of perspectives on it make any study of the undergraduate curriculum a daunting prospect, but if this book can be accepted as a beginning, an opening up of a hitherto largely untilled field and a basis for more systematic, empirical work, then I shall be satisfied.

1

The Undergraduate Curriculum

The final report of the SRHE/Leverhulme Programme of Study into the Future of Higher Education, *Excellence in Diversity* (SRHE 1983), called for a wide-ranging debate about the content of undergraduate courses in the light of contemporary needs. Yet in a recent OECD* report, *Universities under Scrutiny*, William Taylor remarks that 'Curriculum is often the missing chapter' in studies of universities (Taylor 1987, p. 42). This book is an attempt to supply that chapter and stimulate that debate, not only in terms of universities, but of all forms of higher education in the UK.

On the face of it, the absence of such studies is surprising. If education is about anything, it is surely about what is taught: the curriculum. It would seem as if people were ready to write about every aspect of higher education – its aims, policies, governance, finance, organization, staff, students – except the one thing that gives all these their *raison d'être*. However, as Taylor goes on to point out, there are cogent and even forbidding explanations for the apparent neglect. The differences between institutions are, he argues, negligible compared to the differences between disciplines; even specialists within the same discipline often find communication difficult. Hence:

> Most of those who write and speak about universities are themselves specialists – in speaking and writing about universities. If their origins were in an academic discipline, they are often no longer able to identify themselves with it – or are discouraged from doing so by their more specialised fellows. They make no claim to understand other subjects and professional fields, and are in no position to describe, analyse, comment upon or evaluate what goes on there. So the debate on curriculum can only proceed through the statement of generalities, kept aloft by aspirations for change which invoke openness, flexibility, breadth, coherence, progression and other high-inference notions. To

* For all titles and acronyms, see Glossary pp.163–4.

hard-nosed sceptics among the scholars, researchers and professionals, such language is empty of meaning, or cloaks a sinister political ideology, or is the last resort of those denied success and
promotion in their own discipline – or sometimes all three.

(Taylor 1987, pp. 42–3)

Such comments explain why there can be so much discussion of undergraduate courses within specific disciplines, and yet so little of the undergraduate curriculum as a whole. A subject association or professional body
provides a natural forum for debates about degree courses in that subject.
There is a good deal of informal communication about courses in particular subjects, some of it passing along the external examiner grapevine,
some of it through the 'invisible colleges' of research networks. There are
periodic official surveys of courses in particular subjects or fields, usually
when major changes are being contemplated (as at present), and there are
the regular activities of CNAA committees and boards and their counterparts, such as they are, on the university side of the binary line. Some of all
this specific debate surfaces in the pages of the *Times Higher Education Supplement*, and even on occasion in the general 'quality' press.

By contrast, there is remarkably little discussion of the overall pattern
and content of undergraduate studies. As Taylor rightly says, most academics simply do not feel competent to comment on what goes on outside
their discipline, and even if they do, there are powerful professional and
institutional demarcations which deter them from doing so. Of course, this
does not mean that lecturers do not have stereotypes of, and views about,
other disciplines which may be well or less well informed. It does not rule
out habitual sniping or genuine interest, preclude competition for students, or prevent the longer-term struggles for academic territory or pres-
tige which characterize the development of the 'map of knowledge'. But
little of all this results in rational or systematic debate about what people
should study during the three or four years that lead to their first degree.

The official reports are also reticent. Robbins (1963) – comprehensive
and thorough in many respects – had relatively little to say about the undergraduate curriculum, beyond some general statements about the aims of
higher education, and recommendations about the balance of arts and
science and single and combined honours courses. Recent policy statements have been even more succinct. *The Development of Higher Education
into the 1990s* (DES 1985b) does have a short section on higher education,
the economy and subject balance, but is in general much more concerned
with access to and management of the system, and subsequent documents
have tended to reinforce that emphasis. Even the SRHE/Leverhulme enquiry carried out during the early 1980s was arguably weakest on the curriculum, and although the Society has organized conferences on curricular
issues (most recently that on *Education for the Professions*; Goodlad 1984), it
has not attempted to tackle the overall questions of what is taught and what
ought to be taught.

Wisely, perhaps, given Taylor's cautions. Yet the questions cannot be avoided, least of all by students who are faced with a largely predetermined set of choices. The undergraduate curriculum could be otherwise. There may be good reasons for it being as it is, but it could be different, and *is* different in other countries. Even the fact that it could be different, let alone any evidence that it might be capable of improvement, justifies study of it. However, the difficulties of thinking about it as a whole are considerable. The differences between disciplines which Taylor refers to are compounded by differences between sectors, institutions and even departments. And the largely monodisciplinary pattern of higher education reproduces itself in the writing about higher education, most of which adopts the particular perspective of one discipline, be it philosophy, history, sociology, economics or psychology.

The aim of this book is to create a broad, multidisciplinary framework for thinking about what students are taught and ought to be taught on first degree courses. I shall explore three frames of reference for thinking about the undergraduate curriculum: in terms of knowledge, in terms of the relationship between curriculum and society, and in terms of the development of individual potential. I shall try to show that these three frames of reference are complementary rather than self-sufficient or mutually exclusive. In each case, I shall try to identify useful concepts and models, and discuss some of the arguments associated with them. And although I move on in the final chapter to consider some of the policy implications of the analysis, the main aim will be to clarify rather than prescribe.

The differences between disciplines to which Taylor refers mean that the discussion will to some extent be an abstract one, moving at a level at which one can identify general ideas, characteristics and trends. No doubt one can only really understand a discipline from the inside. But it is debatable whether one can wholly understand it from the inside. We already use concepts and ideas which cut across or transcend specific disciplines: words such as 'arts', 'science', 'pure', 'applied', 'liberal' and 'professional'. Higher education policy is couched in such terms, and higher education institutions and undergraduate courses are structured in ways which embody certain curricular concepts, models and assumptions. The language for talking about the undergraduate curriculum already exists; it is a matter of using it.

The nature of curricula

The term 'curriculum' is generally understood but not widely used in higher education; academics are more likely to speak of undergraduate studies in terms of courses, programmes, syllabuses/syllabi or content. It is necessary, therefore, to offer some definitions of the term, and to explore some of its connotations.

The Latin origins of the word refer to a course in the sense of race-course, but its current meaning in education has moved some way from that. The simplest definition of the curriculum is 'what is taught' (Taylor and Richards 1985, p. 2) and the study of the curriculum is concerned with what is taught (description) and what ought to be taught (prescription). There are fuller and wider definitions. For example, Kerr (1968, p. 16) defines the school curriculum as 'all the learning which is planned and guided by the school, whether it is carried on in groups or individually, inside or outside the school'. This emphasizes the intentional nature of the curriculum, and the various forms and settings it can have. Other definitions refer to the totality of what students experience during their course of studies – the learning rather than the teaching – stressing the effects (foreseen or otherwise) of curricular plans and intentions. One ambiguity which runs through most definitions, as it does with the word 'course', is whether one is referring to the total package of studies or only one element in it; thus one can speak of the undergraduate curriculum or the history curriculum. The American usage of referring to the parts as courses and the whole as the programme seems to be gaining ground here.

But what does the word curriculum denote or connote that 'course' does not? How does it differ from a syllabus? In what way does it go beyond 'content'? Why use what seems like jargon? Perhaps the simplest way to answer these questions is to explore the planning of a curriculum, any curriculum. Academics who are planning or revising a curriculum have to address three kinds of questions.[1] The most obvious questions have to do with the *elements* or *components* of the curriculum: the things that go to make it up (see Figure 1.1). There will need to be an initial prospectus which states the overall aims, content and form of the course. Decisions also have to be taken about the admission of students: how many and on what basis? A syllabus needs to be worked out, specifying in varying degrees of detail what is going to be covered and in what order. The syllabus may influence and be influenced by the matter of staffing: who is going to teach what? And when (timing) and where (location)? The matter of teaching also raises questions about the methods to be used, and the learning materials (including facilities and equipment) which will be needed. Finally, there are the questions to do with the assessment of the course, including any examinations.

Such questions may not be addressed in quite this form or this order. While a formal prospectus is normally issued for each degree course, such statements vary considerably in the amount of detail they give, and how explicit they are about the aims of the course. The process of admissions also varies, not only from one course to another, but between younger and older students, and from one institution to another: for example, the Open University is 'open' in terms of admissions, and there are normally special regulations relating to mature students (on undergraduate courses, typically but not always those aged over 21 on entry). A syllabus may be more or less fixed or negotiable; apparently rigid courses can in fact be

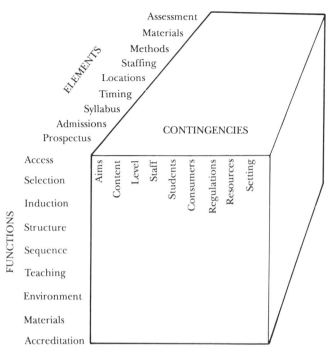

Figure 1.1   A model of curriculum planning.

quite flexible in detail. Teaching methods vary from subject to subject. The pattern and timetabling of courses varies greatly, as do the pattern, timing and methods of assessment. Moreover, those planning a curriculum may find that they proceed not in a linear fashion, but by moving back and forth among the various headings, since these affect one another. The list given here is intended only as a general guide.

However, in order to answer such questions properly, curriculum planners need to address two other kinds of questions.[2] The first of these concerns the *functions* of the curriculum, any curriculum. What does a course do for students that they would find difficult or impossible to do on their own? What advantages does it offer over independent study? Why formalize the learning process in a curriculum at all? These are difficult questions, which go to the heart of the educational process, but the headings in Figure 1.1 suggest some answers. Perhaps the most basic function of organized education is to give students access to something which they would not otherwise have. A curriculum, any curriculum, makes available human and physical resources which the student can use to facilitate or enhance his or her natural capacity to learn. But any particular curriculum goes beyond such generalized access in a number of ways. In selecting the student for the course, and (implicitly) the course for the student, it should offer a certain guarantee of mutual appropriateness in terms of aims, content and level. It should help to induct the student not only into the field of study but the approach to studying. It should provide a measure of structure and sequence in what is learned, though that measure may vary a good deal from subject to subject and even student to student. It should provide teaching (which can itself be analysed into a number of more specific methods, functions and contingencies; see Squires 1988). Beyond the provision of overt, timetabled teaching, it should create an environment which is conducive to learning, and the materials and facilities which are needed for study. And, finally, it can officially accredit students' learning, thus giving it public recognition and status in a way that is simply not possible for the autodidact.

Again, the way such headings work out in practice may vary a good deal from course to course. Some curricula are more tightly structured or sequenced than others. Teaching may involve expository or participative methods. The part-time or 'distance' student does not have the same environment as the full-time one. The accreditation process differs in different sectors of the system. And one must not forget that many of these functions can become dysfunctions, and assume a negative or pathological form: faulty selection, awkward induction, rigid structure, poor teaching, inadequate materials, invalid assessment, and so on. But the headings indicate the kinds of functions that a course can and should perform, if it is to justify its existence as an improvement on independent study.

These functions are not carried out in a vacuum; they are affected by certain key *contingencies* or variables. The answer to many questions about the curriculum is: 'it depends'. It depends on who, what and where one is teaching. The nature of the curriculum will need to reflect its general aims, its content and the level at which it is pitched. Thus liberal arts courses might be expected to have different aims from vocational or professional ones, theoretical courses will differ from applied ones, and undergraduate courses will differ from those in the same subject at A level. Likewise, the 'who' matters. The nature and shape of the course will often be affected by those who plan and teach it, the nature of and changes in the student intake, and any indirect consumers (such as employers or professional bodies) it may have. Where a course takes place is important not only in terms of regulations and resources (or the absence of them), but in the more subtle aspects of the setting: the traditions, norms, ethos, style and habits of particular departments, institutions or sectors.

There is not room here to discuss these various components, functions and contingencies in any detail, but the model presented in Figure 1.1 should at least suggest some of the ways in which the concept of the curriculum goes beyond mere 'syllabus' or 'content'. It involves, for example, some consideration of the overall aims or purpose of a course, though this does not necessarily mean that such aims have to be explicitly formulated or prespecified. It involves thinking about differences in 'level' which is a familiar though complex concept.[3] It points up the importance of admissions, and suggests that the assessment of a course may 'wash back' on its content and aims. It implies that the 'content' of a course may be intimately intertwined with its 'process': the way it is taught, the staff who teach it, the environment it takes place in. It alerts one to the importance of contextual factors such as those relating to the institution's regulations, resources and ethos.

Above all, it highlights two aspects of the curriculum. The first is that a curriculum is not a plan but an experience, not a script but a play. Heyman (1981) has stressed the importance of seeing the curriculum not only as a set of structures and functions, but phenomenologically, in terms of the kind of experience that its various participants together create. This is easy for lecturers to forget in the concern with syllabuses, materials and all the paperwork that curriculum planning involves. The overt, explicit aspect of the curriculum coexists with a less obvious, implicit or tacit side, which has been dubbed the 'hidden curriculum' (Snyder 1971; Cornbleth 1984) and the curriculum plan is always open to a degree of interpretation and even reconstruction by those involved.

Secondly, the model implies that curriculum planning is always to some extent a contingent matter, in which there will be few across-the-board answers. Much depends on the who, what and where. In interviews and written responses to questions, the academics contacted in this study referred, in their comments on courses, to factors such as student numbers, student quality, student age, changes in A level syllabuses, staff losses, changes in funding, changes in regulations, the influence of professional bodies, changes in graduate employment and developments in research, as well as purely 'internal' changes in the subject itself. Planning a course is not an abstract exercise, but one which is intimately affected by the participants, content and setting.

We have discussed briefly the various kinds of questions that curriculum planners need to ask, in order to clarify the idea of a curriculum. But who asks these questions, and who takes the decisions that follow from the answers? Becher and Kogan (1980) have identified four structural levels in the higher education system: individual, basic unit, institution, and central authority. (The basic unit is typically an academic department or comparable unit.) Elaborating a little on this, we can say that curricular decisions may be made by students, individual lecturers, departments, faculties, academic senates or institutional committees, and central authorities in or near government. The influence of professional bodies and other indirect 'consumers' is also relevant in some cases. One of the interesting questions that can be asked about the curriculum has to do with the relative power and influence of these various actors in the planning process; for example, in their study, Boys *et al.* (1988) detect shifts in some cases (but not all) towards higher level and external influences. On the other hand, the generally low 'compliance observability' of the teaching–learning process means that a good deal of power and influence is likely always to remain with those who actually operate the system, i.e. the lecturers and students. Again, it is not easy to generalize; much depends on the institution, the subject and the general framework of regulation and control.

Figure 1.1 sets out a general model for the planning of courses. However, in this book our main concern is not the actual planning of courses, but the basis, or rather bases, for that planning. The very headings in the model presuppose some kind of conceptual framework for thinking about what is to be taught; what is usually referred to in the literature as 'curriculum theory' rather than 'curriculum development'.[4] How do we decide what to teach? How do we decide how to decide? The three main theoretical frames of reference will be explored in the three middle chapters. First, however, something must be said about the existing patterns and trends of the curriculum in higher education.

The curriculum in higher education

The system of higher education in the UK is usually described in institutional rather than curricular terms, and even in a book on the curriculum something must be said about the pattern of institutions since this affects what is taught. Classifying and even counting these institutions is by no means as simple a task as one might think. One has to decide whether federal universities are singular or plural; what proportion of an institution's courses have to be 'advanced' to justify its inclusion in the higher education sector; and whether to include a number of small, specialized institutions (for agriculture, technology and the arts) and voluntary colleges (mainly church-affiliated) in the list. Military colleges might be included on curricular grounds, but are usually excluded on financial ones. The one private university (Buckingham) is excluded from the official statistics, and will be here. The situation is further complicated by recent and impending institutional mergers.

According to the most recent Green Paper (DES 1985b) there were at that time 184 institutions engaged wholly or mainly in the provision of higher education courses, and another 372 in which some provision was at this level − a total of 556 (10 fewer than given in Annex A of that document). Higher education or 'advanced' courses are normally distinguished from 'non-advanced' courses by being beyond A level, Scottish 'Highers' (not the same) or the equivalent in technical qualifications (such as BTEC National), though recent trends towards more flexible access have tended to erode this demarcation at the point of entry, particularly in relation to mature students. It should also be noted that many universities offer extra-mural courses which have no fixed entrance requirements, that the Open University is open entry in terms of prior qualifications, and that many institutions are now developing 'access' courses which provide non-standard routes of entry to first degrees.

The 184 main providers are divided into two sectors: 46 universities (including the Open University) and 138 polytechnics and colleges. The universities are not formally sub-divided, but informal groupings based on origin and type distinguish between Oxbridge (Oxford and Cambridge), the large federal university of London founded in the early nineteenth century, the larger 'civic' universities established later in the nineteenth century in provincial cities (e.g. Manchester, Birmingham, Leeds, Bristol), the smaller civics such as Exeter, Hull or Leicester, the 'new' universities founded *ab initio* in the 1960s, such as Lancaster, Essex and Sussex, the 'ex-CATS' such as Aston, Salford and Bradford, which were upgraded from Colleges of Advanced Technology at around the same time, and the Scottish, Welsh and two Northern Irish universities. While this kind of breakdown does help one to comprehend the various strands and stages that go to make up the current system, it is rather crude. It does not distinguish between the older Scottish universities, such as Edinburgh and St Andrews, which predate all the English ones except Oxford and Cambridge, and the newer ones, such as Heriot-Watt and Strathclyde, which like the English ex-CATS were upgraded from existing technical institutions, but ones with a more prestigious history. It does not show that Wales unlike Scotland has a federal multi-campus university, or that the University of Ulster is the result of recent merger between a university and a polytechnic. And it does not accommodate certain institutions, such as Durham, Keele or the Open University, which because of origin or nature, are *sui generis*.

The non-university institutions are however, formally sub-divided, by location and partly by type. In England and Wales there were 30 polytechnics and 82 colleges or institutes of higher education in 1985. There is no difference between colleges and institutes, but that between the polytechnics and the colleges/institutes is largely a matter of the scale and level of provision – polytechnics tend to be larger, and provide more high level courses, including some postgraduate ones. Many colleges were originally teachers' colleges which diversified their provision in the 1970s to include broad-based arts, social science and science degrees. In Scotland, the 16 'Central Institutions' correspond roughly to the polytechnics in the rest of the UK, but in Scotland and Northern Ireland the colleges are typically 'monotechnic' (concentrating exclusively on technology, education or art, for example), whereas in England and Wales they are now almost entirely multi-subject.

Three general changes are now modifying what has until recently been described as a 'binary' system of higher education. The first is that universities appear to be becoming less autonomous than before, and the polytechnics and some of the larger colleges more, although it is difficult to decide whether the latter, recently removed from local government control and granted corporate status with central funding, are being 'nationalized' or 'privatized'. (The Scottish Central Institutions remain under the aegis of the Scottish Education Department.) This change erodes the distinction between university and what were previously known as 'public sector' institutions, and may blur what Burgess (1977, pp. 23–32) has argued is a contrast between the 'autonomous' (university) and 'service' (polytechnic/college) traditions. This distinction, as we shall see later, is partly a curricular as well as an institutional one. The most recent White Paper, however, firmly places all institutions in the service of the economy (DES 1987).

The second change is the increasing differentiation among universities in terms of funding, based initially on surveys of research performance, but now becoming widened to include a much broader range of performance indicators. This seems unlikely now to lead to the formal designation of the three types of universities ('R' for research-based, 'X' for mixed, and 'T' for teaching only) that has been mooted, but it seems probable that in practice the university system will become more overtly stratified than before; there has always been an element of covert stratification, although this has often related to departments rather than whole institutions. Compared to some continental countries, the levers of higher education policy in the UK are often financial rather than legislative, and this can lead not so much to a change of title as a gradual dissociation between title and reality.

The third major change is the advent of self-validation of courses for a number of polytechnics and colleges, which like all the other 'public sector' institutions, have until now had their degree courses validated and degrees awarded by the Council for National Academic Awards (CNAA), a national body established in 1964 to develop and regulate courses and qualifications in public sector higher education. The CNAA has always embodied a mixed, bureaucratic-collegial model of regulation, but the emphasis seems now to be moving towards the latter as its validation role declines. (This process in some ways parallels the emergence earlier in this century of the smaller civic universities – and some overseas ones – from under the wing of London University.) The changes currently taking place in the system are thus multiple and complex, but they point away from the existing binary pattern towards one that is perhaps more unitary and certainly more differentiated.

How far does the curriculum map correspond to this institutional map? Do the institutional headings referred to above indicate parallel differences in the pattern and content of first degrees? How far is the binary system binary in terms of curricula as well as organization? There is a *prima facie* case for thinking that it is. While each university plans and validates its own degree programmes in the light of a general awareness of policies, constraints and demands, the CNAA sets out general principles for first degree courses under its aegis. Many of these are couched in terms which would be unexceptional in universities. The institution, it says, 'should provide a cultural environment which stimulates a wide-ranging interest among students, and in which rational debate is encouraged' (CNAA 1986, p. 21). There is a reference to 'debate within a wide academic community', and, echoing Robbins (1963), to the development of the student's 'intellectual and imaginative skills and powers'. However, there are also two general principles which seem to signal a particular emphasis in the public sector. The first concerns the application of knowledge:

The student must also be encouraged to develop the ability to see relationships within what he or she has learned, and to relate what he or she has learned to actual situations.

(CNAA 1986, p. 23)

The second implies some breadth of study:

The student must be encouraged to appreciate the nature of attitudes, modes of thought, practices and disciplines other than those of his or her own main studies. He or she must learn to perceive his or her main studies in a broader perspective. As part of this process he or she must be enabled to develop an informed awareness of factors influencing the social and physical environment.

(CNAA 1986, p. 23)

Such principles are rather general, and the concrete nature of the validation process together with the general English distaste for 'philosophizing' will have limited their impact. However, they have been quite widely discussed within the CNAA over the years, particularly in the science and technology boards and committees.

It may be that, in practice, the norms and practices of the various CNAA subject boards count for more than such general sentiments. Nevertheless, there is nothing comparable on the university side, unless one refers to the general aims of higher education enunciated by Robbins (1963) and endorsed by the recent White Paper (DES 1987, para. 1.2): 'instruction in skills, the promotion of the general powers of the mind, the advancement of learning, and the transmission of a common culture and common standards of citizenship'. Again, however, one wonders how far this was mere rhetoric in the original or mere gesture in the repetition; although it may have some influence on the 'mission statements' that some institutions are now struggling to formulate.

On the university side, the main curricular differences are geographical rather than institutional. Although all UK universities (except the Open University) comprise a single system with common admissions procedures, first degree courses in Scotland, and to a lesser extent in Wales and Northern Ireland, are broader than they normally are in England. The reasons are largely historical, and in the case of Scotland have been chronicled and defended by George Davie in his books on 'the democratic intellect' (Davie 1961, 1986; see also Burnhill and McPherson 1983; Bell 1987). In the Scottish universities, students normally enter at 17 rather than 18, after taking five 'highers' subjects rather than three A levels, belong initially to a faculty rather than a department, and proceed to either a three-year ordinary or a four-year honours degree. [The norm in England and Wales is three years to honours, and in Northern Ireland there is a mixture of three- and four-year courses; although it has recently been claimed that as many as 40 per cent of all British university undergraduates are on courses lasting four or more years, in modern languages, medicine, engineering, architecture and some business subjects (Institute of Physics 1988).] Whereas in Scotland over 36 per cent of graduates obtained a pass, ordinary or general degree in 1986, the figure for the UK as a whole was only 12.7 per cent, with the majority of pass degrees in England being in the fields of medicine, dentistry or veterinary science (Source: USR). The relatively broad ordinary degree has an important if subsidiary place in the Scottish system. The first two years of study there will normally involve between three and six subjects rather than the one, two or three typical of the English university, and specialization does not really begin until the third year of the honours course.[5] In Wales and Northern Ireland too, three subjects in the first year is common outside professional degree subjects such as law and engineering. This broader pattern is more typical of the pattern in other anglophone countries than the relatively specialized English university one, and indeed in some cases contributed to it historically. But it is worth noting also that Scotland has had a relatively strong tradition of technical education for the last century, in contrast to the rather patchy developments south of the border (Argles 1964).

There are thus geographical and sectoral differences within the general pattern of curricula in higher education. But what is that general pattern? It may be useful to begin with some general figures. Table 1.1 gives the numbers for all higher education students (sub-degree, undergraduate and postgraduate) in the UK between 1975 and 1987. It shows the steady increase in both sectors and modes of study over that period, to the current total of about one million.[6] It also shows that whereas the universities and polytechnics/colleges had almost the same number of full-time students in 1987, part-time students were mainly concentrated in the latter and the Open University.

As regards undergraduates, Table 1.2 shows the numbers of full-time and part-time students enrolled over the same period, and Table 1.3 the number of first degrees awarded in each sector. Part-time enrolments have grown somewhat more rapidly than full-time ones, but the trends in first degrees awarded are more complex, with a slight decline in the universities and a steady increase in the polytechnics/colleges in recent years. The long-term growth in the latter has been enormous. Table 1.3 also gives the figures for higher degrees, over 90 per cent of which are awarded by the universities.

Such broad figures give a general sense of overall patterns and trends, but more detailed information is necessary for a discussion of the undergraduate curriculum. First, one has to identify what it is that undergraduates actually study. Table 1.4 lists current full-time sandwich and part-time first degree courses in the UK. Two points should be noted. First, although Table 1.4 is intended to give a general picture of provision it is not exhaustive; some of the variants and sub-divisions of subject headings (such as types of history or engineering) have been conflated in order to reduce the overall length of the list. Secondly, many of the subjects in the

Table 1.1   Higher education: full-time and part-time students

United Kingdom	*Thousands*								
Academic year beginning in	*1975*	*1979*	*1980*	*1982*	*1983*	*1984*	*1985*	*1986*	*1987*
Type of institution									
Full-time									
Universities	268.7	300.5	306.7	304.0	300.6	305.0	310.0	316.3	320.9
Polys and colleges	247.6	223.2	227.3	263.7	279.6	284.2	289.6	296.4	304.6
Total	516.3	523.7	534.0	567.7	580.2	589.2	599.7	612.7	625.5
Part-time									
Open University	56.0	69.6	67.8	74.6	76.3	77.4	78.7	81.1	85.8
Universities	26.2	31.3	33.1	34.8	36.1	40.5	42.3	44.5	46.0
Polys and colleges	136.5	171.3	184.3	192.0	198.7	196.6	212.1	230.2	232.7
Total	218.7	272.2	285.2	301.4	311.1	314.5	331.1	355.8	364.5
All modes									
Universities (incl. Open University)	350.9	401.4	407.6	413.4	413.0	422.9	431.1	441.9	452.7
Poly and colleges	384.1	394.5	411.6	455.7	478.3	480.8	501.7	526.6	537.3
Total	735.0	795.9	819.2	869.1	891.3	903.7	932.8	968.5	990.0

Source: Department of Education and Science
Department of Education Northern Ireland
Notes
1 Open University statistics for calendar year following academic year starting in year indicated
2 1987 figures for Northern Ireland further education colleges not available due to industrial dispute

list can be studied in pairs, in 'joint' or 'combined' subject degrees, so that the overall pattern of studies is less specialized than it appears.

Despite these *caveats*, Table 1.4 gives an interesting overview of first degree courses in two respects. First, the sheer range of degree subjects is striking. Whereas a comprehensive secondary school might offer some 30 subjects for all its pupils, and about a dozen subjects account for the great majority of A levels, the curriculum explodes in higher education, part of a post-school explosion even greater when one takes into account the vast number of technical and vocational courses that exist in non-advanced further education. The university list is longer than the polytechnic/college one partly because of the greater range of degrees, and partly because of the greater number of more specialized degrees in the universities, although it should be remembered that specialized patterns of options may exist within broad degree programmes.

Secondly, Table 1.4 gives some sense of the different distribution of subjects in the universities and polytechnics/colleges. While the spread of degree subjects varies a good deal among institutions *within* each sector, one can see some broad differences in the overall pattern. Quantitative

Table 1.2   First degree courses: full-time and part-time students

United Kingdom				Thousands					
Academic year beginning in	1975	1979	1980	1982	1983	1984	1985	1986	1987
Mode of course									
Full-time	287.3	376.9	386.9	416.5	420.9	428.4	432.2	441.2	454.7
Part-time	60.0	80.4	79.8	88.9	90.8	93.8	94.4	97.7	103.2
All modes	347.3	457.3	466.7	505.4	511.7	522.2	526.6	538.9	557.9

Source: Department of Education and Science
Department of Education Northern Ireland
Notes
1 Open University statistics for calendar year following academic year starting in year indicated
2 Figures for Ulster Polytechnic not available in this breakdown

Table 1.3   First and higher degrees awarded

United Kingdom				Thousands					
Year of completion	1975	1979	1980	1982	1983	1984	1985	1986	1987
Universities									
First degrees	55.6	66.0	67.4	71.9	74.0	73.0	71.9	69.9	71.6
Higher degrees	15.8	18.4	18.9	20.1	21.3	21.6	23.5	24.6	26.6
Polys and colleges									
First degrees	10.5	32.0	30.7	36.5	40.0	45.2	49.6	51.5	52.7
Higher degrees	0.5	1.0	0.9	1.2	1.4	1.8	2.0	2.4	2.3
Open University									
First degrees	5.5	5.8	6.3	6.4	5.6	5.9	6.7	6.6	6.4
All degrees									
First degrees	71.6	103.8	104.4	114.8	119.6	124.1	128.2	128.0	130.7
Higher degrees	16.3	19.4	19.8	21.3	22.7	23.4	25.5	27.0	28.9

Source: Department of Education and Science
Department of Education Northern Ireland
Notes
1 For sources of GB figures see DES *Statistical Bulletin 4/89,* Table 8
2 For details of Open University higher degree students see *Open University Statistics 1987: Students, Staff and Finance,* Tables A3 and 10
3 Figures for degrees other than teacher training degrees at Ulster Polytechnic not available in this format

Table 1.4   First degree courses in the UK: Full-time, sandwich and part-time

Universities	*Polytechnics/Colleges*
Accountancy, Banking and Finance	
Accountancy/Accounting	Accountancy/Accounting
Actuarial Science/Studies	Accounting and Finance
Banking	
Finance/Financial Analysis/ Management	
Acoustics	
Acoustics/Electroacoustics	
Administration	
Public/Social Administration	Public/Social Administration
African Studies	
African Studies/History/Language/ Culture	
Agriculture and Forestry	
Agricultural Economics	
Agriculture/Agricultural Science	
Agricultural Biochemistry	
Agricultural Botany	
Agricultural Chemistry	
Agricultural Zoology	
Animal Science	
Crop Protection/Crop Science	
Forestry	
Horticulture	
American Studies	
American Studies/US Studies	American Studies
Anatomy	
Anatomy/Anatomical Studies	
Anthropology	
Anthropology	
Social Anthropology	
Archaeology	
Archaeology/Archaeological Studies	Archaeology
Architecture	
Architecture/Architectural Studies	Architecture/Architectural Studies
Art and Design	
Art/Fine Art	Art/Fine Art
Design	Design
History of Art	Art and Design

Table 1.4—continued

Universities	*Polytechnics/Colleges*
Visual Arts	Graphic Design
	History of Art
	Interior Design
	Three-dimensional Design
	Visual Arts
Asian and Middle Eastern Studies	
Arabic/Arab Studies	
Chinese/Chinese Studies	
Hebrew	
Japanese	
Ancient Near East Studies	
Astronomy and Space Science	
Astronomy	
Astrophysics	
Bacteriology and Virology	
Immunology	
Biochemistry	
Biochemistry/Biochemical Sciences	
Biological Chemistry	
Biomedical Sciences	
Medical Biochemistry	
Biology	
Biology/Biological Sciences	Applied Biology/Biological Sciences
Botany	Biology/Biological Sciences
Zoology	Life Sciences
Animal Biology	
Applied Biology	
Cell Biology	
Ecology/Ecological Science	
Human Biology	
Marine Biology	
Molecular Biology	
Plant Biology	
Plant Science	
Biophysics	
Biophysics	
Biotechnology	
Biotechnology	
Building Science and Technology	
Building/Construction Management	Building/Construction
Building Services Engineering	

Table 1.4—continued

Universities	*Polytechnics/Colleges*
Business and Management	
Business Administration/Studies	Business Studies
Industrial Relations	Commerce
Management (Science)	Management
Marketing	European Business Studies
Chemistry	
Chemistry/Chemical Sciences	Chemistry
Analytical Chemistry	Applied Chemistry
Applied Chemistry	
Industrial Chemistry	
Medical Chemistry	
Classics	
Ancient History	
Byzantine Studies	
Classics/Classical Studies	
Greek (Studies)	
Latin (Studies)	
Roman Civilization/Studies	
Computer Science and Technology	
Computer Science/Computing	Computer Science/Computing
Artificial Intelligence	Information Technology
Computational Science	
Computer Engineering	
Computer Systems/Engineering	
Information Systems/Science	
Information Technology	
Software Engineering	
Dentistry	
Dentistry	
Development Studies	
Development Studies	
Dietetics and Nutrition	
Nutrition	Dietetics
Drama and Theatre	
Drama	Drama (Studies)
Theatre	Theatre (Arts)
Economics	
Economics/Economic Science	Economics
Business Economics	
Econometrics	
Economic History	
Industrial Economics	
Mathematical Economics	

Table 1.4—continued

Universities	*Polytechnics/Colleges*
Education	
Education	Education
Education and Society	Educational Studies
Educational Psychology	
Educational Policy	
Engineering	
Engineering (Science)	Computer-Aided Engineering
	Engineering
	Engineering Technology
Aeronautical Engineering	
Agricultural Engineering/Technology	
Chemical Engineering	Chemical Engineering
Civil Engineering	Civil Engineering
Electrical/Electronic Engineering	Electrical/Electronic Engineering
Control Engineering	
Communications Engineering	
Electronics/Systems	
Information (Systems) Engineering	
Microelectronics	
Systems Engineering	
Marine Engineering/Technology	
Mechanical Engineering	Mechanical Engineering
Production Engineering/Technology	Production Engineering/Technology
Manufacturing Engineering/Systems	Manufacturing Engineering/Systems
English	
English Language	English (Studies)
English Language and Literature	
English Literature	English Literature
Medieval English/Studies	
Environmental Studies	
Environmental Science/Studies	Environmental Science/Studies
Environmental Biology	
Environmental Chemistry	
Environmental Engineering	
Estate and Land Management	
Estate/Land Management	Estate Management
	Urban Estate Management
European Studies	
European Studies	European Studies
Food Science and Technology	
Food Science	Food Science
	Food Studies

Table 1.4—continued

Universities	Polytechnics/Colleges
French Language and Literature/Studies	
French Language/Literature/Studies	French (Studies)
Combined and General Studies	
Arts and Humanities	Arts and Humanities
Combined Studies	Combined Studies
	Contemporary Studies
	Creative and Performing Arts
Independent Studies	Independent Studies
Literature/Literary Studies	
Methodology	Modern Studies
Multidisciplinary Studies	Multidisciplinary Studies
Science	Science
Social Science	Social Science
Twentieth-Century Studies	
Genetics	
Genetics	
Geography	
Geography/Geographical Studies	Geography/Geographical Science
Human Geography	
Physical Geography	
Geology	
Earth Sciences	
Geology/Geological Sciences	Geology
Geochemistry	
Geophysics/Geophysical Sciences	
Germanic Languages and Studies	
Dutch	
German Language/Literature/Studies	German (Studies)
Scandinavian Studies	
Swedish	
Modern Greek	
Modern Greek	
Health	
	Environmental Health
	Health Studies
History	
History	History/Historical Studies
Local/Regional History	
Medieval History/Studies	History of Ideas
Modern History	Modern History
Scottish History	
Social History	

Table 1.4—continued

Universities	Polytechnics/Colleges
History and Philosophy of Science	
History and Philosophy of Science	
Home Economics	
	Home Economics
Hotel and Institutional Management	
Catering Administration/Management	Accommodation Studies/Management
Hotel Management	Catering
	Hotel and Catering Administration
Irish, Scottish and Welsh Studies	
Celtic Languages/Literature/Studies	
Irish (Studies)	
Scottish History/Historical Studies	
Scottish Literature	
Welsh (Studies)	
Welsh History	
Italian Language/Literature/Studies	
Italian Language/Literature/Studies	Italian
Landscape Architecture	
	Landscape Architecture
Language Studies	
Computational Linguistics	
Language/Language Studies	
Linguistics	
Latin American Studies	
Latin American Studies	
Law	
Law	Law/Legal Studies
English Law	Business Law
European Law	
French Law	
Librarianship and Information Science	
Librarianship/Information Studies	Librarianship/Information Studies
Materials Science and Technology	
Materials Science and Engineering	
Materials Engineering/Technology	
Materials Science	Materials Science
Mathematics	
Mathematics/Mathematical Sciences	Mathematics/Mathematical Sciences
Applied Mathematics	
Engineering Mathematics	
Pure Mathematics	

Table 1.4—continued

Universities	Polytechnics/Colleges
Media and Communication Studies	
Communications (Studies)	Communications (Studies)
Film Studies	
Media Studies	
Medical/Health Physics	
Medical Physics	
Medicine	
Medicine/Medical Sciences	
Metallurgy	
Metallurgy	Metallurgy
Microbiology	
Microbiology	
Mining and Mineral Sciences	
Mineral(s) Engineering Technology	
Mining (Engineering)	
Music	
Music	Music
Nursing	
Nursing (Sciences)	Nursing (Studies)
Operational Research	
Operational Research	Operational Research
Ophthalmic Optics	
Ophthalmic Optics	
Parasitology	
Parasitology	
Pharmacology	
Pharmacology	
Toxicology	
Pharmacy	
Pharmacy	Pharmacy
Philosophy	
Philosophy	Philosophy
	History of Ideas
Photography	
	Photography/Film/Video
Physical Education and Sports Science	
Physical Education	Physical Education
Sports Science	Sports Studies/Science

Table 1.4—continued

Universities	*Polytechnics/Colleges*
Physics	
Physics	Physics/Physical Science
Applied Physics	Applied Physics
Chemical Physics	
Electronics	
Mathematical Physics	
Opto-electronics	
Physical Electronics	
Theoretical Physics	
Physiology	
Physiology/Physiological Sciences	
Physiotherapy	
	Physiotherapy
Political Science	
Politics/Political Science	Politics/Political Science
Government	Government
International Relations	
International Studies	
Polymer Science and Technology	
Polymer Science and Engineering	Polymer Science and Technology
Portuguese Language and Literature	
Portuguese	
Psychology	
Psychology	Psychology
Applied Social Psychology	
Social Psychology	
Public Administration and Finance	
Public Administration	Public Administration
Recreation Studies	
Recreation/Leisure Studies	Recreation (Management)
	Travel and Tourism Studies
Religious Studies	
Biblical Studies	
Comparative Religion	
Divinity	
Religious Studies	Religion/Religious Studies
Theology/Theological Studies	Theology/Theological Studies
Slavonic and East European Studies	
Czech/Polish Studies	
Russian Language/Literature/Studies	Russian
Serbo-Croat	

Table 1.4—continued

Universities	Polytechnics/Colleges
Social Work	
Social Work	Social Work
	Applied Social Studies/Sciences
Sociology	
Sociology/Social Studies	Sociology/Social Studies
Social Administration	Social Administration
Social Policy	Social Policy/Policy Studies
Soil Science	
Soil Science	
Spanish Language and Literature/Studies	
Hispanic Languages/Literature/Studies	
Spanish Language/Literature/Studies	Spanish (Studies)
Speech Therapy	
Speech Therapy/Pathology	Speech Therapy/Pathology
Statistics	
Statistics/Statistical Science	Statistics
Mathematical Statistics	Applied Statistics
Surveying	
Quantity Surveying	Quantity Surveying
	Building Surveying
Textiles	
Textile Design	Textile Design
	Textiles/Fashion
Textile Engineering	Fashion
Town and Country Planning	
Planning (Studies)	
Town/Country/Regional Planning	Town/Country/Regional Planning
Urban Studies	Urban Studies
Veterinary Medicine	
Veterinary Science/Medicine	

Sources: Association of Commonwealth Universities (1988), Tight (1987), Open University
    Guide to the BA Degree Programme 1989 and institutional prospectuses
Notes
1 The inclusion of a course indicates that the student can specialize in this subject/field, and
    sometimes take it in combination with one or more other subjects/fields. The actual
    nomenclature of any particular degree course may differ from the headings given
2 In order to shorten and simplify the list, only courses provided by at least three institutions
    in either sector have normally been included; the list is not therefore intended to be
    exhaustive
3 Open University courses, which follow a foundation plus unit pattern, are grouped here
    according to the headings given in the *Guide* (pp. 23–4)

data bear out these differences of emphasis between the two sectors (*DES Statistical Bulletin* 4/89, Table 7; Tight 1986). Education is a much more common first degree subject in the polytechnics and colleges than the universities, whereas courses in medicine and agriculture are heavily concentrated in the latter. The universities have a preponderance of students in arts, languages and pure science, the polytechnics/colleges in professional/vocational studies. The latter also have more engineering/technology and business/social studies students. Art and design are largely concentrated in the polytechnics and colleges, some of which incorporate previously autonomous colleges of art.

Table 1.4 also gives some sense of the differences of emphasis within these broad subject categories, showing that polytechnic/college courses are often 'applied', whereas those in the universities are (by implication) often 'theoretical' or 'pure'; although one must not rely too much on labels in higher education. Some of these differences can be explained by the historical fact that 'public sector' institutions incorporated previously distinct colleges of teacher education, technology and commerce. Some may be attributable to the initial aim of the binary policy to create a sector with a more applied or vocationally relevant emphasis and ethos, although the extent to which that was eroded in the 1970s by 'academic drift' is open to question (Pratt and Burgess 1974; Donaldson 1975; Neave 1978, 1979b). But in some ways the universities have themselves been subject to a countervailing 'vocational drift' in the 1980s, as a result of both government pressure and student demand.

Within the degree course headings in Table 1.4, there are many variations in the *structure* of courses. The appendix of the Robbins Report (2B), which dealt with the undergraduate curriculum, attempted to classify courses in terms of one, two or three main subjects with one, two or three related or unrelated ancillaries. Thus many students would take a single, combined or (more rarely) a tripartite subject degree, with one or two ancillary or subsidiary subjects in the first two years, and some main subject options in the final year. This classification fits some university courses well, but it is now inadequate for the system as a whole. It does not suit professional courses, such as those in medicine, law, engineering or business studies which can be thought of as composite subjects, and which therefore tend to have few external ancillary courses. Nor can it cope with the more general interdisciplinary and modular patterns which have emerged in the last two decades; and it is university-biased in its assumption that the basic academic unit is the subject-department, whereas composite departments offering broader programmes of study are common in the polytechnics and colleges.[7]

How far does the general pattern shown in Table 1.4 vary with time? A comparison of the prospectuses for 1980–81 and 1986–87 of a number of institutions for this study suggested that, contrary to the arthritic stereotype purveyed sometimes by the press and others who should know better, degree provision in higher education is by no means static. Typically, the

Table 1.5 First degree students from home and abroad (000's): Subject and mode of study

United Kingdom

Thousands

Subject group	1979–80			1981–82			1982–83			1983–84			1984–85			1986–87		
	FT	PT	T	FT	PT	T	FT	PT	T	FT	PT	T	FT	PT	T	FT	PT	T
1 Education	29.9	6.8	36.7	26.7	7.2	33.9	27.0	7.2	34.2	27.2	6.7	33.9	29.1	6.5	35.6	29.4	5.9	35.3
2 Medicine, Dentistry and Health	32.0	0.4	32.4	32.8	0.2	33.0	33.5	0.3	33.8	33.8	0.5	34.3	34.1	0.6	34.7	34.3	1.1	35.4
3 Engineering and Technology	54.8	2.9	57.7	58.4	3.2	61.6	59.2	3.3	62.5	59.3	3.6	62.9	60.2	4.1	64.3	64.6	5.1	69.7
4 Agriculture, Forestry and Veterinary	5.3	–	5.3	5.4	–	5.4	5.4	–	5.4	5.2	–	5.2	5.1	–	5.1	5.2	–	5.2
5 Science	70.6	2.8	73.4	80.4	3.2	83.6	83.0	3.2	86.2	85.0	3.5	88.5	88.1	4.1	92.2	91.2	4.4	95.6
6 Administrative Business and Social	91.3	5.6	96.9	98.8	5.8	104.6	101.4	6.2	107.6	103.1	6.9	110.0	104.1	8.1	112.2	107.3	9.7	117.2
7 Architecture and other Professional	11.9	0.6	12.5	13.2	0.6	13.8	14.2	0.7	14.9	15.0	0.9	15.9	15.7	1.0	16.7	15.9	0.9	16.8
8 Languages, Literature and Area Studies	36.7	1.2	37.9	38.8	1.5	40.3	38.8	1.6	40.4	38.6	1.6	40.2	38.8	1.7	40.5	39.7	1.7	41.4
9 Arts other than Languages	30.5	1.0	31.5	34.3	1.7	36.0	29.1	1.6	30.7	29.5	2.1	31.6	26.6	2.2	28.8	25.7	2.5	28.2
10 Music, Drama, Art and Design	20.4	0.2	20.6	22.8	0.4	23.2	30.7	0.8	31.5	30.9	0.9	31.8	31.9	1.4	33.3	32.6	1.8	34.4
11 Other	–	–	–	0.1	–	0.1	0.2	–	0.2	0.2	–	0.2	–	–	–	2.1	–	2.1
All subjects	383.4	21.6	405.0	411.7	23.9	435.6	422.7	25.0	447.7	427.7	26.8	454.5	433.8	29.7	463.5	448.1	33.2	481.3

Source: DES, *Education Statistics for the United Kingdom* (annual)

Notes

1 Data for 1980–81 and 1985–86 not available in this form

2 Excludes Open University

3 FT, Full-time and sandwich; PT, part-time day and evening; T, full- and part-time aggregate, not full-time equivalent

4 1986/87 University figures estimated

broad changes are gradual, the addition or subtraction of a handful of courses or course combinations in any one year, the first usually reflecting potential student demand or research developments, and the second often stemming from resource and staffing problems. In some universities which were hard hit in the 1981 cuts, the changes were more dramatic; one university lost 25 and gained 3 degree courses over the period. Generally, however, the pattern is one of gradual, rolling, incremental change.

This pattern manifests itself even more clearly in the detail of courses. Many of the prospectuses and some of the accompanying letters noted changes in the content of courses, e.g. at the research frontiers of the natural sciences, in the pattern and interrelation of the social sciences, in the new enhanced and extended engineering degrees, in the structure of courses (new combinations and in some cases modular schemes), in project-based options in the final year, in the pattern of teaching and assessment, and in the development of work placements, European links or part-time degrees. One must be careful about making judgements about the capacity of the system to innovate and adapt, because the UK system operates to a considerable extent in an informal, pragmatic mode which makes reliance on labels and formal accounts hazardous. A course may change radically without changing its title; conversely, re-titling a course may simply be an exercise in re-packaging it for external consumption. Trow's (1975) distinction between the 'public' and 'private' lives of higher education, although American, is crucial in understanding the British system.

Nevertheless, quantitative data do provide some guide to changes in the subject balance of first degree courses over recent years. Table 1.5 gives the figures for full-time, part-time and total degree enrolments in 11 subject groups between 1979–80 and 1986–87, excluding the Open University where degree courses cannot be grouped in this way because of the structure of foundation plus optional courses (Open University 1989). In interpreting these broad trends, one should remember that the first two groups of subjects, education and medicine, are subject to what passes in the UK for manpower planning. What the unfettered demand for such subjects would have been, one can only guess. The other subject groups, however, represent a largely demand-led pattern of provision, following the Robbins principle, although there are manifold factors which sully the pure concept of demand in practice. What one sees in general terms are substantial increases in science, technology, administrative, business and social studies, and creative arts enrolments, but stasis or decline in languages and humanities. There are of course significant subject variations within these broad groups.[8]

How far does the pattern of subject choice vary by sex? Table 1.6 gives the male/female enrolments in the 11 subject groups for 1979–80 and 1986–87. It shows that the proportion of female enrolments has been growing steadily, though it is still some way short of parity. It also shows women are over-represented in education, languages and literature and

Table 1.6   First degree students from home and abroad by subject group, sex and mode of study

United Kingdom	Thousands							
	1979/80				1986/87			
	Male		Female		Male		Female	
Subject group	FT	PT	FT	PT	FT	PT	FT	PT
1 Education	7.1	3.2	22.8	3.7	5.8	2.1	23.6	3.9
2 Medicine, Dentistry and Health	18.4	0.2	13.6	0.1	16.2	0.3	18.1	0.7
3 Engineering and Technology	52.0	2.8	2.9	0.1	56.7	4.8	7.9	0.3
4 Agriculture, Forestry and Veterinary Science	3.5	–	1.8	–	2.9	–	2.3	–
5 Science	48.4	2.2	22.0	0.7	57.9	3.0	33.3	1.4
6 Administrative, Business and Social Studies	55.0	4.0	36.3	1.6	56.1	5.6	51.4	4.1
7 Architecture and other Professional/ Vocational Subjects	7.5	0.5	4.4	0.2	8.7	0.6	7.1	0.3
8 Languages, Literature and other Area Studies	12.1	0.3	24.6	0.9	12.8	0.5	26.9	1.2
9 Arts other than Languages	13.6	0.5	16.9	0.5	12.0	1.0	13.7	1.5
10 Music, Drama, Art and Design	9.1	0.2	11.5	0.1	13.4	0.8	19.2	1.0
11 Other	–	–	–	–	0.2	–	1.9	–
All subjects	226.7	13.8	156.6	7.7	242.6	18.6	205.5	14.5

Source: DES, *Education Statistics for the United Kingdom* (annual)
Notes
1 Excludes Open University
2 1986/87 estimated subject breakdown for universities
3 Rounding of figures creates some discrepancies with totals in Table 1.5

music/drama/art/design, whereas men are over-represented in engineering and technology and science, and that this pattern has not changed a great deal over the period, despite attempts to even out the balance, and in particular to attract more women on to science and technology courses. (The rounding of figures in this and the other tables creates some slight discrepancies in aggregates.)

Tables 1.6 helps to provide an overall picture of the content, pattern and distribution of first degree courses, but once one begins to look at courses in any detail, the picture becomes much more complex. While in many ways the UK system is a homogeneous one, with centralized application procedures, common though varying admissions requirements, and a national system of student support through grants and now loans, its often decentralized and pragmatic mode of development has led to great variation in detail. It is unusual outside some strictly regulated professional courses to find two courses covering the same content; it would be difficult to find two that have exactly the same pattern of assessment; and impossible to find two that are taught in precisely the same way.

There are also variations in the institutional patterns. The relatively broader Scottish, Welsh and Northern Irish patterns have already been mentioned. Some universities, such as Queens University Belfast, offer a preliminary year in some subjects; and a common foundation year is an important feature of art and design courses in the polytechnics and colleges. Some universities, such as Cambridge and Nottingham, divide first degree courses into 'Part I' and 'Part II', the former usually but not always occupying the first two years, with some transfer between subjects possible at the second stage. There are three different patterns of curriculum within London University: university-wide, college-based and course unit. One can obtain a degree (largely) through an individualized scheme of 'independent' study at Lancaster University and North East London Polytechnic. There are institution-wide modular degree schemes at Oxford and City Polytechnics, as well as within faculties in other institutions (Squires 1986). About 30 per cent of polytechnic/college graduates and about 5 per cent of university graduates are the products of 'sandwich' courses which include either one (year) long placement or several shorter ones (AGCAS 1989). The Open University has a unique combination of foundation courses followed by a modular course structure. The University of Keele offers its students the option of an initial broad, foundation year before embarking on the three-year course (Iliffe 1968). The University of Essex has a multidisciplinary first year, and the University of Sussex an initial two-term preliminary course. In some polytechnics and colleges students can proceed from a two-year Diploma in Higher Education to a first degree, and the CNAA has set up a Credit Accumulation and Transfer Scheme (CATS) which allows students to accumulate credits not only from a variety of higher education institutions but from accredited employer-based and experiential learning. Many of the colleges and institutes of higher education have established broad-based curricula in the arts, social sciences and to a lesser extent natural sciences. Some institutions offer theme-based rather than subject-based foundation courses in the first year, e.g. the Polytechnic of Central London's social science foundation course. A few institutions, such as Stirling University, operate on a two-semester rather than three-term year. Once one begins to examine the system in any detail, the institutional variations seem virtually endless; and standardized titles and labels often conceal even more informal variety.

The homogeneity or variety of the system is thus largely a matter of the level of magnification. Taken as a whole, it appears relatively standardized, particularly if one compares it with that in the USA. In its detail, however, it is extraordinarily diverse. This fact alone suggests that a purely descriptive approach to first degree courses is likely to be unproductive or excruciatingly boring. Besides, the variations in the pattern and emphasis of such courses seem to have grown up largely pragmatically, as a function of the organizational 'discretion' that both institutions and academics have in responding to the needs, pressures and priorities they have perceived over a long period of time. It would be possible to trace the evolution of first degrees .historically in this way, as has been done in the histories of particular institutions or particular subjects. That would be an interesting task, but one for which this author is singularly ill-equipped. Instead, I shall draw on some of what has evolved over the last half century as 'curriculum theory' in education to try to suggest some frameworks and perspectives for analysing the wealth of detail which the system displays. This involves not only asking 'What is taught?' but 'How do we ask what is taught?'

The three dimensions of the curriculum

The need for some kind of frame of reference for thinking about the curriculum, and asking what is and should be taught is most obvious in the schools. The fact that education (though not schooling) is obligatory up to the age of 16 forces one to try to justify and legitimate in curricular terms such a major act of social compulsion. One justification commonly offered is that the schools exist to provide children with a good basic or general education; the problem is basic to what and general in what sense? (Squires 1987a).

One obvious way of conceptualizing generality is in terms of *knowledge*. Children, it is argued, should receive a good grounding in the main forms or types of human knowledge, for both practical and abstract reasons. If they do not have such a grounding, it will be difficult for them to pursue more advanced studies subsequently, especially in 'vertebrate' subjects such as mathematics and science; also, a merely partial or incomplete exposure to such forms of knowledge sells them short in terms of human thought, indeed of the very concept of mind. Perhaps the best known exponent of this model of general education in the UK is Hirst (1969; 1974), but it is familiar in most countries, and results in the relatively academic type of secondary school curriculum that one finds in the English grammar school, the French Lycée or the German Gymnasium, with appropriate national differences of emphasis (the English have always stressed 'process' rather than 'breadth'). Whereas philosophers such as Hirst (1974) and Phenix (1964) have attempted to classify knowledge in terms of logical forms or groupings, the knowledge-based curriculum in the schools tends to be organized in more familiar, traditional subject categories: mathematics, physics, history, geography, English, etc. The influence of this view is apparent in the new National Curriculum soon to be implemented in the schools. It is worth pointing out that advocates of such a curriculum do not see knowledge as inert and impersonal but as something which can deeply affect the way an individual thinks, behaves and views the world.

A second approach to conceptualizing a general education is in terms of the society or *culture* of which it is a part. Children, it is suggested, need to be inducted into the main forms or aspects of the culture they live in, partly because this will equip them to lead full adult lives, and partly because culture seems to some as inclusive a concept as one can find for planning a general education. There have been several important variants of this model of the curriculum, ranging from the American pragmatists (notably Dewey) to the Marxist theories of 'polytechnical education', but a recent formulation in this country is that of Lawton (1983) with his notion of general education as a selection from the eight aspects or 'sub-systems' that any culture has: social system, economic system, communication system, rationality system, technology system, morality system, belief system and aesthetic system. Such an approach overlaps to some extent with the 'knowledge-referenced' curriculum, but it also results in the inclusion of elements related to health, economics, civics and other 'relevant' topics which one would not normally find in an academic-style secondary school. The main examples of general education planned in terms of the society or culture are the American high school and the polytechnical schools in the Eastern bloc countries, but the model has also influenced secondary education in Scandinavia and the secondary-modern type schools in those countries which have a selective secondary system. Advocates of this type of curriculum not only have the problem of deciding who can speak for the culture (or cultures?) and making an appropriate selection from it, but of deciding to what extent the curriculum should attempt to conserve, reform, revolutionize or even reverse cultural patterns and trends.

An education may therefore be thought of as 'general' either in terms of types of knowledge or the culture to which it belongs. However, the term general can be conceived of in a third way, in terms of the all-round development of the individual. The schools are expected to provide the stimuli and security which will allow children to grow, develop and mature. But develop in what sense? The most obvious form of development is cognitive, in terms of the mastery of ever more complex forms of thinking and consciousness. But there is a strong tradition in this country that education (including higher education) should go beyond cognitive or intellectual development, that it should draw out, through its curricula, teaching and environment, the entire range of types of ability and talent – intellectual, artistic, physical and social – and set these in the context of the whole person, of 'character', 'autonomy' or 'maturity'. As Hargreaves (1982) has pointed out, much of this is rhetoric rather than reality, especially when secondary education comes within the orbit of public examinations, which have hitherto largely emphasized cognitive development, but it does constitute a strong element in 'progressive' models of primary education, and has influenced the content, teaching and assessment of courses leading to the General Certificate of Secondary Education (GCSE). The importance of recognizing the 'total package' of a person's abilities and development becomes obvious once again when one enters the world of employment, as we shall see in the discussion of graduate employment and the notion of 'education for capability' in Chapters 3 and 4.

There are thus three distinct frames of reference which we can bring to bear on the concept of basic or general education: knowledge, culture and student development. Each of these in isolation produces a form of curriculum which embodies its own emphases; but it is surely better to consider them as the three necessary dimensions of any truly general education (Squires 1987a). Logically, they cannot exist separately: all knowledge involves some kind of mental processing and exists in a cultural context; all cultures are conceptualized in terms of knowledge and involve abilities and skills; all development has a content and a context. In practice, too, all three dimensions are always present; the differences between school curricula reflect the relative priority accorded to one dimension or another.

This three-dimensional model can also be used to analyse the undergraduate curriculum, and will provide the three broad frames of reference for the three chapters that follow, which examine first degree courses in terms of concepts of knowledge, the economy and society, and the development of student ability or potential. However, the working out of these three dimensions in the undergraduate curriculum is bound to be rather different from their manifestation in the school curriculum because higher education comes at a different *stage* in the educational life-cycle.

The notion of educational 'stages' is useful as long as it is not interpreted too rigidly or schematically (Squires 1989a). Broadly, one can distinguish five main stages in an individual's educational life-cycle. Compulsory education constitutes the initial *basic* and *general* stages, the difference between the two being mainly a matter of scope and level rather than intention or function, though it sometimes corresponds to the transition from primary to secondary education. The years that immediately follow the end of compulsory schooling can often be seen as a *foundation* stage providing a relatively broad base for work in a particular occupation (as do many craft and technician courses) or for more advanced studies in a specialized field. The foundation stage is then followed by, or merges into, a more *specific* stage which provides a more specialized education or training, which may be on or off the job, or a mixture of both. Beyond that, we are into the final, *open* stage of adult or continuing education, which may go on intermittently for many years, compensating for missed opportunities, updating and extending existing skills, or opening up new fields of interest and expertise altogether. Of course the length of the various stages may vary from person to person (not to mention country to country) and some people's general education may go on well into their higher education, whereas for others it ends early in secondary school.

Some current trends reinforce this linear pattern, whereas others modify it. The rising threshold of competence needed in the job market and the relative decline in traditional semi-skilled or unskilled jobs means that the compulsory school can no longer hope to provide a marketable, vocational education as it did for some (usually lower-achieving) children in the past. It may well include pre-vocational elements in its curriculum; however, these are primarily there for purposes of motivation and orientation rather than vocational training in its traditional form. The generalist function of compulsory education seems thus to be becoming clearer. (This might lead one to approve the technical but question the vocational element in TVEI.) Beyond school, the traditional idea that craft and technician courses can turn out 'finished' workers is being undermined in many occupations by the rapid changes in work skills, and hence the *foundation* function of the 16–19 stage seems to be becoming more obvious. The pattern of labour in an advanced economy means that many jobs and roles now require *specialized* education and training to a higher level than before, though this co-exists with 'de-skilling' in other jobs. The desirability of and necessity for *continuing* education throughout the lifespan is now widely accepted in principle, although in practice there still exist many barriers, not least of cost, which limit adult participation in education and training. There is a good deal of rhetoric in this field, and as regards higher education institutions, the increased (self-)interest in mature students has been prompted partly by the decline in the 18-year-old age-group by about one-third between 1982 and 1995; although for various reasons that decline does not simply translate into a comparable decline in intake (Fulton 1981). Nevertheless, all these broad trends seem to reinforce the notion and distinctness of the various educational stages, and lend substance to the idea of an educational life-cycle.

In other ways, however, the pattern is becoming less rather than more linear. There are second chances to get one's initial basic or general education, through everything from adult basic education classes through to GCSEs and A levels in further education colleges. The age regulations governing access to training are becoming more flexible, on paper if not always in practice, and there is increasing emphasis on 'access' courses of various kinds for adults. A quarter of all full-time home first-year students on first and sub-degree courses were aged over 21 on entry in 1987 (DES *Statistical Bulletin* 4/89, Table 6), and the proportion of part-timers is much higher (see DES *Statistical Bulletin* 11/88 'Mature Students in Higher Education'). The development of more flexible systems of access and qualifications (in particular modular credit schemes) means that the educational life-pattern for any one individual is likely to be less rigidly linear than in the past, a situation which is foreshadowed by developments in the USA (Stacey *et al.* 1988). While one must distinguish between formal access and real accessibility, there are more second routes and second chances, and fewer dead-ends and irreversible choices than in the past, and the whole notion of 'stages' has to be interpreted in the light of the individual's self-perception and the increasing fluidity of age-roles. Some men and women may be acquiring their foundation skills in their 30s, others discovering what a general education can be in their retirement.[9]

Nevertheless, the notion of educational stages helps one to place the undergraduate curriculum in a longer perspective, and to explain the phenomenon of *specialization* which typifies the undergraduate curriculum in this country. Some degree of specialization is a characteristic of undergraduate curricula everywhere. Even in the broader US system, students 'major' in something; but the British, and in particular the English, system is unusually specialized in international terms. As noted above, A levels or Scottish highers typically constitute the foundation stage which precedes undergraduate studies – a foundation in terms of process as much as content – and it is significant that non-A level-based degrees often begin with 'foundation' courses. Indeed, the very notion of student access implies curricular foundations. As regards degree courses themselves, some are broader than others, and in effect provide a foundation for subsequent specialized postgraduate education or training; indeed, it may be more accurate in some cases to see the whole process as a four-year not three-year one, consisting of three foundation years followed by a specialized professional post-graduate year. Many degree courses, on the other hand, clearly belong to the *specific* stage in a person's educational development, after which his or her interests and horizon may narrow further, in specialized research or employment, or broaden out again.

We have now looked at the general patterns and trends of first degree courses, while acknowledging that there are manifold variations in detail. We have explored a general, if somewhat schematic, framework which allows us to analyse rather than simply describe what undergraduates are taught during the three or four years that lead to their first degree. It has been argued that such courses come somewhere around the foundation or specific stage in most people's educational development, although the increasing proportions of mature students must make us wary of too linear a model. And we have sketched out three broad frames of reference for thinking about the undergraduate curriculum: in terms of knowledge, society and student development. It is time now to move on to consider the first of these.

Notes

1 The model presented here is of course an analytic one; the actual planning process in higher education may be very different. It probably lies somewhere between Lindblom's 'incremental' and 'rational' planning approaches (Lindblom 1959; 1979). The first is pragmatic, evolutionary and relies on comparison rather than theory; the second goal-directed, systematic and as far as possible grounded in theory. Much of the writing on higher education tends to advocate the latter 'systems approach' (see Beard 1976; Miller 1987), but actual accounts of

curriculum planning often seem nearer the first (see *inter alia* Parlett and King 1971; Billing 1978). At a guess, the university pattern tends to be more 'incremental', the CNAA-influenced polytechnic/college pattern somewhat more 'rational', and the Open University most 'rational' of all, at least in its early years (Rowntree 1974). However, generalization is extremely hazardous, and differences in subject ethos and departmental and even individual style may be more important than sectoral or institutional ones. The move to self-validation in the polytechnics and larger colleges could lead to greater variation in curriculum planning styles in those institutions.

2   Most models of curriculum planning (and evaluation) have been developed in and for the school sector. The model presented here differs from these in two main ways. First, because higher education is not compulsory, a case has to be made for the existence of a curriculum *per se*, hence the attempt to identify functions. There is little incentive to do this in the compulsory sector, but in post-school education independent study or non-formal education may be a real alternative to a formal course, and in higher education there is a widespread assumption that the responsibility for learning is ultimately the students', and that one should not 'spoon-feed' them. Therefore, it seems appropriate to assume a natural capacity to learn as a starting point; the justification of a course must be that it adds to or enhances this in some way. Secondly, although some schools writers have developed 'situational' models of curriculum development (see Skilbeck 1984, pp. 230–40), the emphasis on contingencies here reflects the greater variety of settings and contextual factors in higher education. Contingency models are familiar in management, but not in curriculum studies; I have attempted to spell out the rationale for this one in a recent paper (Squires 1988).

3   Bloom's attempt to classify different levels of cognitive and affective objectives (Bloom (ed.) 1956; Krathwohl *et al.* 1964) has been criticized on various grounds, but in particular for dissociating level from content (Sockett 1971; Pring 1971). Despite this, modified or simpler forms of his scheme have had some influence on curriculum planning, perhaps because there is little else, although Gagne's taxonomy of types of learning is to some extent a parallel (Gagne 1969, 1975). The NCVQ classification of four levels of competence is simpler, indicative and geared more to employment than education (NCVQ 1988), but could in future influence higher education at Level V (professional).

4   The various subdivisions of curriculum studies are laid out in Richards' useful bibliography (Richards 1984), although typically the references are almost entirely related to the schools. Curriculum 'theories' in fact tend to be analytic models rather than what a natural scientist might expect of the word; there are nuances of difference between curriculum development, design and planning, but on the whole they reflect the difference already referred to between incremental and rational planning models. However, the different perspectives brought to bear on the study of the curriculum – philosophical, sociological (and within that various approaches), psychological, economic etc. – have resulted in different interpretations of what the curricular reality is, and indeed whether one can speak of one at all (see, for example, Reid 1978 and Lawn and Barton 1981).

5   One must be cautious about generalizing about the 'Scottish Universities', since they are less homogeneous than they were, the ancient institutions having been joined by newer technological ones, and one 'green-field' institution (Stirling). Although the common intake of 'Highers' students (together with a substantial

number of non-Scottish ones in some cases) leads to an identifiably broad Scottish curricular pattern, typically with admission to a faculty rather than a department, there are important differences between and within institutions. For example, while arts/social science students at Edinburgh or St Andrews will normally follow three subjects in their first year and two in the second, Dundee has a unit system which allows relative breadth or depth, Stirling a semester-unit system which permits the study of between three and five subjects over the first year and a half, and at Strathclyde students may study up to five in the first year and two in the second. At Glasgow, arts students normally take five subjects over two years, social scientists six, and natural scientists three. The structure of 'vocational' [*sic*] degrees at Edinburgh (divinity, law, medicine) is different again (*source:* Institutional Prospectuses). A perusal of the curricula in institutions in other parts of the UK would probably reveal just as much variation in the fine detail of the system.

6   International comparisons are frequently used as a yardstick in discussions of the size of the UK system and its possible expansion, and both DES *Statistical Bulletin* 4/87 and OECD *Education in OECD Countries* (1988) provide some useful measures. However, such comparisons are tricky for several reasons. First, a good deal depends on the age at which one makes the comparison; for example, a higher proportion of 19-year-olds are enrolled in education in Germany than in the USA (Squires 1989a), but by the age of 20 the order is reversed. Secondly, the distinction between full- and part-time study is by no means as sharp in some countries as it is in the UK. As many as one-third of French and two-thirds of Italian higher education students are involved in some kind of employment; but they may retain full-time registration because tuition fees are low and registration brings fringe benefits in terms of travel, entertainment, meals, etc. In the USA too, working during or through college is quite common, although it has not been shown to have any clear academic benefits (Stacey *et al.* 1988). However, as Cerych (SRHE 1983) notes, the existence of *de facto* part-timers in other countries may contribute to a relative over-estimate of the size of those systems, and make the UK system appear relatively smaller than it really is. Thirdly, much higher proportions of those who initially enrol for degrees in the UK actually graduate than in some countries. This is because the UK system selects mainly at entry, whereas on the continent, partly for constitutional reasons, entry to higher education is relatively easier, but more students fail or are 'cooled out' along the way. Thus while the UK system enrols a lower proportion of the relevant age-group at entry than most of the OECD countries, it actually graduates a comparable or higher percentage than many: 144 per thousand of the relevant age-group as compared to 155 in Australia, 134 in Denmark, 120 in Germany, 154 in France, 146 in Belgium (1985 figures except for Germany 1984) (OECD 1988, table 5.5). The figures for Japan and the USA are higher, but these cases raises the problem of comparing levels of achievement, and in particular whether some of the work in the Japanese two-year colleges and US Community Colleges is not comparable with some courses in the UK *further* education sector, e.g. BTEC Higher National or even National courses. Those who argue for the expansion of UK higher education to something approaching North American levels of participation are thus basing their case on dubious comparisons, although it is perhaps as much the flexibility of the American system, and the impression that it seeks to include rather than exclude (especially with adults and under-represented groups), as size *per se* that people find attractive. However,

Astin (1977) argues that the more accessible parts of the US system have less impact on students in certain ways; and there is the quite separate case for the expansion of technical/vocational education in this country to be considered (see Chapter 3, note 2).

7 This is partly because of the way some departments were originally formed in the polytechnics and colleges, assembling the multidisciplinary resources that were already there rather than starting from a single discipline base. But it also reflects the fact that the basic curriculum units in the CNAA sector are the course and the programme, whereas in the universities the unit is often assumed to be the subject or discipline. There seems to be no consistent difference of usage as between discipline and subject in either sector, and hence I have used the words interchangeably, but the common addition of the term 'studies' (i.e. French Studies rather than French) in the polytechnics and colleges may reflect a less purely mono-disciplinary approach. However, as always, one cannot read too much into labels.

8 How typical is the distribution in Table 1.5 of other industrialized countries? Comparisons are difficult to make because subjects and levels of qualification are classified differently in different countries. DES *Statistical Bulletin* 4/87 (Table 6) gives the percentage of all qualifications for seven subject groups in seven countries for the early 1980s. The UK pattern seems comparable to that in at least some other countries, e.g. Science (France 16%; Germany 7%; UK 14%); Engineering (France 12%; Germany 15%; UK 16%); Law/Business/Social Studies (France 29%; Germany 18%; UK 25%). However, as regards Engineering, Prais (1989) calculates that at the Masters/'enhanced' level, the UK produces about half the German total and one-third of the French, and at Bachelor's level, almost as many as France but only two-thirds as many as Germany. However, he points out that the UK falls short mainly at the craft/technician level.

9 These pages draw heavily on two previous studies I have made of mature access (Squires 1981b) and 16–19 education (Squires 1989a), where I have spelled out some of the ideas at more length. Even so, I recognize the difficulty of generalizing about the situation in both sectors, which are extremely complex and variegated in their own right, and in particular of distinguishing between apparent educational or training opportunities and actual patterns of enrolments; in the OECD study I draw the distinction between formal access and real accessibility. However, at the risk of simplification here, I think it is important to attempt to relate the undergraduate curriculum to what comes before and goes after and to see it in the context of the rest of post-school education.

2

The Curriculum as Knowledge

'The cow is there', said Ansell, lighting a match and holding it out over
the carpet. No one spoke. He waited till the end of the match fell off.
Then he said again, 'She is there, the cow. There, now.'
'You have not proved it,' said a voice.
'I have proved it to myself.'
'I have proved to myself that she isn't,' said the voice. 'The cow is *not*
there.' Ansell frowned and lit another match.

E. M. Forster, *The Longest Journey*

Debates about the nature and structure of knowledge can seem incurably
rarefied, the preserve of a certain species of philosopher or the indulgence
of earnest and callow undergraduates, like those in the opening of Forster's
novel. Certainly, one does not overhear such debates every day in the
senior common room or students' union, and any analysis of the curriculum as knowledge is likely to appear remote from the priorities and
concerns of the average lecturer or student. But it is not. Assumptions
about the nature and structure of knowledge are built into the language of
higher education policy, the statistics of higher education, the structure of
institutions, the identity of academic professions, the planning of courses,
and the methods and styles of teaching and learning.

It has already been observed that the statistics on higher education group
subjects and courses in certain ways, and this is true not only of DES data,
but other sources, such as the NAB and USR classifications (the latter
recently revised), or the transbinary database being established under the
aegis of the CNAA (Bourner 1984). Such classification is inevitable but
problematic. Perhaps the most familiar grouping is the broad division of all
courses into 'arts' and 'science'. Despite the publicity (and acrimony)
surrounding the 'two cultures' debate in the early 1960s (Snow 1964; Leavis
and Yudkin 1962), the distinction is implicit rather than overt in Robbins
(1963), although the worries about the intake of maths/science-based
students show through in several sections (see, for example, Robbins 1963,

Table 45). However, the report is also concerned with the balance between science and *technology*, noting the relative emphasis on the first in the UK compared to other countries (Robbins 1963, Table 40) and suggesting ways of upgrading the latter. The arts/science distinction is more central to the 1985 Green Paper, particularly in the discussion of 'subject balance'. It is worth noting too that DES statistics sometimes single out 'science' enrolments, implying that this is an important and distinguishable category (see, for example, DES *Statistical Bulletin* 14/86, Table 7).

There are several facets to the arts/science distinction. In other tables in the 1985 Green Paper on staff/student ratios (A11 and A12), the DES distinguishes between arts, science and clinical medicine courses in the universities, but between 'lab based', 'class based' and art and design in the polytechnics. In terms of staff–student ratios and teaching costs and patterns, the distinction seems to be the essentially practical and administrative one of laboratory-based *vs* library-based studies rather than anything more abstract. However, the frequent references to mathematics or numeracy in this connection suggest that the arts/science distinction may also to some extent be a maths/non-maths one, although no doubt some economists and psychologists are more numerate than some engineers and biologists, and numeracy tends nowadays to refer, however inaccurately, to computing as well as mathematics.

The most obvious way of interpreting the arts/science distinction is in terms of the kinds of knowledge involved: broadly speaking, 'arts' refers to humanities subjects and social sciences (although the 1985 Green Paper restricts the latter to 'non-vocational social studies'), and 'science' comprises mathematics, the natural sciences and applied sciences including medicine. The value of such a simple dichotomy is questionable. It lumps together subjects which are in some ways profoundly dissimilar, and erodes distinctions which may in themselves be significant not only conceptually but in terms of policy. For example, the general association of mathematics with 'science' may disguise its potential in relation to other subjects; and the whole question of the relationship between science and technology in the UK has been the subject of a lively debate in the last decade.[1]

Nor does the arts/science distinction make much sense in terms of graduate employment, if it is assumed that the distinction is based on a simple non-vocational/vocational one or 'non-relevant/relevant' one. Evans (1971) properly defines vocational education as being that education which makes a person *more* employable in one occupation than others. For example, DES *Statistical Bulletin* 1/86 (Table 4) gives the percentages of higher education graduates believed unemployed six months after completing their courses in 1979 and 1984, for nine groups of subjects. While the table shows that the worst graduate unemployment in 1984 was among the arts (other than languages) group, it also shows that scientists were more likely to be unemployed than either social studies or language graduates (social studies here includes business, accountancy and law). What is even more striking is the variation within the various subject groups. In 1984, the six-month unemployment rate for electrical/ electronic engineers was 4.2 per cent, but that for chemical engineers 11.1 per cent; 9.9 per cent for physicists but 21.9 per cent for zoologists; 11.4 per cent for economists but 18.4 per cent for sociologists; 9.3 per cent for French graduates but 15.1 per cent for Russian graduates. Even in the professional/vocational group, librarians were four times more likely to be unemployed than architects.

The validity of such first destination statistics as a general measure of graduate employment will be discussed in Chapter 3, and it is important to note that in this case they did not cover the colleges/institutes of higher education, which produce significant numbers of 'arts' graduates who have relatively high unemployment rates. Nevertheless, such figures demonstrate the bluntness of the arts/science distinction in terms of graduate employment.

The structure of knowledge in higher education is, however, not only implied by broad notions such as arts, science and subject balance; it is embodied in the very structure of institutions and the academic professions. This fact becomes clear if one imagines an institution called The Anarchic University or Polytechnic (some academics might think it is a fair description of their own). In such a place, staff would be appointed not to this or that department or faculty, but simply to the institution. They would be responsible for teaching what they liked to whom they liked. They could call their courses whatever they wanted, and make them as long or short as they wished. Students, likewise, would simply be admitted to the institution; they would not belong to a department or faculty. They could study what they chose, in the order they chose, and there would be no distinction between different years, or levels of course. As long as they passed the necessary assessments for each course, they would get their degree at the end of three years.

Even if such an institution were established, it is unlikely that it would remain truly anarchic for long. Staff would begin to cluster in groups, perhaps because they needed common equipment and facilities, perhaps because they discovered common ground in what they taught. Some such groups would become more permanent, establish certain physical and academic territories, begin to call themselves by a common title, and start to defend these against 'outsiders' with vigour and cunning. Students also might begin to cluster in little sub-cultures, small tribes united by a common interest which in due course would become institutionalized and formalized. These groups might enter into semi-permanent contracts with academics who had similar interests, and develop rules about who could and could not take part in a 'course' in a particular 'subject' and how that 'course' should be conducted. Some criteria and methods for 'assessing' and 'accrediting' what had been learned would gradually emerge, serving to validate the teaching contract, regulate entry to the emerging 'discipline' and generally build up its identity and status. No doubt, in the fullness of time, a structured institution would emerge, with all the rituals and

Table 2.1   Faculty and School structures

University of Oxford (faculties)
Anthropology and Geography
Biological and Agricultural Sciences
Clinical Medicine
Education
English Language and Literature
Fine Art
Law
Literae Humaniores
Mathematics

Medieval and Modern Languages
Modern History
Music
Oriental Studies
Physical Sciences
Physiological Sciences
Psychological Studies
Social Studies
Theology

University of Edinburgh (faculties)
Arts
Divinity
Law
Medicine
Dentistry

Music
Science and Engineering
Social Sciences
Veterinary Medicine

University of Bristol (faculties)
Arts
Science
Medicine
Engineering

Law
Social Sciences
Education

University of East Anglia (schools)
English and American Studies
Biological Sciences
Chemical Sciences
Information Systems
Mathematics and Physics

Environmental Sciences

Law
Economic and Social Studies
Development Studies
Education
Modern Languages and European
   History
Art History and Music

University of Reading (faculties)
Letters and Social Sciences
Science

Agriculture and Food
Urban and Regional Studies

University of Loughborough (schools)
Engineering
Pure and Applied Science

Human and Environmental Studies
Education and Humanities

Manchester Polytechnic (faculties)
Art and Design
Community Studies and Education
Hollings (clothing, food, catering)

Humanities, Law and Social Science
Management and Business
Technology

City of London Polytechnic (faculties)
Accounting and Finance

Administration and Language Studies

Computing Mathematics and Allied
   Studies
Law

Table 2.1—continued

Arts	Life and Environmental Sciences
Business Economics and Social Studies	Physical Sciences and Technology

Buckinghamshire College of Higher Education (schools)

Art and Design Furniture and Timber	Humanities Education and Social Science
Building	Management Studies and Languages
Business Studies	Science and Environmental Studies
Engineering	

South Glamorgan Institute of Higher Education (faculties)

Art and Design	Science
Business and Liberal Studies	Technology
Education	

Source: Institutional prospectuses

regulations, and all the academic-territorial demarcations, conflicts and ambiguities, which typify the modern university, polytechnic or college.[2]

However, such a fantasy serves to show just how structured contemporary institutions of higher education are, and how far such structures imply structures of knowledge. It is taken for granted that an institution will be sub-divided into faculties, schools, departments, units and centres; but the epistemological implications of such subdivisions are rarely examined explicitly. Table 2.1 lists the faculty or school structures of a number of institutions. No doubt such structures reflect not only assumptions about the structure of knowledge, but more mundane matters such as the existing groupings of staff, the physical location of sites, historical accident and the current pressures to retrench and regroup. But once one starts looking at such headings, questions arise. If there is a faculty of science and one of applied science why is there not a faculty of applied social science as well as a faculty of social science? Why are engineering, medicine and agriculture not all grouped together as applied sciences? What is or are liberal studies? What kind of knowledge is involved in development studies or urban and regional studies? What is the difference between social science and social studies, or between arts and humanities, or humanities and letters? Or between arts and art?

And when one thinks of individual subjects, why is mathematics typically in the science faculty when it is not a science? Should one speak of biological science or sciences? Why is law sometimes a faculty in its own right, and sometimes a department within a faculty? Why is history, which is clearly a social *subject*, not a social science? Why do the USR undergraduate statistics have two headings each for psychology and geography, one in the natural sciences and one in the social sciences? What kind of subject is geography?

How does it relate to environmental sciences? Why can one sometimes get a B.A. in economics, and sometimes a B.Sc.? Where does architecture belong? And what about computing? Do languages belong inherently to the arts? Is business studies a subject or a collection of subjects? And why should philosophy not be in every faculty?

Such questions seem both searching and naive, searching because they open up a Pandora's box of issues about the nature and structure of knowledge, naive because they are not usually asked, and doubtless cannot be answered, in quite such a simple way. Nevertheless, any account of the undergraduate curriculum has to address such issues, not because the questions must be asked, but because they have *already* been answered – in the institutional, professional and curricular structures that exist – and these answers must be examined.[3] The problem is to come up with an analysis and structure which is not only reasonably clear and self-consistent in terms of concepts of knowledge, but which maps on to and helps to explain the curricular structures that are already in place.

The boundaries of higher education

The first demarcation is between what is and is not 'higher education'; this constitutes the general boundary within which knowledge and curricula are structured. That boundary is itself by no means clear, and is continually being tested, but certain criteria seem to be involved.

First, the curriculum should be based on some body or bodies of knowledge. This in itself involves several things. To begin with, it implies that the curriculum is some advance on pre-theoretical or commonsense knowledge (Berger and Luckmann 1971), treating as problematic what is normally taken for granted.[4] Secondly, it implies some notion of rationality and explicability (Dearden *et al.* 1972), although Schilling (1986) draws a distinction between theoretical rationality and practical rationality. And, thirdly, there is the expectation that the body of knowledge is in some sense developmental or cumulative, though this notion is perhaps easier to relate to the sciences and technology than the social sciences and easier to the social sciences than the arts. Although positivists treat scientific knowledge as the paradigm of all knowledge (implicit in the expression 'hard sciences'), in practice the criteria for judging the development or fruitfulness of bodies of knowledge in higher education seems to be relative to those bodies, and each field is judged largely on its own terms by those who work in it, although outsiders may have other and sometimes more sceptical views. The more organized the body of knowledge appears to be, the more distinct its academic identity, and the more likely it is to be called a 'discipline'. Disciplines which exist only at the intersection of other disciplines may be regarded as merely derivative or parasitic, and their very identity doubted or denied (Albrow 1986).

Secondly, while such knowledge may involve certain skills, it should not merely be a matter of *skill*. 'Skill' is itself an elusive concept, but it implies a degree of routinization or automacity in the performance of perceptual-motor or cognitive tasks (Fitts and Posner 1973). Thus there is some feeling in higher education that courses which involve languages or computing *merely* as skills are not proper 'subjects'. This curricular boundary is sometimes embodied in the fine institutional distinction between a 'department' and a 'centre', though the latter can also indicate a specialized research centre. 'Proper' subjects have to ensure that even if they involve skills, they are not based on them. Historically, engineering has had to distance itself from the sound of metal-bashing, and agriculture has become fiercely scientific and managerial; while the obvious skill element in medicine and veterinary work only comes *after* a thoroughly academic grounding (though it is sometimes pointed out rather unkindly that surgeons evolved from barbers). The same kind of criticism is sometimes levelled at newer, vocationally orientated courses in higher education (such as secretarial studies, catering or nursing) which are perceived, however inaccurately, as being largely a matter of skill acquisition. Such courses have to develop an element of 'theory' or 'analysis' in order to acquire academic legitimacy; which risks producing a counter-reaction from practitioners.

A different kind of criticism is sometimes levelled at courses in creative fields such as music, drama, art and even architecture. It is accepted that such activities are not merely a matter of skill, but questions are asked about how far the 'knowledge' in such fields is capable of being explicated and taught in an explicit rather than tacit, intuitive or mimetic manner, or how far one can develop standard or consensual criteria for judging performance. Again, such subjects typically have to develop a more 'scholarly', conceptual or abstract side in order to gain admittance to and status within the academic fold, although to some extent they can isolate themselves from other faculties and departments – art and design in the polytechnics and colleges often seem to be states within a state, enjoying an autonomy underpinned by their separate location on inherited art college sites. The tension within such subjects between 'theory' and 'practice' remains. But the existence of such fields within the undergraduate curriculum is interesting not least because it raises some of the basic epistemological and educational questions in a particularly sharp form; questions which may have caused some of the digestive problems which the CNAA has had with courses in art and design.

The third aspect of the boundary of higher education is that it should be *higher*. This implies a level of studies which is clearly beyond that which pertains in the schools or non-advanced further education. The term also carries with it certain élite connotations, and quickly generates references to 'standards' and 'excellence'. As we noted in Chapter 1, level is an elusive concept, difficult to objectify without formal procedures of initial admission and final assessment. The main doubts about level and standards in higher education probably relate to new or interdisciplinary courses for which the criteria are not well established, or courses which have atypical entrants (e.g. 'unqualified' mature students) or which are not assessed in conventional ways (e.g. with a heavy reliance on course or project work rather than unseen examinations).

The general 'boundary maintenance' around higher education goes beyond these broad criteria to do with bodies of knowledge, skill and level. Historically, higher education has often seemed reluctant to admit new fields of study and enquiry; witness the problems faced by the natural sciences and professional fields in nineteenth-century Oxbridge, or by the social sciences in the twentieth century. Albrow (1986) has questioned what he calls the 'myth of the heroic struggle' in sociology, but it seems clear that many disciplines had to fight hard to gain entry and become established, especially where they appeared to threaten the hegemony of existing disciplines, as English and modern languages did with classics, the social sciences with history, and now perhaps computing with mathematics. But as Church (1978) has noted, even modern history was accepted only as 'half a degree' initially in conjunction with law, and law itself was slow to become established inside, rather than outside, the higher education system (Twining 1987).

Such struggles have both a positive and a negative side. In one way, they represent little more than the attempts of established disciplines to retain market share in a situation of academic and economic scarcity. In times of expansion, developments can be additive, and it is easier for new subjects to become institutionally – as distinct from academically – accepted (doubts can linger for a long time). However, now that the resources for higher education – both for research and teaching – are limited or declining, more money for one department often means less for another. Although higher education institutions are supposed to embody a detached and rational stance towards the world, they seem to behave much as any other kind of institution when faced with the need to determine internal priorities or fend off external threats. Perhaps because they are relatively loose in conventional management terms, with a good deal of devolved power and individual discretion, they seem relatively 'tight' in normative terms, held together more by values than by structures (Becher and Kogan 1980); indeed, they may constitute an interesting organizational example of the 'simultaneous loose–tight properties' described by Peters and Waterman (1982). It is not surprising, therefore, that those norms sometimes turn into dogma, which pose an internal, as distinct from an external, threat to academic freedom. Because of the intimate and informal way in which the system operates, academics can put one another under a good deal of pressure, whereas they can often find ways of coping with or deflecting external demands.

In another way, however, the difficulties experienced by new courses or fields in gaining acceptance are functional and desirable. It takes time for the validity or fruitfulness of any academic development to become clear, and too rapid a response to intellectual fashions could leave institutions with an embarrassing residue of dubious courses, which once installed are difficult to dislodge. The history of 'communications' as a field of study is perhaps a case in point. This was much in vogue in the 1960s, due not only to the fashionable ideas of Marshall McLuhan, but the more serious earlier work by Wiener (1948) and Shannon and Weaver (1949), but as time has passed doubts have grown not so much about its existence, but rather whether it does not constitute two distinct fields of machine and human communication, for which information theory *cannot* provide a unifying paradigm. Similar doubts were expressed about the study of the environment, which took off about the same time, but this seems to have gained a much firmer academic foothold, despite the fact that such courses range from the physical to the social with, as one CRAC Degree Course Guide put it, almost nothing in common between these two extremes. The general growth of awareness of environmental problems may have provided a problem-centred focus which helps to overcome any sense of theoretical looseness.

The mere passage of time, however, seems of itself to help legitimize fields of study, perhaps as much through growing indifference as acceptance. The study of the discipline does not often include a study of its own academic evolution; indeed, one suspects than an ahistorical attitude is sometimes projected by lecturers, as if the discipline had always existed in some vague Platonic sense, and could not possibly not have been there. (Of course, the history of the discipline can be used not to question it, but to try to establish the canon, and to legitimate authority based on it.) Institutional and professional continuity seems to allow established disciplines to contain epistemological doubts or crises which might kill off the fledgling. For example, one wonders if the doubts about the unity of geography are any less profound than those that afflict environmental science, but geography has been around for much longer and has developed powerful institutional, professional and curricular structures, not least in the schools. Such structures also seem to provide a kind of elementary momentum in periods where a discipline is in the doldrums, and not a great deal is happening at the research level. Or in the end the crisis may become a fact of life.

There are thus general if disputed boundaries to the undergraduate curriculum as currently conceived. It should be based on or at least draw from coherent bodies of knowledge which go beyond mere skill and are capable of being explicated and taught at a high level. Within such broad parameters, the curriculum is worked and fought out in terms of the structures of disciplines, fields and courses. It is not possible here to attempt to unravel the many strands of thought and practice that have historically influenced the contemporary curriculum in this way, but it may be useful to refer briefly to some of them before going on to consider the current pattern.

The structures of knowledge

Much of the writing on education and the structure of knowledge refers not to higher education but to the schools, and in particular to the concept of general education at the secondary level. This makes it less relevant than it might be here, partly because the undergraduate curriculum is relatively more specialized than the secondary school one, and partly because distinctions or dimensions which are important in higher education – for example, between the pure and the applied – are less so in the schools. Nevertheless, there are certain major figures who stand behind curriculum thinking at both levels. Plato's theory of knowledge, as elaborated in the *Republic*, seems an inescapable point of departure. As Schwab (1964) has pointed out, one of the features of Plato's scheme is that it does not primarily classify knowledge in terms of what it is of or about but in terms of its quality – its degrees of reality. Thus the physical, biological or social can all be apprehended or known as images, things, hypothetical ideas or real ideas, with each level of knowing more real than the previous one. These different 'levels' of knowledge in turn involve different states of mind in the knower: conjecture, belief, understanding and pure reason. There is thus an interaction between the nature of knowledge and the process of thought, a notion which, according to Schwab, underpins modern curricular concepts such as problem solving, concept formation and enquiry, and leads to a general emphasis on 'process' rather than 'content'.[5] This is a distinction which has been at the heart of a good deal of post-war curricular reform in the schools both in the USA and the UK (see, for example, Bruner 1960), and which will be explored further in due course. The influence of Plato, though difficult to exhume from the centuries of interpretation, seems to relate more to the 'process' and 'quality' of studies than to their 'object' or 'content', though it is worth noting the paradigmatic nature of mathematics and the primacy of philosophy in his scheme of things.

The other major Greek influence, Aristotle, classified all thought into the theoretical, practical or productive, concerned broadly with knowing, doing and making (Ross 1928; pp. 993b, 1025b). Mathematics and the natural sciences constitute examples of the first, ethics and politics of the second, and fine arts and engineering the third. We seem to have lost the distinction between the second and third, which seems to depend on the existence of an identifiable artefact in the latter case. But although Lobkowicz (1967) cautions us against assuming that Aristotle's distinction between theory and practice is similar to today's usage, and suggests that it was as much a matter of the context as the content of knowledge – types of life as well as types of thought – the dichotomy is still very much with us. It is not, however, as clear-cut in this country as it is on the continent. Although one does find parts of courses labelled 'theory' or 'practice' in some subjects, more often the contrast is attenuated, perhaps by an often unconscious empiricism.

The medieval period sometimes attracts people who are looking for some general structure for the undergraduate curriculum which goes beyond a mere aggregation of subjects (see, for example, MacCabe's 1982, proposals for a 'modern trivium'). In medieval times, the curriculum was divided into the *trivium* of the three verbal arts (grammar, rhetoric and logic or dialectic) and the *quadrivium* of the four mathematical arts (arithmetic, music, geometry and astronomy) (Wagner 1983). The central position of theology as the 'queen' of disciplines was paralleled in later centuries by the similar position occupied by philosophy in Scottish universities (Davie 1961). The generally utilitarian function, if not rationale of medieval universities (Cobban 1975), is acknowledged even by those such as Veblen (1957, p. 3), who argued that the best principles for academic endeavour are 'an Idle curiosity, and the Instinct of Workmanship', and provides ammunition for Bell (1971) and others who contend that the liberal tradition is based largely on an historical myth. But the issues are complex and it is difficult in general to assess the real strength or continuity of influence of these classical or medieval models on the modern curriculum. One wonders, for example, to what extent the original distinction between theory and practice was reinforced or modified by the later Christian one between the contemplative and the active, or when and why the word 'pure' came to be used of certain types of knowledge.[6] It may be that such historical exemplars, rather like foreign comparisons, are largely used to legitimate a particular contemporary point of view, rather than constituting a real and unbroken tradition.

Subsequent centuries brought more layers of thought and tradition to ideas about the undergraduate curriculum. British empiricism, and to a lesser extent German idealism, must have entered the bloodstream of at least some subjects. Kant's distinctions between analytic and synthetic judgements and between the *a priori* and *a posteriori* are obviously important to the philosophy of knowledge, but their influence on the structure of the curriculum is not obvious, except perhaps in reinforcing the general sense that mathematics is somehow unlike all other subjects. On the other hand, the influence of Comte's *Positive Philosophy* seems to have been pervasive if often unacknowledged, and still surfaces in odd places (see Alexander 1988). Comte (Martineau 1853) proposed a hierarchy of positive sciences which classifies knowledge in terms of its objects, what it is of or about. The hierarchy begins with mathematics, and then moves up through astronomy, physics, chemistry and biology to sociology at the top. Setting aside mathematics for the moment, the different levels can be seen in terms of scale (which Hodgson 1985 neatly gives in centimetres), in terms of envelopes (Needham 1969) or perhaps best in terms of levels of organization (since physicists argue that they relate to 'all levels of scale'; Institute of Physics 1988, p. 2). Comte's hierarchy is more often expressed nowadays in terms of a spectrum running from 'hard' to 'soft' sciences (spectra are less contentious than hierarchies), but its influence is still apparent at the undergraduate level, although the picture at the postgraduate and research level in the sciences seems to be becoming ever more complex and many-faceted.[7] Probably few people would adhere strictly to Comte's scheme nowadays if it was presented to them in its original form, but nevertheless it does still seem to underpin the structure of first degree courses in the main natural sciences (physics, chemistry, biochemistry, biology) and the typical faculty demarcation between the natural and the social sciences. It does of course raise serious questions about reductionism (Peacocke 1985), although it is worth noting that reductionism between levels (e.g. from the social to the biological or from the biological to the biochemical) is different from reductionism within a given level (e.g. the psychological as against the sociological, or the sociological as against the economic), which is a matter of perspective or aspect rather than level in Comte's terms. Perhaps the confidence of physicists noted by Becher (forthcoming) has something to do with their apparent irreducibility.

Apart from the issue of reductionism, Comte's scheme raises two other major problems. The first is the place of mathematics in any scheme of 'science', a problem not only for positivism but for any theory of knowledge; as Schwab (1964) notes, mathematics is one of the perenially puzzling disciplines. The paradox is that while mathematics appears to be based on axioms rather than empirical knowledge (although some have argued that it is rooted ultimately in the 'one-twoness' of things), it has nevertheless turned out to be remarkably fruitful in enabling us to understand the physical and to a lesser extent social world; it is as if we had invented a game which turned out to be real. The second major problem with Comte's positivism lies at the other end of his hierarchy, at the level of the social. Comte's scheme covers, in his own terms, what would now be regarded as the main social science disciplines, together with philosophy, theology and history. The problem comes with the arts. Comte does not ignore the arts; indeed his work ends with a call to 'aesthetic action':

> One of the least anticipated results of this working out of opinions, morals, and institutions under the guidance of positive philosophy, is the development which must take place in the modes of expressing them. For five centuries, society has been seeking an aesthetic constitution correspondent to its civilization.
>
> (Martineau 1853, p. 559)

Comte's view of the arts was primarily an instrumental one; they were to be harnessed to, and take inspiration from, the new scientific, moral and political order he proposed. Such a view implies the incorporation of the arts or humanities into the broad domain of the social or human sciences, a development which has to some extent occurred in France with the concept of *sciences humaines* and in Germany under the rubric of *Geisteswissenschaft*. However, in both countries, the creative arts also maintain a distinct existence under the headings of *Kunst, lettres* and *beaux-arts*. In this country, where the concept of science has always been the narrower one associated with the paradigm of the natural sciences, there is still in most institutions a very firm institutional demarcation between arts or humanities on the one hand and the social sciences on the other, a demarcation which will be explored later.

If Comte's positivism provides an example of the apparent continuing influence of one nineteenth-century idea on the undergraduate curriculum, the notion of a liberal education, and in particular its expression by Newman in *The Idea of a University* (initially in 1852 and later in 1873) provides another. Of course, the concept of a liberal education goes back to the Greeks, and Newman's lectures and books were only one more interpretation of an idea which as Rothblatt (1976) clearly shows has demonstrated a remarkable adaptability and longevity. Nevertheless, Newman's was an important interpretation, even if it influenced the rhetoric of higher education more than the reality (Bell 1971; see also Slee's 1986, interpretation in relation to the growth of history as a discipline). However, there were important differences between the classical and nineteenth-century forms of the idea. In its classical form, the concept of liberal education was grounded in the doctrine of metaphysical realism: that there was a Reality, that that Reality could be known, and that the purpose of education was to lead people towards that knowledge. Such knowledge was not only desirable in itself, but would liberate and transform the life of the individual, and through him [*sic*], the life of the society, since such individuals would or should be the appropriate leaders or rulers, a notion which would become democratized in modern ideologies of liberal education to include 'leaders' in any walk of life (especially the working-class) and indeed the ordinary, democratic citizen.

However, as the belief in metaphysical realism declined in the nineteenth century in favour of more nominalist, relativist or generally hesitant views of knowledge, the concept of a liberal education seemed to lose its firm epistemological foundation and become not so much a theory of knowledge as a theory of ignorance. There could be little agreement any longer on the nature of reality or truth, but this did not prevent a wide if vague consensus about the undesirability of dogmatism, superstition, parochialism, unexamined assumptions and unthinking lives. Such ideas have probably influenced the process of teaching more than the content of courses in higher education, although they had a direct bearing on the original terms of reference of university extra-mural departments. It is sometimes argued that certain subjects are better vehicles for a liberal education than others, because they are concerned with the human rather than merely the natural, or are reflexive rather than merely instrumental; hence the term 'liberal' has been most often associated with the arts, and in this century social sciences, though it has been used of some science courses as well (e.g. 'Liberal Studies in Science'). However, once one begins to argue the toss about the liberal value of various academic subjects, it becomes difficult to exclude any of them: Do not medicine and engineering raise profound questions about life? About society? About what is good or beautiful or true? And do not such disciplines go further and focus such questions in real-life judgements, decisions and actions? Compared to the USA, where there is a long tradition of debate about general education (Squires 1976; Gaff 1983), the main influence of the concept of a liberal education in British higher education has probably been on the *enactment* of the curriculum – on the methods and styles of teaching, the role models and relationships involved, and the general learning ethos and environment. This emphasis reappears in the 'process' justifications of higher education, advanced both by its providers and consumers, in terms of training the mind, learning to think, developing autonomy and so on, notions which are to some extent 'subject-free', and which will be explored further in Chapter 4.

Among more recent writing on knowledge and the school curriculum, two of the most interesting examples are Hirst's discussion of 'forms of knowledge' and Phenix's 'realms of meaning.' Again, it is not possible here to do these justice in the space available. Hirst (1969, 1974) divides knowledge into seven or so distinct or irreducible forms: mathematics, the physical sciences, the human sciences and history, literature and the fine arts, morals, religion, and philosophy. His later work has tended to modify the distinctness of each of these, as well as exploring problems which arise with particular forms of knowledge; for example, the fact that the social sciences may involve truths of several different logical kinds, or the difficulties of explicating the kind of knowledge embodied in literature and the arts. While Hirst's analysis addresses the nature and structure of knowledge in general, and can be related to the undergraduate curriculum, it has nevertheless been debated mainly in terms of the schools.

Likewise, Phenix (1964) identifies a number of basic categories, but his approach differs from Hirst's in two important respects. First, he takes 'meaning' rather than knowledge or rationality as his point of departure and, secondly, his headings are less closely related to conventional subject headings: symbolics (including language, mathematics and other non-discursive symbolic forms), empirics (natural and social sciences), aesthetics (the arts), synnoetics (personal knowledge), ethics, and synoptics (history, religion, philosophy). The use of these somewhat esoteric labels may obviate the difficulties of using terms which have a common and often imprecise meaning for a precise purpose – a problem which has afflicted the understanding of Hirst's work – but it has also limited their circulation, and outside the rather enclosed world of curriculum theory, Phenix's work is largely unknown. The relationship between the two approaches has been discussed by Hirst (1974), and both writers have stimulated further thinking in the field of curriculum theory, particularly in relation to the schools (see Richards' bibliography, 1984).

But what of higher education? Concern with the nature and structure of knowledge is a continuing if not always explicit aspect of many subjects, but few discussions go beyond the single discipline or field. Oakeshott's (1962) distinction between technical and practical knowledge, which itself echoes Aristotle, has been used by Eraut (1985) in a discussion of professional knowledge. Plumb announced a 'crisis in the humanities' as long ago as 1964. An issue of *New Universities Quarterly* in 1980 [Vol. 35(1)] contained several papers on the arts. The Leverhulme study also devoted one volume specifically to the arts in higher education (Robinson 1982), but although this contained much interesting material, particularly on social and anthropological views of the arts, it did little to establish their epistemological base. The Scottish challenge mounted by Davie (1986) continues. The OECD (1972; Levin and Lind 1985) volumes on interdisciplinarity inevitably raise questions about the nature of disciplines. Levine and Weingart (1973) and Levine (1978) have provided accounts of the undergraduate curriculum in the USA, and Boyer (1987) a contemporary discussion. Bergendahl (1984) has edited a colloquium which includes foreign as well as Swedish speakers (see, for example, Scott 1984b, and Silverman 1984), and Scott (1984a, 1987) has also advanced more general analyses. There have of course been innumerable discussions of developments within particular disciplines. But the two most systematic modern contributions to our general thinking about the undergraduate curriculum are the recent paper by Donald (1986) and the book by Becher (1989a), which itself reviews some previous attempts.

Of the two, Donald's approach is the more abstract. Knowledge is categorized in terms of four parameters: the nature of the concepts involved, the logical structure of the discipline, the truth criteria used, and the methods employed. Each of these can be analysed further. For example, concepts are analysed for their generality or degree of abstraction; and logical structure is a matter of either similarity or dependency relationships, which in turn can be sub-divided into associational, functional and hierarchical, or procedural, logical or causal. The paper is rigorous and thought-provoking, but it does not map easily on to existing curricular structures, and the very complexity of the model may limit its diffusion in higher education.

Becher is more concerned to develop ways of analysing the differences between disciplines which will allow him to explore their particular 'cultures'. He reviews various previous attempts to categorize different kinds of knowledge, some of which have been mentioned above, and devotes particular attention to Pantin's (1968) distinction between restricted and unrestricted sciences, Biglan's (1973) three dimensions of hard/soft, pure/applied, and life/non-life and Kolb's (1981) typology of abstract/concrete and active/reflective. Drawing on such work, Becher arrives at a four-part typology of hard/pure, hard/applied, soft/pure and soft/applied. Although he stops short of locating particular disciplines within this typology, one can see that for example the natural sciences would tend to be hard and pure, engineering would be hard and applied, the arts are likely to be soft, and so on. However, he also stresses the differences that exist within disciplines, for example, physical geography may be placed on the hard side of the line, but human geography on the soft side, and in any case the line itself is not sharp. He argues that most individual subject areas themselves turn out on closer examination to contain a diversity of research styles and epistemological characteristics.

A rapid review such as this of theories of knowledge and the curriculum cannot hope to do justice to the various concepts and models, and risks inducing a kind of conceptual vertigo. It does, however, serve to establish two points. The first is the basic realization that knowledge can be 'carved up' in different ways, depending on what criteria or parameters one employs.[8] It is easy for us to slip into the assumption that the institutional, professional and curricular structures with which we are familiar are somehow natural or inevitable. In any case, it is usually easier to think in concrete terms than abstract ones; easier to reify knowledge and turn it into a *thing*. Secondly, it is significant that several recent writers – such as Kolb, Donald and Becher – have moved away from unidimensional classifications of knowledge to multi-dimensional typologies, which seem to map on to the undergraduate curriculum better. The model that follows involves three such dimensions.

Object, stance and mode

The most obvious dimension of the curriculum as knowledge is the 'object' of study, i.e. what the course is about (see Figure 2.1). In this simple sense, we talk about a course in physics, history, medicine, music or whatever. Here, in the natural sciences, despite the complex patterns that exist at the research level, it still seems appropriate to use the broad categories identified by Comte and embodied in the nomenclature of undergraduate degrees – the physical, the chemical, the biological – while recognizing that there are gradations between these (physical chemistry, biochemistry) and foci and links within and across them (geology, biophysics, physiology or ecology). The main problem with the 'object' dimension arises when one moves beyond the biological to the social and human.

The label 'social science' has always been something of a misnomer, because in addition to the obviously collective perspectives of economics, sociology, anthropology and politics, it also includes a concern with the individual, in particular in some branches of psychology. The term 'human' might therefore be preferred, and is more common in some other countries, but that brings another problem, namely the relationships between the concepts of 'human science', 'humanities' and 'arts'. Setting aside for the moment the human science/humanities distinction we need to decide whether there is any real difference between 'humanities' and 'arts'. Institutional labels would suggest not; it seems to be largely a matter of historical accident whether a university, polytechnic or college has a faculty/school of humanities or one of arts (or even letters). As noted earlier, we should not perhaps take labels too seriously.

However, there lies a problem beneath the labels. There is a strong tradition in the UK, deriving partly from Matthew Arnold, that the arts are essentially *human* in their capacity to develop human sensibility, and moral and social awareness. In this sense, the modern humanities were taking on the mantle worn by classics in earlier centuries, as a central cultural frame of reference. On the other hand, there is also the view that art-objects are

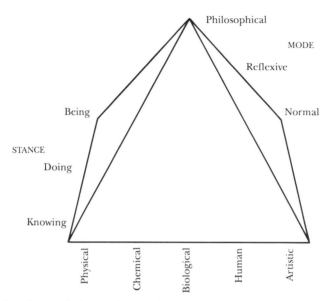

Figure 2.1   The curriculum as knowledge.

different from all other human artefacts and phenomena in that judgements about them have to refer partly to the medium and form of that artefact. In this sense, a novel or symphony has to be judged partly in relation to the overall system of language or music, and to the specific 'grammar' of that particular linguistic or musical form. Words such as system and grammar suggest something remote and rational, but as Abbs (1989) points out, they constitute 'a fundamental sensuous mode of human response and interpretation'. They are intimately bound up with sense perception and consciousness. The conflict between these two views of the arts currently takes the form, in the case of English, of the struggle between those academics who represent the 'humanistic' Arnoldian tradition, often as interpreted by Leavis (1952), and the more recent continental influences, such as structuralism, which emphasize the systemic or formal properties of art-objects (Welch 1987). (The work of Hoggart 1957 and others on popular culture seems to me to constitute largely a variant of the first tradition, though with some Marxist influence in some cases.)

The issue here is whether the arts can be subsumed under the 'humanities' or whether they require their own heading, as being different in kind from other human phenomena. The emphasis on medium, form and aesthetic grammar would suggest that, whatever their 'content' or 'effect', they are somehow different; at the simplest level, saying that a history or sociology book is badly written is different from saying that a novel is badly written. Of course, it may be objected that the very notion of an 'art-object' is a cultural construct peculiar to certain traditions, but that notion is so deeply embedded in Western culture that it is difficult to dismiss it. Provisionally, therefore, Figure 2.1 distinguishes between the 'human' and the 'artistic'.

The work of Becher and others, however, suggests the need for a second dimension in classifying curricula. It is not enough to say what a course is about; physicists and engineers, biologists and doctors, economists and managers may each be concerned with the same phenomena but for different reasons and in different ways. This difference is usually formulated in terms of a difference in knowledge (pure as against applied, theoretical as against practical) but it may be more accurate to see it as a difference of *stance*.[9] It is a matter of intention or angle rather than data. We can distinguish broadly between the intention of knowing, and the intention of doing, which correspond roughly to the conventional distinction between pure and applied. To say that the stance is one of knowing does not necessarily imply a belief in 'objectivity'; the process may be thought of as a hermeneutic, interpretative one in which objective knowledge is not possible. However, the idea of 'knowing' does suggest a concentration on the nature of the object or phenomenon. By contrast, the stance of doing is concerned with acting upon those phenomena to bring about change, although the capacity to react or respond to phenomena may be a precondition of successful action in some cases, for example in the diagnosis of human problems and situations, as Ryan (1984) points out in relation to medicine. Nevertheless, responsiveness or sensitivity in such instances is only a means to the end, which is to effect change of some kind.

The distinction between knowing and doing is by no means clear-cut, but the real problem arises with the third stance identified in Figure 2.1, that of 'being'. Being is rejected by many linguistic philosophers as a meaningless or misleading term, a conceptual chimera; but it is central to the phenomenological tradition. The problem is that both 'knowing' and 'doing' seem largely to exclude the knower or doer from the equation; they tend to excise the subjective, and direct attention away from it. Knowing typically excludes the experience of knowing, doing the sensation of doing. 'Being' in this sense is not synonymous with the self or the subject; it implies being-in-the-world, a kind of subject-objectivity. 'After all', remarked Merleau-Ponty, 'the world is around me, not in front of me' (1964, p. 59). Nor is being a passive notion, although the nature of its projects or problems is difficult to express. We can say that the purpose of knowing is truth (however conceived) and that the purpose of doing is effectiveness (Horner 1985). We could perhaps speak of coming to 'know' being, but it may be that in this case 'knowledge' is itself a metaphor. Words such as illumination, actualization and realization come to mind. Such language seems vacuous to some, but if we are to comprehend the nature of the arts in particular, being is a concept which it seems difficult to do without. It does not necessarily imply essence or totality, but merely a derestriction of the stances of knowing and doing. It does not exclude anything; but that is not to say that it can attain everything.

Two other points should be made about the notion of 'stance'. The first is that despite what was said earlier about the unique nature of art-objects, the stance of being suggests why the arts are so frequently associated with the human, and are therefore regarded as central to the 'humanities'. One can thus see gains and losses in the two broad approaches to the study of literature described by Welch (1987). The Arnoldian tradition relates art firmly to being in all its existential, moral and aesthetic modalities, but in so doing perhaps diminishes our awareness of the unique properties of the arts as arts; conversely, while the continental schools in various ways direct our attention to the formal or technical properties of the arts (even when contesting them), they perhaps risk losing the human frame of reference.[10]

Secondly, the notion of stance may help us to locate the study of mathematics, computing and language (*qua* language) in the curriculum as a whole. These three disciplines sometimes relate to the objects of study (physical, biological, human, etc.) in the lowly status of 'service courses', in which they play a limited functional role (statistics for social scientists, computing for chemists, languages for management students). Service courses, to judge by what one hears, are a frequent source of irritation on both sides, with the provider unhappy about cannibalizing or trivializing his or her discipline and the consumer complaining that the course is not geared or geared down to his or her needs.

However, mathematics, computing and language go far beyond such a service role; they are disciplines and objects of study in their own right, with an intrinsic as against merely instrumental status in the academic world. The model being offered here suggests that far from merely being tools or means, they to a large extent *constitute* our stances in and towards the world; in this sense, they lie across the base of the pyramid in Figure 2.1. There are arguments about whether we have some 'primordial' sense of the world which is in some way independent of the symbol systems we use, or to what extent our visual or aural perceptions of painting or music depend on or are penetrated by the knowledge we have through such systems. However, setting aside such issues, we can say that the very stances of knowing, doing and being are inconceivable – literally – without the symbol systems of language and mathematics. It is in this sense that one can argue that our consciousness of the world is consciousness of the symbols we use.

It may seem odd to add computing to mathematics and languages as another basic symbol system, since computing is often regarded (not least by mathematicians and linguists) as something less profound, more purely instrumental. However, its use in a wide variety of disciplines has grown dramatically in recent decades, to the point where it seems not only to be facilitating what was done before, but to be creating new possibilities. In particular, it appears to be forging links with philosophy, linguistics and psychology in what are increasingly referred to as 'cognitive sciences', and establishing itself not simply as a tool but an object of study in its own right. It would be unwise to set limits to its march.

Two dimensions of the curriculum as knowledge have now been explored: the 'objects' of study, and the stances that people can adopt in relation to those objects. The need for a third dimension arises most obviously from what may be called the problem of philosophy. Philosophy, in the undergraduate curriculum, can be regarded in two ways.[11] On the one hand, it can be seen as a discipline, indeed perhaps the oldest of all disciplines, with its own core of sometimes highly technical activities which are peculiar to it, and the normal organizational manifestations of departments, chairs, courses, degrees, and so on. However, philosophy is also closely related to many other disciplines. Science evolved out of natural philosophy (indeed the term is still sometimes used in Scotland) as did psychology. More recently, philosophy has had very close links with mathematics and artificial intelligence. There is the philosophy of science and of social science, political philosophy, aesthetics as an aspect of the arts, jurisprudence in law, and ethics impinging on a range of applied fields such as medicine and education. Degrees in such fields may include courses or options on the 'philosophy of' the field, and in a looser sense still, people may refer to any fundamental statements or questions in a field as 'philosophical'. So where does philosophy belong? And is its typical location in faculties of arts or humanities appropriate?

One useful way of looking at this problem is to recall Kuhn's notion of 'normal' science (Kuhn 1962; Lakatos and Musgrave 1970). Normal science, according to Kuhn, is science which proceeds along and within the lines that have become established as orthodox, for the moment. It aims to elaborate and refine rather than overturn; it is evolutionary rather than revolutionary. Kuhn argued that the comparatively long periods of normal science were punctuated by crises when the existing paradigms broke down and a new paradigm, and eventually orthodoxy, would become established; the Copernican revolution was a prime example of this. This theory of scientific development has been contested; others have pointed to more incremental patterns, or to cases especially in the social sciences where paradigms do not displace each other but simply accumulate as alternative perspectives. This aspect of Kuhn's argument is not at issue here. What is useful is the idea that research and study in a particular field or discipline can proceed for many people for quite long periods in a relatively routine or normal way, without continually digging up the roots. Such 'normality' can surely apply not just to the sciences, but to any discipline; it refers to the working acceptance of current assumptions and procedures. Indeed, it is difficult to see how knowledge would advance if people did not get on with 'normal' work much of the time.

However, few disciplines or academics are ever wholly 'normal'. The fundamental questions may be shelved for the moment, but they are always there; it is a matter of foreground and background rather than distinct modes of operation. Most undergraduate courses claim at least to encourage students not·only to learn, but to think about what they are learning; to challenge the assumptions, to question the questions, to consider the alternatives. If this process becomes more than sporadic, we may label it 'critical' or 'reflexive', in the sense of turning thought back on itself. There may be references to 'second-order questions' or 'meta-theories', and if the process becomes sustained and systematic, the word philosophy tends to creep in. What this suggests is a third dimension of the curriculum as knowledge, which refers to the *mode* of work, and the extent to which it is normal, reflexive or philosophical. To be sure, these are gradations not distinctions, and it is difficult to say where one ends and the other begins. But such a dimension does help to explain why philosophy can be seen both as a mode of thinking in any discipline, and also a discipline in its own right; for it is at least arguable that the 'questions about questions' in every field eventually converge·on certain basic questions and concepts which we recognize as the traditional domain and concern of the philosopher. This allows Figure 2.1 to rise up to a satisfying and unifying point, and has implications for the role of philosophy in the undergraduate curriculum which will be explored in the final chapter.[12]

Object, stance and mode are broad terms, and in the undergraduate curriculum they take more precise and concrete forms. The object of study does not usually encompass the whole physical, biological or other field, but focuses on certain phenomena, problems, aspects or themes. The physicist concentrates on the behaviour of certain particles, the economist on a particular type of firm, the literature student on a certain period or genre. Stance manifests itself in the adoption of certain approaches, methods or techniques: the experimental method of the scientist, the survey method of the sociologist, the close reading of the student of literature. Methodological arguments may reflect deeper disagreements about stance, for example between empirical sociologists and ethnomethodologists. 'Mode' may be reflected in either a course title (philosophy of, critical theory, foundations of) or in the subtle detail of teaching and learning which may assume or encourage a 'normal' or 'reflexive' process.

There are daunting epistemological problems involved in the ideas of object, stance and mode. However, Figure 2.1 does seem to clarify several aspects of the undergraduate curriculum at a more practical level. First, it allows one to see and establish broad relationships between different groups of disciplines and faculties. One can see that the natural sciences are in the main concerned with the 'knowing' of physical, chemical and biological 'objects' in a largely 'normal' or operational mode. This is not to say that the sciences are 'objective' or even that all scientists suppose them to be so, nor that they do not sometimes have an active or applied emphasis, or that they are not sometimes reflexive and even philosophical, although in practice the 'philosophy of science' seems to be marginal to the mainstream of scientific activity. Whether the stance of 'being' makes any sense in the natural sciences is an interesting question, but it is worth noting that some physicists talk of a phenomenological or holistic approach. The so-called applied sciences, such as engineering, agriculture and medicine, are concerned with much the same objects, but from a different stance: they are largely concerned with 'doing', although again this does not necessarily preclude 'theorizing' or 'philosophizing'. The social sciences embody a range of sometimes conflicting stances towards the human world. In their empirical modes, they seem concerned with 'knowing', conceptualizing, modelling and theorizing about human phenomena. However, 'applied' social sciences are ultimately concerned with doing, with action or deliberate change. And there are traditions within the social sciences which include the knower or the subjective in the equation, in the tradition of *verstehen* in sociology, in ethnomethodology, and in phenomenological psychology. The arts, as noted above, can be viewed both in terms of properties of the art-objects and in relation to the stance of being. But within the arts, and indeed within any one discipline or medium, one can distinguish the 'scholarly' emphasis on textual and historical accuracy from the more interpretative and responsive 'readings', which in turn differ from the active, creative mode of 'doing' the arts. And while work and study in all disciplines can range from the routinely normal through the critical and reflexive to the philosophical, philosophy exists as a distinct field of concerns.

The model does not provide answers to some of the curricular problems which concern us, but it may help us to frame our questions more accurately. For example, it suggests a way of looking at the relationship between science and technology which focuses not on the subject matter of the different disciplines, but rather the stance towards it and use made of it. Both scientist and engineer, biologist and doctor, chemist and agriculturist may be handling the same kind of data, but where the first intervenes in the world in order to understand it, the second has to understand the world in order to intervene in it. It is surely a simplification to see the latter simply as 'applied' sciences; they embody a different stance and intention, which may in turn generate its own 'theories of action', which will be explored in Chapter 3.

The model also goes some way to clarify the problem of the 'humanities'. It suggests that of the subjects that usually comprise the humanities, philosophy need not necessarily be identified with the humanities at all, literature and the other arts are defined by their concern with art-objects and history arguably belongs to a broader conception of 'human sciences'.[13] Such observations may help to explain the protracted sense of crisis in the humanities; but the model also offers the possibility of regrouping the traditional concerns of the humanities around the notion of 'being', if that concept can be allowed. It is worth noting that Holbrook, writing about the arts, (1980) quotes Husserl's phrase 'functionaries of mankind'.

Thirdly, the model suggests one way of accounting for the peculiar nature of mathematics, computing and language, as the disciplines which constitute our stances in and towards the world, and for the way they relate to other disciplines, both servicing them at a mundane level and pervading them at a profound level. It shows why philosophy may penetrate so many disciplines and yet remain a distinct discipline itself. It also suggests why 'interdisciplinarity' may occur not simply at the notional boundaries of contiguous disciplines, but as a subtle and often unpredictable flow of information and influence from one part of the model to another. It is not a question of disciplines and their boundaries being 'natural' or 'artificial', but rather that (inevitably perhaps) our conceptions of knowledge become overly reified in their institutional and professional structures and we need to be reminded of their fluidity within the whole epistemological space.

Disciplinary spaces

More fruitful perhaps than such broad categorizations is the implication of Figure 2.1 that it is better to think of disciplines as occupying a certain space in a universe of knowledge, rather than a certain level in a hierarchy or place on a map. That space has to be defined and defended along three dimensions, not one, and the strongest disciplines in academic terms are usually those which can indicate quite clearly what stance they adopt towards what objects and in which mode of enquiry. (Other aspects of the discipline, such as methodology and equipment and even physical location on the campus, can provide subsidiary means of self-definition.) However, the situation is always to some extent fluid, and the dimensions of the disciplinary space may change, expanding here or contracting there, sometimes under pressure from a contiguous discipline. Moreover, different stances and modes of enquiry can exist in respect of the same object, and this helps to explain why considerable ambiguities and tensions can exist *within* disciplines as well as between them. The pure economist may see himself or herself as occupying a different space from that of the applied economist; the 'scholarly' critic from the 'responsive' one; the 'objective' social researcher from the 'interpretative' one; the doctor who 'delivers' health care from the one who 'responds' to his or her patients.

The flows of information and the patterns of influence in and among the various disciplines are extremely complex. With a broad historical perspective, one can see the influence of the 'paradigm' of the natural sciences on the emerging social sciences, and also certain pressures exerted on the arts by the latter. But sometimes it is a case of a more specific influence; a concept, technique or even piece of equipment which acts as an exemplar, parallel or metaphor in another field. Notions such as quantum leap, entropy, feedback and software spread far beyond their original habitats; indeed, whole languages and ways of seeing the world spread out and colonize other fields, in the way that experimental method, rational planning models, and computer terminology have done. The spread of disciplinary languages is a measure of their relative influence, but such epistemological imperialism is not always an index of their essential academic strength and status. Physics appears a strong, fundamental discipline; computing a strong, pervasive one; history, a strong adaptable one; law, a strong self-contained one.

How do these rather abstract dimensions and headings work out in concrete terms? How does one get at the identities of and relationships between disciplines in the actual curriculum? It was mentioned in the preface that a number of written questions were put to academics as part of this study.[14] Four of these questions concerned (a) the size of the compulsory core of their discipline, (b) the boundaries of the discipline, (c) the structure of the discipline, and (d) the culture of the discipline. The purpose of these questions was to try to get some sense of the spaces occupied by each discipline, how well that space was defined, and to what extent disciplinary identity or integrity was a matter of epistemological structure (unifying theories, concepts, methods, etc.) or a more elusive matter of disciplinary 'culture', involving academic norms, ethos or styles. Some responses to such questions are cited here by way of example.

The size of the compulsory core of a discipline might tell us something about the strength of its identity, and the extent to which it constitutes an organic whole or, to use a common expression, 'seamless web'. How large was that core?

For students who specialise in economics, about ⅔ of the degree is 'core'. It could be smaller – maybe as little as ⅓.

(Economics)

100%. Could not really be modified.

(Pre-Clinical Medicine)

Approximately two-thirds. This seems to be about right.

(Music)

This is not a very easy question to answer. Approximately 95% of lecture material is compulsory core. However, do you count things like our final year project which occupies 25% of our third and final year? Students have a very wide choice of projects to select from, indeed they can suggest projects of their own.

(Engineering)

About 80%. I would hate it to get larger, but it could not be smaller because it *is* a specific professional education and training.

(Social Work)

About 20%. It is generally held that it should be larger but no agreement on enlarging it seems attainable.

(Philosophy)

95% of the degree course is devoted to compulsory subjects. We feel that this is too high, but past experience has shown that undergraduates will only apply themselves to subjects which they perceive as relevant to their future careers.

(Engineering)

30%. Could be anything 20–40%.

(Sociology)

The range in the size of the core is striking, and may reflect various factors: the 'internal logic' of the discipline, professional requirements, student attitudes, even staff shortages. Whatever the reason, it is likely that disciplines with large or strong cores are less easy to displace than ones with smaller cores. Another way of getting at the question of disciplinary spaces is to ask about the *boundaries* of the discipline. This is a complex notion in itself, because as Figure 2.1 suggests, there may be several kinds of boundaries, demarcated in different kinds of ways; and the nature of the boundaries may be as much as institutional or professional as epistemological. Nevertheless, the questions (Have the boundaries of your subject altered much in the last decade? Is it more, or less distinct from other subjects than it used to be?) produced some interesting answers:

Generally it has resisted (both academically and administratively) the challenge of other disciplines. It has been changed by the influence of sociology and anthropology but it has not surrendered its distinctiveness to them. It is a self-confident subject. 'Political history' and 'narrative', previously considered outmoded, have undergone a renaissance.

(History)

Sociology has expanded enormously over the last decade in terms of the body of significant literature. It has always had significant overlaps with Anthropology, History, Psychology, Economics, Politics, Social Geography, etc. The boundaries certainly haven't become any *more* distinct lately.

I don't think the boundaries of Business Studies have ever been particularly clear. Natural sciences and humanities are not included. There is a real blurring between Business Studies and Management Studies and there is a much greater computing/I.T. input.

The boundaries have changed markedly from a close affinity with physical science (providing an understanding of theory and explanation) to a close affinity with engineering (knowing what, and how, specifying, designing solutions to specific technical problems, and technology).

(Metallurgy and Materials Engineering)

Other responses described both change and stability in the boundaries:

> Linguistics is regarded as an 'autonomous' discipline in the mainstream tradition, a notion to which I do not subscribe. There has been in the last decade a considerable strengthening of links with philosophy, sociology, cognitive science, discourse analysis, literary criticism. Our interdisciplinary aims have always led [us] to concentrate on such links, but I think this is unusual in linguistics departments generally.

> The boundaries of physics constantly change as new discoveries are made, e.g. the discovery of new fundamental particles. However, the boundaries have not changed over centuries in terms of what is regarded as Physics. This is because Physics is a basic, probably the basic, science. It is, I think, concerned with the nature of the inanimate world – not just facts but their explanation. It is about the interaction of energy and matter, cause and effect, understanding phenomena.

> My subject [English] now incorporates a larger amount of theory – that is, questioning the nature of its own activity – than it used to do. Courses which relate English literature to other subjects are perhaps commoner than they used to be. . . . In my own department, I should say that, although some members still believe that literature is best studied in isolation, looking simply at 'the words on the page', most of us now like to contextualise it in some way, often historically, and are inclined to ask students to read some texts which are not 'literature' in the conventional sense. Most of these developments might be seen as making English *less* different, but the kinds of changes that go on in 'literary theory' are unlikely to be familiar to anyone but a philosopher.

> Although Computing Science (or Computer Science) as a field has changed dramatically in the last ten years and will continue to do so in the next ten, I do not believe its boundaries have altered significantly. It is becoming more of an engineering discipline, but numerical methods are less important, so that the range of mathematical skills required is changing. The applications of computers to other subjects have resulted in a significant commitment to computing in those subjects, but the subject of Computer Science itself remains at the centre: 'systematic approaches to the development of computer based systems (hardware and software)'. It is this general systematic approach which keeps it distinct from the application areas of computing.

The next comment presents a changing view of physics which contrasts with the earlier one which stressed its stability:

> The applications of physics have widened and continue to widen at an incredible rate. However, all the important branches of physics are now seen as engineering subjects in their own right and are often taught without much of the underlying physics. Thus undergraduate

physics is always being decapitated – once an aspect grows to be important, it is lopped off and becomes an engineering subject (electronics, semiconductor devices, fibre optics, acoustics, quantum electronics, electron microscopy, etc., etc., etc.).

The final comment emphasizes the continuing distinctness of law as a subject:

There has been very wide extension in the sense that a large number of new course options are being taught involving new specialisms. In theory one might say that the problems have always been there and we have now just started to recognise them. In general one might say that Law has become marginally less distinct from other subjects than it was in that quite a few people are doing cross disciplinary research, e.g. in law and economics and law and society. But overall it remains a pretty distinct subject.

Questions about the 'core' and 'boundary' of a discipline imply a spatial or territorial metaphor; but another way of getting at the nature of disciplines is to explore their internal structure. Again, this is a complex notion in itself, so it is hardly surprising that some respondents found it difficult to reply to the questions: Has the conceptual map of your subject changed much in the last decade? Is it more or less unified than it was? Nevertheless, again, the replies help one to identify some of the aspects of the structure and unity of a discipline:

Ours is essentially a Basic Medical Sciences course, with some emphasis on morphology and with a scientific rather than clinical approach. The conceptual map of the basic medical sciences has changed remarkably in recent years with developments in immunology, molecular genetics, biotechnology and the neurosciences, to name a few. These changes are reflected in an evolving undergraduate curriculum.

An economist painted a picture of growing unity within his subject:

There has been a progressive unification of the theory of the behaviour of individual consumers and firms (microeconomics) on the one hand and theory of the behaviour of the aggregate economy (macroeconomics) on the other. The idea of rational behaviour – or behaviour modelled as if rational – and the careful modelling of information and expectations (of future quantities or events) has become much more pervasive. There has been a continuing move in the direction of making economic theory mathematically and logically more rigorous and developing statistical methods to test and measure theory using what data is available.

Economists working within the tradition of 'political economy' might disagree with this interpretation. But such differences of interpretation are surely intrinsic to the pursuit of knowledge; they are the essence, not accidents, of academic work. For example, a lecturer in English dismissed some of the theoretical incursions referred to earlier:

> Not much change. The recent fashion for dubiously coherent theoretical approaches has made little impact, beyond occasional outbursts of rant and cant which no one takes seriously. A few university colleagues . . . have from time to time shown some loss of nerve.

An engineer took a longer view:

> I am not convinced that the 'conceptual map' of our subject has changed a lot in the last decade. Certainly over the last quarter of a century it has changed quite a lot. When engineering was first introduced into universities in a large way, then the departments bent over backwards to try to show that engineering could be taught as an academic subject. Engineers were not just people who got their hands dirty mending cars! However, recently, perhaps the conceptual basis for the teaching of engineering has shifted somewhat from that of an academic subject to a professional subject and indeed the professional institutions of engineering, and the Engineering Council have influenced a lot the ways in which the subject has grown up. For example, most engineering degrees must now be accredited by the engineering institutions and ultimately by the Engineering Council if graduates wish to become chartered engineers and members of those institutions, so the way in which courses develop is very much dictated by the whims of the engineering institutes. To some extent then the 'conceptual map of our subject' has been altered in ways beyond our control.

Another writer, responding to a general question about changes in his discipline, described a long-term cyclical or pendular motion which may suggest parallels in other subjects:

> . . . having myself graduated in Business over 40 years ago, there seems to be a remarkable cycle in which we return to particular models every few decades. The present pattern of Business Studies degrees, in many respects, reflects the state of thinking of commerce degrees of the late 30s, most of which had disappeared by or soon after 1950, in favour of a more discipline-oriented approach in which there were substantial new elements, with the appearance of sociology and politics, both of which were to acquire greater prominence. With the 60s the dominance lay in two apparently contradictory pressures; one emphasizing sociology and organizational behaviour, the other quantitative methods and the beginning of the impact of the computer/ information technology revolution. The past ten years have seen striking changes which reflect social changes. There has been a further growth in the importance of information technology, to the state where entire curricula have been revised on the assumption that

students coming up from school can programme quite complex computers within their first year. The emphasis in the teaching of economics has moved from macro-economics to an emphasis on micro-economics and in particular decision-taking at the level of the firm. This involves close connections with operations analysis. Side-by-side with this has been a greater emphasis on the link with organiz-ational behaviour and decision analysis, with a growing recognition of the importance of political processes within firms, quite apart from those around them. The so-called functional areas, such as marketing, production and personnel have given way to a more problem-centred approach, but within this there has been a notable decline in the significance accorded to industrial relations, and still more, to the field of personnel management. The new subject clusters, as they are sometimes termed, have grown in importance, such as policy studies, and there is a much greater emphasis on the development of personal and social skills as opposed to concentration on conceptualization and theoretical analysis.

(Business Administration)

Another writer on engineering distinguished between subjects and themes:

There has been a move away from the narrow field of Production Engineering into the broader field of Operations Management. . . . More use of open ended case studies is made from the second year onwards and the subjects have been unified under broad themes rather than treated as separate subjects.

Even these few quotations show that the notion of the 'map' or 'structure' of a subject is by no means straightforward, and involves not only the theoretical or conceptual unities which are referred to in the literature on the nature of disciplines (OECD 1972), but the approach, emphasis and even methods of teaching.

A fourth question related to the 'culture' of the discipline. The notion that disciplines, being not only bodies of knowledge but bodies of people, might develop their own norms and patterns of beliefs, attitudes or behaviours, which constitute a kind of sub-culture within the general academic milieu, was originally put forward by Gaff and Wilson (1971) but has been most thoroughly explored recently by Becher (1989a). The very idea of 'disciplinary cultures' is itself problematic, involving as it does not one but two rather elusive concepts; and many disciplines appear less homogeneous to insiders than they look from the outside. A discipline that is structurally diverse, and consists of a loosely related collection of sub-fields might nevertheless be held together by a common ethos or set of norms, attitudes and habits; even by a common style. On the other hand, disciplinary cultures might, on closer inspection, reveal a set of sub-cultures which view one another with varying degrees of animosity, warmth or indifference. Despite the difficulty and unfamiliarity of the concept, it seemed worth asking academics if they thought the 'culture' of their subject had changed much in recent years. Some found the question opaque or meaningless; others responded as follows:

> History as a body of knowledge which all people who claim to be 'historians' must share has collapsed. Its 'norms' now tend to be based on methodology.

> Sociology is a pluralistic discipline with different norms, etc. prevailing in relation to a variety of different approaches. Overall, the discipline in the UK has become more heavily dominated by those who espouse sociology's political role.

> Medicine does have a culture of shared norms but on the whole I do not think that this has changed much.

In contrast to the last comment, a metallurgist, philosopher and zoologist all noted significant changes in the norms or emphases within their disciplines:

> Yes, because of the change described (above), from the norms of science (free enquiry, publications, respect for truth, resistance to argument from authority) to the norms of commerce (cost conscious-ness, restriction to profitable study, limited publication and need to retain commercially valuable technology secret, respect for adequate solutions, acceptance of the authority of 'current good practice' and standards and specifications – 'doing it by the book').
> (Metallurgy and Materials Engineering)

> The culture has changed greatly – from an emphasis on precise analysis to one on evaluation of overall views or theories. Also attitudes towards quality of work have changed. As university funding has come to hinge on publication, this has been encouraged for its own sake.
> (Philosophy)

> Shift from taxonomic, structural approach to a functional, quanti-tative approach involving an appreciation of statistics and increasing computer literacy, i.e. of a shift from the culture of a 'knowledge of the cranial nerves of dogfish' to a knowledge of the growth, dynamics and exploitation of fish stocks.
> (Applied Environmental Zoology)

Again, in physics, a rather more stable picture was presented:

> The culture of Physics has not changed greatly in recent years. It is about establishing *simple models* to *explain events* and the applications of these models to predict the outcome in unexplored situations.

Experimentation is crucial in confirmation of predictions and estab-lishment or elimination of theoretical models. Students are en-couraged to believe that they must be broad and hopefully able to cope with any Physical problem.

One English lecturer described both academic and political tensions which affected the ethos of her discipline:

This is the area of greatest conflict in my subject at present. Teachers of English can be fairly divided into 1. those who think that some literary works are inherently and self-evidently superior to the rest and 2. those who think that such value-judgements are only the product of an ideology which itself is the product of material circumstances. These views often correspond to the political views of their holders: conservative and left-wing, respectively. I should say that the current ethos of most departments is relatively left-wing as far as the teaching staff are concerned, but that many of the students hold views considerably further to the right.

A political scientist was sceptical of the whole idea of a shared disciplinary culture:

I do not really accept the underlying assumption about a 'culture' of shared norms. For what it is worth, my view is that the student of political science is exposed to a wide range of somewhat superficial opinions, most of them barely distinguishable from the prejudices daily expressed in newspapers. But fortunately there is much diversity in this muddle.

(Political Science)

Another lawyer spoke of long-term rather than short-term shifts:

In overall terms it is difficult to say that the culture of a law degree has changed. That depends very much on the approach of some individ-uals. Some want more 'Law and Society' teaching. I can't say I have noticed any change in the last few years. But over the last twenty years one could identify changes.

Such comments give some idea of what some academics understand by the idea of a disciplinary 'culture', a notion which we will explore in more depth in Chapter 4. But the general limitations of questions and responses such as these should be stressed. The above quotations represent excerpts from the briefly stated views of particular academics to some very general questions, typically in relation to their own course; others in the same discipline might or might not agree with them. Moreover, there is no room here to explore the comments further, to probe the reasoning behind them or to see to what extent they represent a wider consensus. They constitute no more than pointers towards an agenda for more detailed, empirical research.[14]

However, what the questions and responses *do* illustrate is that the notion of a discipline or subject, which is the basic building-block of the undergraduate curriculum, far from being straightforward and clearly defined, is in fact extremely complex. We have tried to approach it through four general questions, about the core, boundaries, structure and culture of subjects. The responses to those questions show just how problematic a concept it is, and makes phrases such as 'the map of knowledge' begin to seem decidedly simplistic.

Figure 2.1 offers one attempt to locate disciplines within a general model of the curriculum as knowledge. But how does knowledge manifest itself? What forms does it take? What kind of existence does it have? Who creates it, who knows it, how is it used? We have tended to speak as if it existed in some obvious and consistent way in higher education, but as some of the above quotations pointed out, the undergraduate curriculum may be influenced by other manifestations of organized knowledge, in particular research and professional practice.

Research and scholarship are concerned with the pursuit and advancement of knowledge. At this level knowledge is classified not into hundreds of disciplines but thousands of specialisms, and although many specialisms can easily be located within a discipline, there are many others which are difficult to locate and are interdisciplinary or even transdisciplinary (OECD 1972; Squires *et al.* 1975; Cotterrell 1979). On the other hand, some kinds of knowledge are organized as practice, most notably in the traditional professions such as medicine, law, engineering and teaching, but also in the newer ones such as accountancy, architecture, management, social work and now psychology. Others again, such as physics, chemistry or history, have important professional associations or societies without being full-blown professions.

The influences of knowledge-as-research and knowledge-as-practice on knowledge-as-curriculum (and vice versa) raise some interesting and topical questions. How closely linked are research and teaching? Does research provide a constant curricular stimulus, or does it tend to reinforce authority and hierarchy? Is its impact confined to final year courses, or diffused through the whole curriculum? Does it necessarily have a fissiparous effect? And what about the influence of the professions and organized practice on undergraduate studies? Do professional requirements cover more or less of the curriculum in any given field than they did ten years ago? Does the seniority structure of the professions tend to make professional courses conservative and traditional, not only in the overt but the hidden curriculum? Or does practice provide a constant flow of real-life problems and approaches which helps to set the agenda for curricula and research, and which may even run ahead of theory? Such questions go well beyond the scope of this book, but they point us away from the epistemological frame of reference of this chapter towards the socio-cultural one of the next.

Notes

1 The debate has been partly about numbers. Ahlstrom (1982) provides evidence that this country was producing fewer engineers than its competitors at the turn of the century, and Prais (1989) identifies some similar current shortfalls, partly at the Masters/enhanced level, but mainly at the lower technician and craft levels. There is also a debate about the general relationship between science and technology (see *inter alia* Keller 1984). But the nagging UK question has more to do with the identity and status of engineering both *vis à vis* science, and in industry and society generally. Here, several writers have argued that there exists in Germany and Sweden a 'third' culture of *Technik* which is independent of, though related to, the culture of science, and which enjoys a considerable measure of both academic and social status (Fores and Rey 1979; Finniston 1980; Fores and Pratt 1980), an idea which helped to give birth to the 'Education for Capability' movement sponsored by the Royal Society of Arts in the 1980s. However, this notion of a third culture is rejected by a German writer (Horner 1985) who suggests that it was precisely the bringing together of academic science and technical efficiency which allowed the *Technische Hoch-schule* to establish its own status in the German system. Hutton and Lawrence (1981) tend to regard the status problem in the UK as a symptom rather than a cause, and place the whole issue in a wider cultural context which draws a distinction between 'profit-centred' British industry and 'product-centred' German industry, and ultimately the historical emphasis on financial rather than manufacturing capitalism in this country.

2 Bodies of knowledge are also bodies of people, and hence the structure of disciplines can be subjected to sociological analysis in the way that any other form of social organization can. As Becher (1989a) notes, most of the attention so far, from Merton (1973) on, has been focused on the natural sciences. Glover (1980) takes sociologists to task for not paying much attention to engineering; and there seems to have been less done on the social sciences, although a current study of the sociology curriculum itself is under way (Gubbay, personal communication). While such analyses provide a good corrective to *in vacuo* epistemology, and illuminate the development and maintenance of knowledge-professions, they do not seem to me to solve the basic problem of why certain kinds of knowledge seem to have developed and to be more fruitful than others. Indeed, there is sometimes an element of evasion (for example, in Berger and Luckmann 1971; Barnes 1974) of the basic epistemological issues, and an unquestioning assumption of nominalist or relativist theories of knowledge.

3 Such questions could be approached historically, and one can explore the uses and meanings of terms such as arts, science and philosophy in previous centuries, although that will not be the approach here. But it is also worth noting that librarians have to find answers willy-nilly to questions about the structure of knowledge because they have to organize the resources of study. Most higher education institutions in the UK use the hierarchical Universal Decimal or Library of Congress classifications, although at least one university (Leeds) classifies its materials according to its undergraduate departments. More specialized libraries (including the University of London Institute of Education) sometimes use faceted classifications which allow retrieval under several headings, but these and the standard classifications are both being modified by newer computerized forms of access such as keyword searches.

4 Playfair (1852, p. 6) noted the tendency of the English to rely on 'empirical experience', rather than acquired skill or theory in relation to production, and detected an anti-theoretical bias. He is not the only one; but the question is why this should be so if it is. In my experience, the idea of 'common sense' has greater force and resonance in this country than it or its equivalent have in either the USA or France. Has this something to do with the early development of democratic forms of life (we still talk about a 'moot point') or a demotic rather than court literature? The evolution of common rather than code law, the possession of a book of Common Prayer rather than something more hieratic? The existence of common land, common rights of way, a Commonwealth, a House of Commons? Whatever the reasons, the centrality of the belief in common sense, which may have protected the country against extremist ideologies, may have nevertheless undercut the demand for and belief in education, since parents, employers and workers have all been apt to regard skilled jobs and tasks as requiring 'just common sense'. Higher up the social scale, this translates into a suspicion of professionalism and devotion to the amateur. If all this was counterproductive in 1852, it is potentially catastrophic in a knowledge-led late twentieth-century economy.

5 In that part of the *Republic* which deals with the education of the philosopher, Plato speaks of subjects which 'naturally stimulate thought', 'draw men to the truth', 'provoke the mind and turn it to the vision of reality', and knowledge that 'draws the mind upwards and forces it to argue about pure numbers', and 'compels the mind to think in order to get at the truth' (Lee 1955, pp. 289–93).

6 I am indebted to my colleague David Walker who informs me that although there are several references in the Lee translation of the *Republic* to 'pure thought', 'pure numbers', 'pure reality' and 'pure knowledge', the Greek does not in fact contain the word pure (*katharos*) but phrases such as 'by thought itself', 'in the true number', 'into what is itself', or quite simply 'knowledge'. There is, however, a reference to the purifying (*ekkathairetai*) effect of studying mathematics, which betrays a Pythagorean influence. Walker comments that there seem to be several distinguishable notions of pure knowledge in the passage: (1) knowledge pursued for its own sake as opposed to knowledge for the sake of its useful and banausic applications; (2) knowledge acquired by the intellect uncontaminated by the senses; (3) knowledge as purifying, i.e. as detaching us from the senses and preparing the mind for the contemplation of the Form of the Good. The latter two reveal Pythagorean influence in their hostility to the body and the senses and in their assumption of the need for purification.

7 A useful corrective to the rather static view of science implied by the persistence of the traditional disciplinary categories at the undergraduate level is the list of new interdisciplinary research centres recently approved by the Advisory Board for the Research Councils: superconductivity; molecular science; surface science; engineering design; synthesis and characterization of semiconductor and novel materials; high-performance materials; polymer science and technology; process simulation integration and control; optical and laser-related science and technology; cell biology; protein engineering; toxicology; transgenic animal biology; population biology; human communications; and microsocial change to the year 2000 (Turney, *Times Higher Education Supplement*, 24 March 1989).

8 It is not only sociology which eases one towards a relativistic view of knowledge,

but history as well. The undergraduate map of knowledge has probably changed as much in the last century as the map of Europe, with the integration of some parts and Balkanization of others (see, for example, Brock and Meadows 1977; Church 1978; Mansell 1984). However, to say this is not to jettison notions of reality, objectivity and truth entirely, because if our knowledge were truly relative one theory or interpretation would be as good as another, and there would be no reason for one to displace another. The relativist is then driven back to argue that it is our criteria for judging between theories which are relative, but that requires criteria for judging the criteria, and so on.

9 In choosing the word 'stance', I want to catch something of what seems to me the intentional quality of Husserl's concept of the natural 'standpoint' or natural 'attitude' as it is variously translated. In fact Husserl uses two words, *Einstellung* and *Standpunkt*. Boyce Gibson (Husserl 1931, pp. 460–1) says that the first refers to the mental and the second the physical but one of the characteristics of phenomenological writing is the interplay of the two. In any case, the word implies an active stance rather than simply a passive location – see also Schutz (1970, p. 116): 'The following considerations concern the structure of what Husserl calls the "life-world" (*Lebenswelt*) in which, in the natural attitude, we, as human beings among fellow-beings, experience culture and society, take a stand with regard to their objects, are influenced by them and act upon them.' Of course, the main difference between the natural stance and the ones described here is that the latter take little for granted, and treat the world as problematic.

10 Abbs (1989) notes a particular unease with the idea of the 'aesthetic'. This could be partly a hangover from late-Victorian aestheticism, but there could be a deeper reason which goes back to the Western Christian tradition which at least in recent centuries seems to have emphasized the truth and goodness of the divine rather than its beauty, which is more salient in earlier classically influenced theologies (e.g. divine harmony). This could have become secularized (in Arnold, for example) leading to an emphasis on the truth content and moral content of art, rather than its aesthetic qualities.

11 In its submission to the UGC, the National Committee for Philosophy (1988, para 52) states: 'Like any other subject, the core of philosophy has its own special place on the academic map. Above all, philosophy is the one subject which involves wholly rational enquiry into ultimate issues concerning human life and society; and such enquiry is arguably one of the distinguishing marks of civilisation, especially as understood in the Western world. But philosophy is also unique in the extent to which it has implications for the whole range of other disciplines. In particular we would emphasise its concern with: (a) reasoning techniques as such; (b) the theoretical dimension of teaching and research in all areas, which differentiates higher education from training; (c) the relationships between different areas of knowledge, such as biology and physics, and science in general and the humanities. Philosophy thus has a major role to play in transcending departmental boundaries and uniting each institution into an organic whole.' The report of the UGC working party on philosophy (January 1989) views it both as a core discipline and one that interpenetrates with an extraordinary range of subjects, although it does place it generally in the context of the humanities.

12 But note Davie's (1986, pp. 172–3) comment on the position of philosophy in

the Scottish universities (in particular Edinburgh and Glasgow): 'As regards the first three-quarters of the century, the question of philosophy certainly had great importance, I think, not only because the main issue of the curriculum was whether philosophy should hold its own against the human sciences, but also because the latter were ultimately able to win out against philosophy only because they took upon themselves the responsibility for the metaphysics and the morals which philosophy had given up.' Davie argues that the influence of analytic or linguistic philosophy narrowed the scope and weakened the influence of Scottish philosophy during this period, although he also notes more recent developments. There is also the hint that analytic philosophy was quite simply too difficult for the mass of students. Be that as it may, the current first-year philosophy options for M.A. General and Honours students at Edinburgh are certainly broad: aesthetics and general philosophy; history and philosophy of science; logic and philosophy of science; metaphysics; moral philosophy. The UGC working party report also remarks that philosophy in Britain is currently much more diversified than it was in the period immediately after the war.

13 Slee (1986) explores the historical emergence and Becher (1989b) the contemporary state of the identity of history in this country, and both remind us of the important currents and conflicts *within* the subject, as distinct from around it. Slee is particularly interesting on the issue of 'method' as a potentially defining characteristic of an emerging discipline. The idea of history as a 'human science' seems to find little favour in this country, but relations with the social sciences are complex and not necessarily antagonistic. Two steps can be hazarded here in what appears to be a minefield. First, there is a certain parallelism between the sub-types of history (constitutional, social, economic) and social science subjects (politics, sociology, economics). Secondly, the fact that history grew up mainly within the ambit and ethos of the humanities, and the social sciences under the influence of the natural sciences, may have led to the first acquiring a particularistic non-theorizing emphasis, and the second a generalizing, theorizing one. But the contrast or conflict may not be as clear-cut as is sometimes portrayed; witness the development of quantitative approaches within history, and of ethnographic or idiographic research methods in the social sciences.

14 These comments are drawn from responses to questions sent out to academics in 1987 at an early stage in this study. In all, questions were sent to 505 academics in 23 subjects or subject groups, in a ratio of 2:1 junior to senior (i.e. senior lecturer and above) staff in 28 institutions (12 English universities, 2 Scottish universities, 1 Welsh university college, 1 Northern Irish university, 6 polytechnics, 2 Scottish central institutions and 4 colleges/institutes of higher education). Each one of four variants of the letter explained the broad purpose of the study, and posed four questions about undergraduate curricula and teaching, covering 16 questions in all, together with one common question asking the person what were the most significant changes of any kind to have taken place in undergraduate courses in his/her subject in the last ten years. The response rate (without any reminder) was just under 32 per cent (161 replies). The purpose of the exercise was not to attempt a formal survey, but to help me to formulate and clarify some of the themes and issues which were emerging from my study of the literature at that stage. Many of the questions were thus rather general and open to wide interpretation, and hence difficult to answer. However, many of the academics who responded did so at considerable length,

and their responses were extremely useful in helping me to focus the themes and issues subsequently, and I am very grateful to them for this. In general, the material from the responses has been used to inform the discussion in all parts of the book, but I decided to quote directly from some responses to some questions, partly because such responses help to relate general concepts and problems to particular disciplines and situations, and partly to enliven the text. However, it should be noted that the responses quoted here have been excerpted from longer replies, and as many respondents pointed out, can only be taken as a brief summary rather than full statement of that person's views. For this reason also, I have avoided making direct comments on the responses myself, letting them rather speak (within these limitations) for themselves. In keeping with my commitment to the respondents not to identify them or their institutions, I have simply indicated the subject category to which the respondent belonged.

3

Curriculum and Culture

The idea that the curriculum can be seen in terms of the society or culture of which it is a part is both ancient and recent. It is there in Plato's writing on education, in the association of certain types of curricula with certain groups of people, and in the notion that education may have certain social functions or effects. It is a recent idea in the sense that systematic sociological analysis of the curriculum is largely a post-war phenomenon, associated in the UK with writers such as Young (1971) and in the USA with the work of Michael Apple (1979, 1981) among others. The bulk of that analysis has, however, been directed towards the schools.

In this chapter, we shall explore some of the ways of analysing the undergraduate curriculum in terms of 'culture'. The word culture is being used here in its descriptive, anthropological or sociological sense, rather than its normative literary or artistic sense. In this sense, everyone belongs to a culture or sub-culture and is 'acculturated'; any distinction between 'cultured' and 'uncultured' represents a particular value-judgement within that culture. One could perhaps use the term 'society' just as well, but the word culture, with its connotations of the way of life of a people, seems preferable because of the potential influence of the curriculum on ideas, beliefs, values and habits. As in Chapter 2, there will be room only to open up a few of the many possible perspectives and issues, and to suggest some ways of thinking about them.

A useful if rather schematic starting-point is Lawton's (1983) division of cultures into eight aspects or sub-systems which he argues can be used to analyse any culture: the social system, economic system, communication system, rationality system, technology system, morality system, belief system and aesthetic system. Such headings are open to a number of objections; nevertheless, they do provide an initial framework for thinking about curriculum and culture.[1]

In terms of the social system, for example, one might look at first degree courses in terms of *social selection* and *access* – one of the functions identified in Figure 1.1. Trow (1974, p. 63) has distinguished between elite and mass systems of higher education and argues that 'Countries that develop a system of elite higher education in modern times seem able to expand it without changing its character in fundamental ways until it is providing places for about 15% of the age grade.' The importance of age-group measures is declining as higher education admits more mature students and becomes less age-specific, but nevertheless the proportion of young people enrolling is some index of the possible social functions and perceptions of first degrees. Kelsall *et al.* writing in 1972 seemed in no doubt that UK graduates then constituted an elite (which is not necessarily a bad thing). However, it is likely that a quantitative shift from elite to mass higher education, such as has happened in the USA and Japan, will bring with it a qualitative change in the undergraduate curriculum. As Furth (1982) points out, this may result in increased status differentiation *within* higher education between subjects or institutions; it may also affect the 'hidden' curriculum of assumed values, perspectives and relationships (Becker *et al.* 1968; Snyder 1971).

This last point also raises questions about another preoccupation of sociologists, namely *socialization*, and the ways in which, to use Bernstein's (1971) framework, knowledge is 'classified' in terms of demarcations, and 'framed' in terms of the teaching–learning relationship. Although this framework has been usefully applied to higher education (see Wright 1988), its main impact has been on studies of the school curriculum. There has also been some interesting work on vocational education and training at the school or post-school stages (Willis 1977; Gleeson and Mardle 1980). However, in general the literature on the sociology of the undergraduate curriculum is limited, and there remains much scope for further work on it in this country in terms of social selection, status and socialization. In the absence of such empirical work, it is difficult to say much about it in sociological terms.

Curriculum and employment

One is on slightly firmer ground when considering the relationship between the undergraduate curriculum and the 'economic sub-system'. Not only does this lie at the heart of current government policies on higher education, but a good deal of empirical work has been done on it, particularly on the relationship between higher education and initial employment. The more general relationship between higher education and the economy is of course extremely complex, but here also there is a substantial literature.[2]

This is not a book about graduate employment, on which a number of important analyses have appeared in the last decade (Lindley 1981; Roizen and Jepson 1985; Harland and Gibbs 1986; Tarsh 1988; Brennan and McGeevor 1988; Boys and Kirkland 1988; Boys *et al.* 1988); nevertheless, something must be said briefly about the factors which complicate the curriculum–employment nexus. Working backwards from the labour market, first of all there are changes in the labour market itself. One can distinguish between cyclical changes, which reflect the buoyancy or depression of the economy, and structural changes, which are longer-term shifts in the pattern of employment. The latter may involve changes in the content of work (for example, the decline in manufacturing and shift to services) and changes in the level of work (upgrading or deskilling). Neither cyclical nor structural changes are easy to predict, and there is considerable debate as to whether, for example, the shift to services will continue, and whether there really is a 'rising threshold of competence' in the OECD economies. Even if the latter is true, it does not automatically translate into increases in higher level educational streams; in some countries the main growth at the 16–19 stage has been not in the pre-academic general streams, but in the intermediate 'technical' ones (Squires 1989a).

When one looks at the use of highly qualified manpower within this shifting labour market, the picture is further complicated by the phenomenon of 'substitution' (Blaug 1983). People are not always working in the jobs for which they were trained. Where there are labour shortages (or sudden crises such as wars) one may find upward substitution – people working above the level they were trained for. Conversely, where there is an oversupply of manpower of a particular kind, one may find downwards substitution, e.g. graduates working in 'non-graduate' jobs, leading sometimes to a 'cascade' effect whereby people who trained for a particular level of work are systematically displaced by those more highly trained. Or there may be lateral substitution, with people moving sideways into kinds of work which are different from, though often related to, their initial training. Substitution is itself affected by various factors, such as both general and specific supplies of labour, the existence of restrictive practices and professional demarcations, the transferability of training, the technical possibilities of substituting capital (i.e. machines) for labour and, increasingly, the availability of continuing education.

In addition to these changes in the labour market, and the possibilities of substitution within it, the curriculum-employment nexus is complicated by a third set of factors related to the selection of graduates. Here, the recent literature suggests that four main things may affect the initial selection of graduates.[3] First, there is their *expertise* derived from the subject content of their degree. This is most obviously important where there is a direct link between the degree subject and occupation. Secondly, there is their general *ability*, inferred from the class and source (i.e. institution) of their degree, and perhaps also from A level grades. This is not simply innate or pure ability, but ability which has been developed through the process of the curriculum; not merely the 'good mind' but the 'trained mind' (See Chapter 4). Such inferred ability may be relatively more important in selection for 'general entry' graduate employment. Thirdly, there are their *personal qualities*, which refer to the various personal (and social) attributes and attitudes which may be relevant to a particular job and which emerge from references, 'biodata' (i.e. biographical information) or during an interview. Finally, there are the identifiable *skills* which they may or may not possess, such as numeracy, computing, communications and foreign languages, which to some extent cut across different degree subjects, and may be acquired on the growing number of 'employment skills' courses in higher education.

The distinction between these four factors is by no means clear-cut. It is not easy to distinguish between high-level cognitive skills and abilities, or between interpersonal skills and personal qualities; nor one can easily sustain the complete disjunction between curricular content and process implied by the expertise/ability distinction, or the notion of 'screening' for ability that depends on it. However, one can see that the relative emphasis on these four factors may vary (and sometimes conflict) not only from job to job (in some cases expertise is of the essence, in others the degree content is virtually irrelevant, and ability and 'personality' are the key things) but from one employer and even personnel manager to another. The whole process involves a complex and perhaps partly unconscious set of trade-offs between various desirable graduate attributes and the more general context of supply and demand. Much depends on whether the employer sees the degree as a screening for general ability, a broad foundation of knowledge and skills for a particular occupation, or as turning out a finished product which he can employ without incurring further substantial training costs. With mature graduates, the situation may be different again, depending on whether the graduate is operating within an internal labour market which he has never left, or is starting out afresh. Many part-time mature graduates are relatively limited to a local labour market rather than a national or international one, and this probably influences the behaviour of both employers and graduates.

These three sets of variables – to do with the labour market, substitution within it, and graduate selection – make the whole curriculum–employment relationship an extremely complex one, and make the interpretation of graduate employment statistics a hazardous business.[4] However, there is one kind of measure which, though still affected by many of the variables mentioned above, may help us to conceptualize the undergraduate curriculum in relation to employment; namely the occupational distribution of graduates in any one subject, which has been analysed in a recent paper by Tarsh (1988) in terms of the relative importance of direct, subject skills, and indirect, general skills.

There are several sources for this kind of data. DES *Statistical Bulletin 1/86* (Table 9) gives the relationship between five subject groups and four types of work for universities (GB) and polytechnics (England and Wales). The annual AGCAS publication *What Do Graduates Do?* gives figures for 18 subjects and 14 types of work for universities and polytechnics, with a less detailed breakdown for colleges. While many of these types of work categories are still very broad, what the tables (and diagrams) show clearly is that there is a marked contrast between subjects such as computing and engineering (civil, electrical/electronic, mechanical) where one type of work absorbs 70 per cent or more of the graduate output, and subjects such as English, history, biological sciences or social studies where graduates are absorbed into a fairly even plurality of occupations; with everything in between these two extremes.

A more detailed analysis of the degree subject/type of work relationship for polytechnic and college graduates has been provided by Brennan and McGeevor (1988), who showed that the percentage of 'specialist' graduates working in the field of their specialism three years later ranged from 97 per cent in pharmacy to only 24 per cent in 3D design, although it should be noted that employment figures for art and design graduates are particularly problematic (Barnett 1989). The authors also show (Table 5.1) that the percentage of graduates in all the 31 subjects in their study employed after three years in the three largest type of work categories for that subject ranged from 100 per cent in three subjects (pharmacy, graphic design, electrical engineering) to under 60 per cent in three others (science, English literature and interfaculty studies). However, the most detailed figures currently available for the degree subject/type of work relationship are in the university sector where the data relate 112 subjects or subject combinations to 121 first destination types of work. Table 3.1 shows the intake of graduates in 25 subjects or subject combinations into types of work which absorbed at least 1 per cent of the total for that subject in one year (permanent UK employment, 1986/87).

The information has to be treated with some caution. It refers only to university graduates, whom some employers may assume (partly on the basis of A level grades) to be more 'able' than polytechnic or college ones, and for whom therefore the 'screening for ability' function of a degree for general graduate employment may be relatively more important (Gordon 1983). Secondly, the figures relate to a time before the recent cutbacks in the financial services sector in the City of London and the intake to such types of work may have declined relatively since then. Thirdly, it should be noted that the proportion of university graduates entering permanent employment itself varies from subject to subject (see AGCAS, annual) between about 40 and 75 per cent of all graduates in that subject, with a mean of 56 per cent; the remainder go into short-term or overseas employment, further research or training, are unemployed or otherwise classified (1987 figures). [For this reason, law has been excluded from Table 3.1, since only 14 per cent of law graduates entered permanent employment, while 64 per cent went into (paid) further training.] Nevertheless, the figures do illuminate the extent to which employment can provide a frame of reference for thinking about what to teach. They give us a highly detailed picture of the initial occupational spread of graduates, and the extent to which they enter occupations which are cognate with their degree (the mere number of type of work categories is a rather crude measure; one has to look at the actual headings).

Table 3.1   Types of work employing at least 1 per cent of university
graduate output in each of 25 degree subjects, 1986–87

---

1 *Clinical Medicine*   *No. of types:* 1   *No. of graduates:* 3417
Medicine (3413)

2 *Pharmacy*   *No. of types:* 1   *No. of graduates:* 627
Pharmacy (622)

3 *Clinical Dentistry*   *No. of types:* 1   *No. of graduates:* 554
Dentistry (549)

4 *Architecture*   *No. of types:* 1   *No. of graduates:* 317
Architecture (303)

5 *Accountancy*   *No. of types:* 3   *No. of graduates:* 558
Financial (9), Accountancy (504), Banking (6)

6 *Computer Studies*   *No. of types:* 9   *No. of graduates:* 970
Management Services (177), Systems Analysis (84), Computer Programming
(458), Management Consultancy (18), Accountancy (29), Research (21), Research
and Development (21), Design (11), Technical Advisory/Consultancy (11)

7 *Civil Engineering*   *No. of types:* 9   *No. of graduates:* 860
Computer Programming (18), Accountancy (67), Engineering (28), Research and
Development (9), Design (19), Technical Advisory/Consultancy (33),
Environmental Planning/Construction (25), Surveying/Cartography (15), Civil
Engineering (549)

8 *Mechanical Engineering*   *No. of types:* 14   *No. of graduates:* 956
Production Management (25), Selling (13), Management Services (13), Systems
Analysis (12), Computer Programming (18), Accountancy (36), Engineering
(314), Research and Development (105), Design (102), Technical Advisory/
Consultancy (54), Production/Process Engineering (105), Technological (10),
Flight Deck/Ships Officer (13), Engineering Technical Support (17)

9 *Electronic Engineering*   *No. of types:* 14   *No. of graduates:* 782
Production Management (8), Management Services (43), Systems Analysis (17),
Computer Programming (57), Accountancy (22), Scientific (9), Research (10),
Engineering (134), Research and Development (141), Design (139), Technical
Advisory/Consultancy (45), Production/Process Engineering (39), Technological
(8), Engineering Technical Support (16)

10 *Mathematics*   *No. of types:* 15   *No. of graduates:* 1330
General Admin. (25), Management Services (63), Operational Research (22),
Systems Analysis (38), Computer Programming (167), Management Consultancy
(15), Statistician (20), Financial (19), Accountancy (370), Banking (42), Actuarial
(244), Insurance Underwriting/Broking (18), Research (37), Teaching/Lecturing
(15), Clerical/Secretarial and Related (20)

Table 3.1—continued

11 *Music*　　　　　*No. of types:* 16　　　　*No. of graduates:* 218
Management Supporting Occup. (5), Admin., Operational Management (5),
General Admin. (22), Selling (14), Combined Buying and Selling (7), Computer
Programming (6), Accountancy (16), Banking (4), Teaching and Lecturing (36),
Social Welfare (4), Pastoral (5), Librarian (6), Acting/Music/Sport (27),
Broadcasting/Stage/Film Production (5), Clerical/Secretarial and Related (17),
Miscellaneous Services (14)

12 *Chemical Engineering*　　*No. of types:* 17　　*No. of graduates:* 527
Unknown (6), Management Supporting Occup. (8), Production Management (32),
Buying, Marketing and Selling (6), Selling (11), Marketing (12), Management
Services (13), Computer Programming (7), Accountancy (37), Development (6),
Engineering (61), Research and Development (33), Design (23), Technical
Advisory/Consultancy (33), Production/Process Engineering (167), Technological
(6), Engineering Technical Support (16)

13 *Economics*　　　　*No. of types:* 19　　　*No. of graduates:* 1244
Management Supporting Occup. (17), Admin., Operational Management (24),
General Admin. (45), Buying, Marketing and Selling (14), Purchasing (15), Selling
(28), Combined Buying and Selling (28), Marketing (44), Computer Programming
(14), Management Consultancy (19), Economist (25), Financial (40), Accountancy
(475), Banking (117), Actuarial (20), Insurance Underwriting/Broking (45),
Investment Analysis (58), Stockbroking/Jobbing (35), Clerical/Secretarial and
Related (21)

14 *Chemistry*　　　　*No. of types:* 19　　　*No. of graduates:* 936
Management Supporting Occup. (10), Admin., Operational Management (16),
General Admin. (19), Production Management (34), Selling (40), Marketing (24),
Management Services (10), Computer Programming (29) , Financial (11),
Accountancy (151), Banking (26), Investment Analysis (10), Scientific (62),
Research (157), Development (70), Technical Advisory/Consultancy (19),
Technological (10), Scientific Technical Support (42), Clerical/Secretarial and
Related (11)

15 *Business/Management*　*No. of types:* 22　　*No. of graduates:* 796
Studies
Management Supporting Occup. (19), Admin., Operational Management (19),
General Admin. (33), Production Management (12), Personnel (23), Buying,
Marketing and Selling (24), Purchasing (21), Selling (54), Combined Buying and
Selling (22), Marketing (77), Market Research (15), Advertising Account
Executive (8), Management Services (25), Systems Analysis (16), Computer
Programming (11), Management Consultancy (14), Financial (25), Accountancy
(191), Banking (47), Insurance Underwriting/Broking (20), Investment Analysis
(17), Stockbroking/Jobbing (17)

16 *Combined Social*　　*No. of types:* 23　　*No. of graduates:* 509
Sciences
Management Supporting Occup. (17), Admin., Operational Management (11),
General Admin. (36), Land Management (9), Hotel Catering Amenity (7), Buying,

Table 3.1—continued

Marketing and Selling (8), Selling (24), Combined Buying and Selling (21), Marketing (11), Financial (8), Accountancy (90), Banking (25), Insurance (13), Investment (7), Stockbroking/Jobbing (9), Teaching and Lecturing (6), Social/ Welfare (48), Nursing (9), Police (8), Non-scientific Research (13), Journalism (6), Clerical/Secretarial and Related (16), Miscellaneous Services (6)

17 *Agriculture*   *No. of types:* 23   *No. of graduates:* 278
Management Supporting Occup. (7), Admin. Operational Management (8), General Admin. (8), Production Management (10), Farming and Fishing (56), Land Management (6), Hotel Catering Amenity (3), Personnel (4), Buying, Marketing and Selling (4), Selling (27), Combined Buying and Selling (8), Marketing (8), Financial (4), Accountancy (16), Research (11), Development (3), Technical Advisory/Consultancy (24), Landscape Architecture (3), Scientific Technical Support (4), Teaching and Lecturing (3), Further Education Advanced (3), Social/Welfare (3), Manual-Making/Growing (26)

18 *Biology*   *No. of types:* 24   *No. of graduates:* 580
Management Supporting Occup. (9), Admin., Operational Management (13), General Admin. (15), Production Management (14), Farming and Fishing (10), Personnel (8), Selling (28), Combined Buying and Selling (14), Marketing (8), Computer Programming (17), Financial (11), Accountancy (53), Banking (16), Insurance Underwriting/Broking (9), Stockbroking/Jobbing (6), Scientific (13), Research (107), Development (7), Scientific/Technical Support (67), Teaching and Lecturing (6), Police (6), Manual-Making/Growing (11), Clerical/Secretarial and Related (9), Miscellaneous Services (15)

19 *Geology*   *No. of types:* 24   *No. of graduates:* 320
Unknown (7), Management Supporting Occup. (6), Admin., Operational Management (4), General Admin. (8), Selling (12), Management Services (5), Computer Programming (19), Data Processing (9), Management Consultancy (4), Financial (6), Accountancy (34), Banking (6), Insurance Underwriting/Broking (4), Scientific (36), Research (15), Technical Advisory/Consultancy (46), Engineering (6), Technological (4), Surveying/Cartography (9), Scientific/ Technical Support (5), Social Welfare (4), Museum/Art Gallery (5), Clerical/ Secretarial and Related (5), Miscellaneous Services (6)

20 *Physics*   *No. of types:* 25   *No. of graduates:* 1008
Unknown (11), Management Supporting Occup. (9), Admin., Operational Management (19), General Admin. (20), Production Management (22), Selling (13), Management Services (40), Systems Analysis (39), Computer Programming (96), Management Consultancy (14), Financial (12), Accountancy (121), Banking (12), Scientific (55), Research (137), Development (28), Technical Advisory/ Consultancy (16), Engineering (73), Research and Development (64), Design (37), Technical Advisory/Consultancy (13), Production/Process Engineering (28), Technological (15), Flight Deck/Ships Officer (13), Clerical/Secretarial and Related (12)

21 *English*   *No. of types:* 25   *No. of graduates:* 892
Unknown (10), Management Supporting Occup. (18), Admin., Operational

Table 3.1—continued

Management (18), General Admin. (98), Personnel (22), Buying, Marketing and Selling (12), Selling (59), Combined Buying and Selling (36), Marketing (21), Advertising Account Executive (15), Public Relations/Promotional (25), Financial (13), Accountancy (64), Banking (18), Insurance Underwriting/Broking (17), Teaching/Lecturing (21), Social/Welfare (31), Librarian (36), Non-scientific Research (10), Journalism (41), Editorial (47), Acting/Music/Sport (16), Broadcasting/Stage/Film Production (17), Clerical/Secretarial and Related (59), Miscellaneous Services (22)

22 *Geography (Human)*   *No. of types:* 26   *No. of graduates:* 686
Management Supporting Occup. (17), Admin., Operational Management (33), General Admin. (47), Transport Distrib. Management (20), Personnel (10), Buying, Marketing and Selling (11), Purchasing (8), Selling (36), Combined Buying and Selling (23), Marketing (27), Market Research (8), Computer Programming (13), Financial (10), Accountancy (118), Banking (32), Insurance Underwriting/Broking (27), Stockbroking/Jobbing (7), Town and Country Planning (9), Surveying/Cartography (9), Social/Welfare (17), Security/Protection (11), Police (9), Non-scientific Research (9), Manual-Making/Growing (7), Clerical/Secretarial and Related (22), Miscellaneous Services (7)

23 *Combined Languages*   *No. of types:* 27   *No. of graduates:* 872
Management Supporting Occup. (16), Admin., Operational Management (28), General Admin. (87), Hotel Catering Amenity (10), Personnel (14), Buying, Marketing and Selling (16), Selling (66), Combined Buying and Selling (32), Marketing (34), Market Research (9), Advertising Account Executive (10), Public Relations/Promotional (9), Computer Programming (18), Management Consultancy (12), Accountancy (86), Banking (71), Insurance Underwriting/Broking (30), Investment Analysis (17), Teaching/Lecturing (27), Social/Welfare (12), Translating/Interpreting (19), Librarian (18), Journalism (20), Editorial (17), Broadcasting/Stage/Film Production (9), Clerical/Secretarial and Related (38), Miscellaneous Services (18)

24 *Psychology (Natural*   *No. of types:* 27   *No. of graduates:* 402
Sciences)
Unknown (6), Management Supporting Occup. (9), Admin., Operational Management (11), General Admin. (13), Hotel Catering Amenity (5), Personnel (21), Selling (13), Combined Buying and Selling (19), Marketing (8), Market Research (7), Advertising Account Executive (6), Management Services (4), Systems Analysis (5), Computer Programming (6), Management Consultancy (7), Accountancy (30), Insurance Underwriting/Broking (5), Research (12), Technical Advisory/Consultancy (5), Teaching/Lecturing (9), Social/Welfare/Religious (7), Social/Welfare (44), Psychology (47), Nursing (17), Non-scientific Research (5), Clerical/Secretarial and Related (15), Miscellaneous Services (15)

25 *History*   *No. of types:* 28   *No. of graduates:* 1220
Unknown (16), Management Supporting Occup. (23), Admin., Operational Management (39), General Admin. (141), Personnel (25), Buying, Marketing and Selling (17), Selling (48), Combined Buying and Selling (33), Marketing (32),

Table 3.1—continued

Advertising Account Executive (13), Public Relations/Promotional (16), Computer Programming (14), Financial (24), Accountancy (200), Banking (85), Insurance Underwriting/Broking (41), Investment Analysis (13), Stockbroking/Jobbing (20), Tax (12), Teaching/Lecturing (15), Social/Welfare (33), Security/Protection (17), Librarian (32), Non-scientific Research (13), Journalism (23), Editorial (14), Clerical/Secretarial and Related (55) Miscellaneous Services (26)

Source: USR Tabulation F21135 – year 1986–7.

Notes

1 Figures are for UK university first degree graduates entering permanent UK employment
2 Combined Social Sciences = Other and Combined Group 9
3 Geography (Human) = Geography Group 9
4 Psychology (Natural Sciences) = Psychology Group 3
5 Combined Languages = Other and Combined Group 12

Such detail will be important in the discussion of transfer of learning in Chapter 4.

Where there is a strong relationship between the degree subject and one or a few subsequent types of work, it is possible to orientate the curriculum towards such work. Where, by contrast, the relationship between subject and type of work is more pluralistic, that possibility does not exist; or rather does not exist in theory. For we have to consider the possibility that curriculum planners might assume an employment relationship where one does not exist (any longer?) and conversely may be unaware of, or ignore, one that does. For example, how many physicists realize that physics is now as 'general' a degree in this sense as English; and how many academics are aware of the significant proportions of graduates in almost all subjects entering the financial and commercial sectors?

Where a strong subject–employment relationship does exist and influences course planning, we may speak of a 'professional' course. This is to adopt a functional definition of professional education, rather than the normative ones which are common in the literature. But what of courses which do not have such a steady relationship? Since they cannot be planned in terms of the students' likely destinations, they must have some other kind of rationale or logic. The most obvious one is in terms of the discipline itself. The titles of such degrees bear this out: headings such as physics, geography, sociology, English and history refer to the well-established and familiar 'bodies of knowledge' discussed in Chapter 2, which can constitute an 'internal' rationale for the course of study without any necessity to refer outside or beyond to the world of work. In this case we can speak (without prejudice) of 'academic' courses in contrast to the 'professional' ones referred to above.

However, in addition to defining 'academic' courses negatively in terms of their 'weak' link with employment, we may also be able to define them positively in terms of their 'strong' link with academic research and postgraduate study. Table 3.2 gives the proportions of graduates in each of 30 subject categories who went on to 'further academic study' after their first degree. Again, certain *caveats* must be observed. The figures are based on a survey sample, although one with a very high response rate. The category of 'further academic study' is a relatively broad one, comprising all full-time further education or training aimed at a higher or other degree at home or overseas.[5] For reasons of classification and sample size, not all the headings in Tables 3.1 and 3.2 are comparable, and law is omitted from the first and medicine from the second. Nevertheless, one finds that on the whole, 'professional' courses such as pharmacy, architecture and engineering (and doubtless law if one classified its trainees as employed) appear in the top half of Table 3.1 and the bottom half of Table 3.2, and 'academic' courses, such as the natural sciences and the 'non-applied' arts and social sciences, appear in the bottom half of Table 3.1 and the top half of Table 3.2.[6]

However, there are some courses which do not seem to fall naturally under either the 'professional' or 'academic' heading. The AGCAS booklet and the USR statistics refer to 'combined', 'interfaculty' or 'general' courses. In the universities, these are mainly the combined or joint honours courses mentioned in the opening chapter, which often come in cognate pairs such as physics and chemistry, economics and sociology, or French and German. Such combinations are perhaps a sub-type of the 'academic' degree course. But the USR statistics also list 'other' and 'general' courses, and combinations which cut across the main course groupings. These may not account for many university graduates (although relatively more in Scotland), but they are rather more important in the polytechnics and colleges, especially in the latter where such multi-subject combined or general degrees are quite common (outside Scotland). Some of these broad polytechnic/college degrees seem relatively 'academic' in content; others are broad in occupational terms.

What is the rationale of such courses? Are they 'professional' or 'academic'? In many cases they seem to be neither, in that they do not have a direct or specific relationship with the labour market; nor do they fit into the conventional, specialized academic categories. They are rather general, although some general degrees allow for considerable specialization within them, and one must always distinguish between what is on offer and what the student actually does. This does not mean that there is no rationale behind them. They may be planned deliberately to give the undergraduate a good general education, for example by sampling or balancing a number of types of knowledge, or they may be planned in terms of an applied, problem focus such as environmental control, or a broad theme such as modern urban society, or in terms of some concept of individual development. But in the prevailing higher education culture they seem to represent neither one thing nor the other.

Such courses also raise questions about graduate employment. There may be the possibility of partial substitution or compensation among the four factors identified earlier – expertise, ability, personal qualities and

Table 3.2   Percentage of graduates in 30 subject categories proceeding to further academic study, 1987

Subject	University	Polytechnic	College
Chemistry	34.5	17.8	
Biological Sciences	28.7	15.2	
Physics	28.4	16.9	
Combined Biol./Phy. Sciences	15.8	11.1	
Environmental Science	15.2	14.2	
Psychology	12.8	9.0	
Mathematics	12.3	9.2	
Electrical/Electronic Eng.	10.4	5.2	
English	10.0	9.1	
Geography	10.0	7.3	
Sociology/Social Studies	9.5	6.6	
Economics	8.9	8.0	
Govt/Public Administration	8.6	3.8	
History	8.5	5.2	
Chemical Engineering	7.9	19.3	
Computing	7.6	1.3	
Civil Engineering	7.4	4.4	
Mechanical Engineering	7.0	6.2	
B.Sc.			6.3
B.A.			5.3
Architecture	5.3	0.5	
Modern Foreign Languages	5.0	1.7	
Art and Design	4.5	6.5	
Law	3.7	5.1	
Business/Management	3.2	2.2	
Other			3.1
Home Economics/Catering, etc	2.8	1.3	
Accountancy	1.2	0.5	
Pharmacy	0.3	2.4	
B.Ed.			0.3
Average	11.0	5.6	3.5

Source: AGCAS, *What Do Graduates Do?* (1989).
Note:
1 College figures are for broad subject groups as follows: B.A. (languages, general arts, humanities, music, drama, art and design); B.Sc. (physical and biological sciences, engineering, technology and agriculture); Other (administrative, business and social studies, catering, architecture and combined studies); B.Ed. (education)
2 Polytechnic chemical engineering is based on small sample

skills – in the case of particular graduates and graduate jobs. More of one may make up for less of another in some circumstances. A more serious problem arises where the applicant does not rate highly in terms of either expertise or ability, that is where the content of the degree is irrelevant, and the quality of it uninspiring. By no means all general degrees are associated with low quality or ability, but some are, and the employment prospects of graduates of such courses appear to be relatively poor, with substantial proportions of them entering 'non-graduate' jobs (see Harland and Gibbs 1986; Tarsh 1988). Such a situation raises two questions about the curricula of such courses. First, to what extent do they (or indeed other courses) really develop the high-level, indirect, general-purpose skills which are implied in the 'trained mind' doctrine? And secondly, would it not be wiser in terms of employment to steer 'low-quality' graduates towards 'high-relevance' courses which would allow them at least to offer some expertise to prospective employers? This is an issue to which we shall return at the end of the chapter; first, however, we must explore the broad classification of degree courses which has emerged from this analysis of their relationship with employment.

There has been an implicit triangularity about much of the preceding discussion which can be explored further, although as with all models of the curriculum, this one simplifies the reality. Figure 3.1 suggests that in relation to employment and the economy, undergraduate courses lie somewhere among three points: the *professional*, the *academic* and the *general*. With the first, the course is planned substantially though by no means exclusively in terms of an external occupation; with the second, the rationale of the course is primarily internal, in terms of the demands of the discipline and implicit preparation for research (and in some cases school-teaching); with the third, the rationale derives from something other than an occupation or a discipline. The three points represent three 'ideal types' or extreme cases; most courses will lie somewhere within the area thus bounded.

How far does the relative emphasis on academic, professional or general courses vary from one part of the system to another? Without a detailed analysis, one cannot be certain, but it appears as if the Scottish universities, with their significant proportions of general courses, are fairly evenly spread in terms of Figure 3.1, whereas universities in the rest of the UK seem to emphasize the academic or professional and de-emphasize the general. Because of its foundation-plus-option course structure, it is difficult to place the Open University in the diagram, but it may tend towards the academic and general at least at the undergraduate level.[7] Brennan and McGeevor (1988) locate polytechnic/college courses on a continuum ranging from the 'occupational specialist' through the 'occupational generalist' and 'generalist plus' to the 'generalist', which suggests that they lie down the professional–general side of the triangle. However, the English and Welsh colleges, apart from their teacher education function, are associated mainly with general courses (Harland and Gibbs 1986), whereas the Scottish central institutions are the most clearly 'professional' of all the institutions in the UK. As Table 1.4 showed, the 'duplication' of the universities and polytechnic/colleges in professional courses is more apparent than real, since certain types of professional courses are largely concentrated in one sector and there may be differences of emphasis between courses in the same subject.

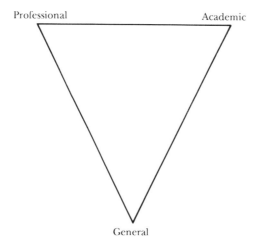

Figure 3.1   Professional, academic and general degrees.

The institutional distribution of types of course has interesting policy implications which, however, go beyond the scope of this book; here we need to explore further the types themselves. In each case, something will be said about the literature on each type, the patterns or sub-types that exist, and the problems and issues associated with them, beginning with the 'professional' course.

Professional curricula

It has already been made clear that the definition of a 'professional' degree course being adopted here is an operational rather than conceptual one: it is a course which has a consistent and fairly exclusive relationship with a particular occupation, exclusive in that graduates from such courses tend not to go into other occupations, and in that entry to that occupation is largely or wholly restricted to graduates from such courses. Traditionally, some occupations such as accountancy and engineering have had non-graduate entry routes, through on-the-job or technician education, though the general drift is towards all-graduate professions. The term 'professional' will thus be used in a looser way than would be indicated by the conceptual analysis of what is or is not a profession.

Nevertheless, the literature on the professions *per se* provides a useful entrée into this type of education, because it identifies some of the main themes which characterize not only those professions but preparation for them: the existence of a body of specialized knowledge and expertise; the influence of professional norms and ethics; the autonomy and responsibility of the professional; the relationships with colleagues, clients and the state. The literature on the professions goes back a long way, but seems to have reached a peak in the 1960s and 1970s (see, for example, Etzioni 1969; Jackson 1970), perhaps because the professions were at an apogee of esteem at that point, before the attacks of Illich (1977) and others who, like Shaw many years before, accused them of establishing a 'radical monopoly' in the name of meeting people's 'needs'. This was essentially a moral critique; the political attack was to come a decade later.

Although there was also a burst of writing on professional education during the same period (Schein 1972; Cook 1973; Turner and Rushton 1976), its central importance in higher education means that it is a continuing, indeed permanent theme. In addition to Jarvis (1983) there have been books and papers emanating from a recent SRHE conference (see Goodlad 1984; Squires 1989b). Professional education is also a recurring theme in OECD studies of higher education. One of the most interesting current lines of research is the exploration of the relationship between professional theory and practice by Argyris (1982) and Schon (1987).

As well as the literature on professions and professional education in general, there are the periodic major reports on specific professions. Whereas the former attempt to generalize across all or at least some professions, the latter deal only with one field, such as medicine, engineering, law, social work, management or accountancy. If the former are sometimes rather abstract and theoretical, the latter often show relatively little concern with trends or issues outside their own field, and tend to draw few parallels.[8] The need for such periodic major reports can perhaps be attributed to the structures of authority and seniority in the professions, which seem to necessitate periodic revolution rather than the research-led rolling evolution which is more typical of 'academic' subjects.

There are three main patterns of professional degree. The first, consecutive pattern, in which a period of theoretical study is followed by a period of supervised practice, is associated mainly with some of the traditional professions such as medicine, dentistry, veterinary science, law and to a large extent engineering. This pattern seems to have emerged historically for a number of reasons. It is of course a plausible pattern in educational terms, particularly in fields where practice involves the application of theory, as is more the case with natural science-based professions. Indeed, the growth of theoretical or basic knowledge in any field would logically push it towards this pattern. A secondary factor may be the need to protect the public by guaranteeing a certain minimum level of competence before the trainee begins to practise (in both senses of the word!). However, the emergence of this pattern may also have been related to the growth of higher education itself, and its increasing involvement in professional fields in the nineteenth and twentieth centuries; for it was the practice element which existed first, in the form of on-the-job training, and the preparatory theoretical elements which were added subsequently, as higher education became more and more involved. Once established, however, the theoretical stage seems to have grown in status and size, and may even have led to a relative decline in the importance and quality of the practical stage.

The second main pattern one finds in professional education is the 'sandwich degree' (Smithers 1976; DES 1985a). Here, theory and practice alternate during the degree stage, in the form of one thick sandwich (T-P-T) or several thin ones (T-P-T-P-T). Again, this is a plausible pattern in educational terms in certain circumstances. Where the relationship between theory and practice is more dialectical than applied it allows a fruitful interaction between the two, although this does not always happen. It may motivate students by allowing them to get their 'hands on' at an early stage. It should counter any academic drift in the theoretical component. It is not surprising, therefore, that one finds this pattern in some of the 'softer' professional fields, such as social work and teaching, where the theory–practice relationship may be less one-way than it is in the 'harder' ones. But the fact that sandwich courses are found in engineering in the polytechnics, colleges and some 'ex-CAT' universities (such as Aston, Bradford and Strathclyde) and in other fields such as architecture, planning and agriculture, points to an economic rather than educational rationale. Many students of engineering and other professional or semi-professional fields were in the past part-time not full-time, and sandwich courses have grown out of a long tradition of first night-school, then day release and then block release – a pattern associated in the post-war period mainly with the non-university sector.

The third pattern is the post-experience one in which students come to theoretical or systematic study of the field after a period of practice. In logical terms, this is the reverse of the first, consecutive pattern, but like it, it seems to have emerged for a mixture of educational and other reasons. It is a defensible pattern in what might be called 'low-theory' fields, where people can learn to practise in some way and with some success without any theoretical preparation for what they are doing, although they may have had some relevant training at a lower level. The post-experience pattern has emerged chiefly in the management and administrative fields, although it is also found in teaching (in post-school education and the proposed 'licensed teacher' scheme) and some other service professions (for example, voluntary social work experience is often a requirement for admission to social work courses). There seem to be several reasons for its emergence: a backlog of untrained practitioners; a desire to certificate practice, for a variety of reasons, including status; labour shortages which require quick solutions; and a growth of theory or technology in the field itself, requiring more systematic training than has hitherto been necessary.

It is interesting to ask how far the particular pattern that exists in each field is the optimum in curricular terms. To some extent, each pattern seems to have grown up for extraneous, though important, reasons to do with institutional or occupational history and student circumstances. To what extent do the differences between these three patterns still make educational sense? Is there any intrinsic reason why medicine should not adopt a sandwich pattern, or management a traditional, consecutive one? Why should sandwich courses in engineering exist in some institutions and not others? The curricular answers to such questions must involve some analysis of the knowledge, skills and norms peculiar to each profession. The preceding paragraphs have tentatively related the different patterns to different theory–practice relationships, associating 'high-theory' or applied fields with a consecutive pattern, 'dialectical' fields with sandwich ones and 'low-theory' ones with the post-experience one. But other factors enter into the equation. How do the different patterns affect student motivation? How do they affect the balance between analysis and synthesis in professional work? How do they relate to the balance between deductive and inductive approaches? Do 'problems' provide a better focus for learning than 'theories'? What are the effects of each pattern on the balance between engagement and reflection, having hands on or standing back?

There are some signs that the three patterns are becoming less distinct. For example, the distinction between pre-clinical and clinical studies has been eroded in some medical courses. The general value of practical placements and projects during the first degree stage is becoming more widely recognized. There are major changes on the way in nursing, as a result of the Project 2000 scheme (UKCC 1986), which will reduce the emphasis on trainee nurses as 'pairs of hands', and emphasize their student status. But perhaps the main shift in all professional fields is the gradual introduction of recurrent, continuing education which implies that a professional degree (or even chartered and qualified status) is only the initial stage in a much longer process. It is difficult to say exactly what impact – if any – this shift is currently having on undergraduate curricula, but its future importance cannot be doubted.

What are the main issues in professional higher education? It is not easy to generalize, because the substantial differences between the various professions or semi-professions translate into differences in professional education. Some problems seem peculiar to each profession: the balance between technology and human relations in medicine; the relationship between the two branches of the legal profession; the status of some branches of engineering; the balance between generic and specialized social work; the growing shortage of young nurses; the low morale in teaching; the uncertain identity of management; the crisis of confidence in architecture. However, at the risk of underestimating such differences, certain current issues can be picked out.

First, there are the changes in the professions themselves which necessitate changes in professional education. The increasing need for continuing professional education, to update and sometimes re-orientate practitioners has already been mentioned. A subsidiary problem here is how or whether to institutionalize this, for example in the form of attendance or credit requirements. But the development of continuing education must eventually have a backwash effect on initial professional education at the undergraduate stage. How should such courses equip people, both cognitively and affectively, to continue to learn and want to learn? One of the problems with continuing education lies not in learning, but in unlearning.

A second change in many professions is the shift away from autonomous, individual practice to teamwork: group practices in law, primary health care teams in medicine, project teams in engineering, team-teaching in education, co-ordination and liaison in social work. In principle, most people are in favour of more teamwork and better co-ordination, but in practise it often proves difficult, perhaps because it is at odds with the image of the autonomous professional who has a private relationship with his or her client. There may also be inter-professional tensions, as well as intra-professional ones, for example in the case of primary health care teams. The relationship between professional and client is also changing in other ways. Members of the public are less deferential, better informed, and more litigious than they used to be. They want to know not only what is to be done, but why.

The relationship between professionals and the state is also changing, as government imposes a more entrepreneurial and competitive pattern on what it perceives as genteel cartels. It becomes more and more necessary for professionals to know about finance, management (including self-management) and even marketing. Technological changes are also affecting not only the content of professional work, necessitating new competences such as computing, but even the structure of professions, in terms of the relationship between the generic practitioner and the specialist technician whose power grows with the growth of specialized technology in medicine, management and other fields. All these general changes in the professions themselves have implications for professional education, even if their impact on undergraduate courses is not yet always apparent.

A second major issue in professional education is, and has always been, the *control* of the curriculum. The main historical tension here has been between the institution (typically the university) and the professional body. In practice, this tension has been modified by the common background, both educationally and socially, of both parties, the existence of 'dual-practitioners' (who both teach and practice), the overlapping memberships of important committees, a long tradition of often discreet negotiation, and the fact that academics are also, in their way, professionals. So the explosions have been rare, the exceptions which proved the rule. But latterly, other policy actors have sought to enter the stage. Government has not only turned its attention to the professions as economic entities, but in the 1980s adopted an increasingly *dirigiste* approach to higher education. This tended to affect the capital-intensive professions, such as medicine and engineering, in the form of regulation of capital spending and student numbers, rather more than the cheaper ones, but there have been direct or indirect consequences for fields such as nursing, teaching and social work as well. Institutions will not gain professional accreditation for their courses if their learning resources – laboratories, libraries, etc. – are deemed inadequate by the relevant professional body. The consumer's voice has been heard, if faintly and intermittently, usually when something goes badly wrong, for example in the medical or social work fields. Student influence seems, by contrast, rather weaker than it was in the 1960s and 1970s, when more radical questions were asked, leading to the inclusion in some cases of courses to do with the social and environmental impacts of professional activities.

Theory and practice

In addition to these issues which arise from the nature of professional occupations and the control of professional courses, there are two other issues which lie at the heart of professional education, so much so indeed that they can be taken as defining characteristics of it. They are the relationship between theory and practice and the balance between conservation and innovation. Each has already been touched on in passing, but something more needs to be said. Of all types of education, professional courses experience the tension between theory and practice most strongly, because they give considerable if not equal weight to each. In craft and technician level courses, theory is seen merely as an adjunct of practice, while in purely academic courses practice, if it is a point of reference at all, is seen simply as a spin-off or by-product of theory. The professional, however, can be defined as a person who practises theory or theoretizes practice; indeed, the very concept of professional expertise implies both knowledge and use. As part of the present study, academics were asked: Is your subject typically conceptualized in terms of 'theory' and 'practice'? If so, has the relationship between these elements changed in recent years? The first response is from an ex-university lecturer now working in industry:

> Pharmacology is basically a practical subject and if anything there is pressure for this part to increase. However due to 'outside influences' the opposite has occurred – practical classes have been greatly reduced in number and academic merit. This makes them cheaper and less time consuming (academics' time). Inevitably this means a reduction in the standard of graduate turned out.

Clearly, resource factors can influence the balance of theory and practice in some subjects, but other responses indicated that 'internal' subject factors and student preferences may be important also:

> It is difficult to divide Business Studies courses so clearly. This is because the subjects taught really fall into three types, namely, appropriate parts of basic disciplines taught on a theoretical basis, e.g. economics, psychology, sociology, mathematics; essentially practical, procedural subjects such as accounting, and problem areas which are a

mixture of theory, practice and problem solving, e.g. marketing, policy studies.

The position in Sociology is well known and I don't think I need to set it out. We have always had a middle range approach (in Merton's sense) at —— though we have always been weighted to social institutions and the applied end. I don't think we have changed over the years in our teaching but student choice has greatly changed and we have found demand for our more theoretical courses has fallen away. The reasons for this appear to be (a) what the students perceive as cashable cheques in the job market and (b) a genuine intellectual concern to understand what is going on in their society. By (b) I'm not of course implying that I would necessarily agree with the judgement that pure theory is no use but I think that's the way the students see it. Nevertheless I must admit to some sympathy with that view. I think that without going into a lengthy treatise, I would have to argue that middle range theory springing out of empirical data is in general the best approach but you will see all the qualifications and nuances involved in such a view.

My own particular academic subject is geography. In recent years it has moved far more towards conceptualization in terms of 'theory' and 'practice', to the extent that in some areas (e.g. locational studies, certain parts of geomorphology) the theory dominates the practice. There is some realisation of this, and many geographers now talk endlessly about 'relevance'.

The curriculum is devised primarily according to the knowledge and skills required by the practising surveyor, and the theoretical content is that required to give the student the necessary understanding. The content and blend has been improved over recent years, but I don't think that there has been a fundamental change.

Yes. I would say it has, primarily as a consequence of the blurring of the distinction between theory and practice by computing and software. There may even be a danger that CAD (Computer Aided Design) for example may largely replace 'practice'.

(Engineering Science)

My subject – civil engineering – is very often seen as divisible into quite separate 'theory' and 'practice' elements. However this reflects more the wishes of the academics than their market and – in recent years – great pressure has been brought to bear to remove this compartmentalisation.

With the advent of BEng courses, the teaching of 'abstract' theory is no longer acceptable or appropriate. Theory is always taught in the context of real-life applications, preferably drawn from examples to be found in industry.

(Engineering)

Even the small number of comments quoted here – which represent the perceptions of individuals – signal a complex situation affected by both abstract and concrete factors.[9] Many professional fields seem to have got more 'theoretical' over time. This can mean several things. It can refer to the growth of influence of the natural and social sciences as bodies of knowledge which underpin practice in fields such as medicine, pharmacy, agriculture, engineering, architecture or social work; it can refer to the increased importance of mathematics or computing in some fields; it can refer to the attempt to develop models or theories of practice itself, for example in the fields of management, nursing or teaching, or it may simply reflect the enlargement of the off-the-job element in professional education.

This kind of academic–theoretical drift can yield benefits in terms of knowledge and academic status, but it can also produce a reaction which attacks the increasing irrelevance or distortion of such studies. Practitioners, it is claimed, have their heads filled with jargon and are no longer adequately prepared for the 'real world'; the 'contributory disciplines' do not contribute much; there is too much emphasis on analysis, not enough on decisions, relevance, etc. Examples of this reaction against academic drift can be found in management (Revans 1982) and education (Hirst 1983). It underlies the continuing tension in engineering between 'engineering science' and 'engineering design', and in social work between the social scientific and case-work elements in training. It seems to lie behind recently announced plans for a new (private) school of architecture which will train mainly through practice. It exists in other professional fields, especially those which deal with people rather than things, and may in time arise in nursing which is currently becoming more academically orientated. In many cases, however, it is expressed as an intermittent grumbling of practitioners rather than as a systematic counter-argument.

The case for re-thinking what we mean by practice and its relation with theory has been made at an abstract level by writers who draw on the two very different philosophical traditions which contest the dichotomy, Marxism with its concept of praxis, and the American pragmatists who direct our attention to the consequences of our actions. The main example of the first is Habermas' *Theory and Practice* (1974), which has had some influence in this country mainly on education, social work and the 'caring' professions, particularly at the radical edge. Theorizing, according to Habermas, is not some free-floating intellectual activity, but has to be socially situated and contextualized just as much as practice; indeed, it is more accurately seen as theoretical practice. The typical denigration of 'practice' arises largely from the social status of practitioners, which tends to be lower than that of theoreticians. According to Habermas, the very distinction between theory and practice is at root a social rather than epistemological one.

The critique which draws on pragmatism is best exemplified by Argyris (1982) and Schon (1987) in a series of joint and individual works, the most recent of which is Schon's *Educating the Reflective Practitioner* (but see also Usher and Bryant 1987; Boreham 1988). Their argument is subtle, depends heavily on examples, and is therefore difficult to summarize, but is based essentially on the idea that practice itself generates approaches, artistries, strategies and operational (as distinct from espoused) theories and concepts which together constitute a kind of knowledge which is general without being abstract. Their examples are drawn from various professions, including architecture, planning and management.

The problem facing writers like Schon who attempt to theorize about practice is that if they fail, practice remains particularistic or intuitive, and if they succeed, they simply generate more theory. However, there seem to be four characteristics of practice – of 'doing' – which tend to distinguish it from theorizing or 'knowing'. First, practitioners, lacking the time and resources to carry out exhaustive analyses, may have to operate on a more limited, *probabilistic* basis. A GP, during a seven-minute consultation, may form a provisional hypothesis early on, rather than running through the whole gamut of possible examinations or tests; the engineer tracing a fault may have a hierarchy of probable causes in his mind and investigate these rather than embark on a text-book linear analysis. Secondly, practitioners may become very aware of contextual factors which affect what they do, and implicitly develop *contingent* models of their work. The doctor or engineer will become aware that the answer to a lot of his or her questions is 'it depends', and will take the relevant factors or variables into account. Practice does not take place in a vacuum, and may be implicitly based on contingent theories which allow few across-the-board answers or approaches. Thirdly, because of the constraints imposed not only by external factors but sometimes by the design problem itself, practitioners may engage in a complex set of *trade-offs*, rather than trying to optimize any one aspect of what they are doing. There is often no optimal design, treatment or solution; better in one way means worse in another. The practitioner may have to balance safety against economy, speed against certainty, appearance against strength, effect against side-effect; and there is no easy answer. Professional judgement comes into play. Fourthly, the pressures and experience of practice may eventually lead practitioners to *condense* – in psychological terms to 'chunk' – the decision-making process to such an extent that it appears from the outside to become a matter of intuition, flair, or artistry.

It may be that the theory–practice issue in professional education has become over-polarized. The notion of theory is itself relative, implying a statement with some degree of generality and some taxonomic, explanatory or predictive power. But the generality and power can vary from the local and tentative to the universal and highly probable. Practice can doubtless yield 'theories' of a limited or weaker kind, but once such theories are seen to apply more generally or with more force, they tend to become dignified with the name of 'model', 'theory' or even 'paradigm'. Practical theories and theorized practice meet somewhere in the middle, and it may be more fruitful to see them as a continuum than as a di-chotomy.

But if this is so, why is the dichotomy such a familiar one in this country, and even more firmly entrenched on the continent? And why are there associated dichotomies such as active/contemplative, pure/applied and even mental/manual which seem to reinforce and complicate the original one? Unless one posits an inherent human tendency to comprehend the world in binary terms, one has to look for more sociological explanations. Lobkowicz (1967) has argued that the original distinction was less epistemological than occupational, the difference between the life of the philosopher and that of the politician. Be that as it may, we should perhaps pay more attention to the context rather than the content of the distinction, and the relationship between the two environments or worlds: the department and the firm, the laboratory and the field, the lecture-room and the ward. As Figure 2.1 suggested, the difference may lie not so much in the knowledge *per se* as in the stance one adopts.

Conservation and innovation

The second major issue in professional courses is the balance between conservation and innovation. It has already been suggested that whereas academic courses tend to change incrementally, perhaps under the influence of research, professional courses seem to need the new broom of a major report every so often to bring about change. To be sure, this contrast is over-stated, and academic fields have periods of relative stagnation and sudden revolution, just as professional ones can evolve almost without anyone noticing in response to shifts in practice. For example, computing has infiltrated most professions now without any great ballyhoo, and in many of the 'people-professions' the attitude to the client has shifted steadily towards a rather less authoritarian one.

Nevertheless, the apparent need for periodic spring-cleaning in the professions does pose some questions. Is it simply that age and authority structures in the professions tend to reinforce stability, whereas in research authority has a dual and sometimes conflicting basis, in publications and seniority, e.g. the brilliant *young* physicist? Is it simply that new knowledge keeps being added to professional fields without old knowledge being taken away? Is it that institutions have to prepare people to work in traditional as well as up-to-date professional settings, and so cannot afford to be too 'progressive'? In any case, one must be aware of assuming that the angels are always on the side of innovation. Intellectual fashions may work themselves through without any very serious consequences (what impact has struc-turalism had outside academe?), but professional fashions (for example, in architecture, child-rearing and teaching) can have far-reaching effects.

The issue points to a more fundamental tension at the heart of professional education, which is that it is concerned not only with knowledge and skills but with norms and attitudes. The problem is that the two may not change in tandem; the first may need to change rapidly, while the latter change only slowly if at all. The notion of a profession implies some continuity of values and attitudes, which form the ground-rules for the transactions between colleagues and between practitioner and client. Professions are sometimes referred to as institutions, but the interesting point is that compared to many institutions they function less on the basis of formal, explicit regulations and codes than on informal, tacit norms and expectations. This makes the attitudinal and affective element of professional education especially important.

However, it is not just the fact that professional education involves value-education which tends to make it conservative; it is the way in which values and attitudes are learned. Whereas knowledge can be acquired through lectures, seminars and reading, and skills are learned through demonstration and practice, the process of attitude-formation depends crucially on two things: role modelling and group socialization. The learning is embodied. The young doctor learns a great deal from what the older doctor is, not simply what he says or does, and from the sub-culture of the little group of medical students to which he or she belongs. Such models and sub-cultures tend to be conservative because they are part of a process of long-term cultural transmission, going back through previous cohorts and even generations.

Academic curricula

If professional courses are geared ultimately to the external world of practice, the pattern and content of academic courses reflect the internal nature, logic or demands of the discipline. But what kinds of demands are they? And in what sense are they internal? And what is a discipline?

There is surprisingly little literature which explores these questions in *curricular* terms. There is of course the whole domain of theories of knowledge which was explored briefly in the last chapter, but there is typically little concrete reference to curricula or courses in such writing; it moves at a much more abstract level. There is also a large and venerable literature on the nature and purposes of higher education, which rings with names such as Newman, Veblen, Ortega y Gasset, and Jaspers [see Powell's bibliography (1966, 1971), and there have been many more recent examples but such writing likewise tends to be rather general, and only by extension addresses the question of what is to be taught in curricular terms; but see Goodlad 1976; Barnett 1985]. Similarly, there is a small body of literature on the academic profession in this country (see Halsey and Trow 1971; Startup 1979; Whitburn *et al.* 1976), but again this deals only indirectly with what academics teach. The most sustained recent discussion of the nature of the 'academic' is to be found in the journal *Minerva* (see Shils 1984; Lobkowicz 1984; Ruegg 1986) where it is explored in relation to concepts such as truth, inquiry, research, culture (*Bildung*), community, rationality, disinterestedness, voluntary solidarity and equality among researchers; though one should not overlook Broady's (1978–9) stimulating attack on mere academicism. The bulk of writing about academic disciplines is, however, specific to each discipline, and there are relatively few examples of attempts to extract generalities about the nature of the academic or the nature of disciplines. Paradoxically, some of these attempts have arisen out of challenges to the very notion of a discipline, through 'interdisciplinary' work or 'modular' schemes. In general, however, the concept of an academic curriculum has been less well explored in recent years than that of a professional curriculum, and what follows here will reflect that fact.

Like professional courses, academic courses come in several sub-types. First, there is the single-subject course, variously labelled (single honours, special honours, etc.) which concentrates on the study of a single academic discipline (e.g. mathematics, chemistry, economics, history, fine art) after shedding some ancillary or subsidiary courses in the first or second year. The basic rationale for such courses derives from the discipline itself, and can be seen in its pure form in disciplines which have no obvious employment destination, such as philosophy or history. However, many academic courses have or had an implicit point of reference in school-teaching, and many are organized in institutes or professional or subject associations. There is thus no clear dividing-line between the 'academic' and 'professional' degree.

Robbins (1963) presented dual-subject courses (joint honours, combined studies, etc.) as a variant on the single-subject pattern for those students who do not want such a specialized higher education, but that represents a university view, and a dated one at that. The combined subject degree has a firm place in the polytechnics and colleges in its own right. However, there seems to have been little empirical work done on such courses. There is some anecdotal and a little firm evidence that dual-subject degrees are less well regarded by some employers (Gordon 1983). There is again some anecdotal evidence that such degrees are less likely to lead on to postgraduate research, and some of the figures in Table 3.2 suggest this; but such assertions need to be tested empirically. On the other hand, a broader education may provide a better preparation for some jobs and certain kinds of research. It is also difficult to understand how what is sometimes believed to be the essential 'minimum' syllabus of the three-year single subject degree can be halved without loss of disciplinary integrity. Presumably it can be done only where the essential core of each subject is no greater than half the total; or where the subjects overlap in some way; or where students are prepared to do more than 100 per cent of the work. Of course, all this assumes that three years is a 'natural' rather than arbitrary period in which to reach 'degree standard'.

Some of these issues surfaced in the responses of academics to the question: Would you favour an increase or decrease in the proportion of students taking combined/joint degrees?

At present employers tend to see joint degrees as second class. This is a pity. Many companies want to employ specialists (e.g. statisticians, computer experts). Only in 'management' is a broader course valuable.

(Mathematics)

I would very much favour an increase in the proportion of students taking joint degrees. It does seem to me that philosophy is much more effective when combined with some 'first order' discipline, than when taught in isolation.

(Philosophy)

It depends on the subjects of the degree. I think the proportion of students following joint honours physical science courses (physics/maths, chemistry/physics, etc.) is about right, but there is room for more students on combined biological/physical science degrees.

(Physics)

I would favour a very substantial increase in the proportion of students taking combined and joint subject degrees where Business Studies are an important element. I see every reason with the recent Handy report (NEDO/MSC/BIM) and other such reviews for a provision of Business Studies in adequate depth in combined degrees with any technology, with languages, and possibly with such other disciplines as history and geography.

The concept of the student with a broad scientific base is fine but in practice it does not work. Combined degrees in e.g. Physiology and Pharmacology mean that the student (except for the very good ones) is master of neither and in terms of future employment (Ph.D. or industry) is starting from a weak base. On the other hand I do favour a greater amount of 'non-scientific' components – e.g. philosophy, history of science – which if taught well put the practical science into proper context.

(Pharmacology)

I think that the study of two languages concurrently is quite academically acceptable and may be of benefit to students with a strong linguistic interest. I believe that it is important in most cases for each language to have parity; a language studied as a subsidiary subject seldom reaches a proper university standard. I think that the continuing growth in demand for foreign languages justifies an increase in this type of degree.

One social scientist pointed out that the weighting of the two subjects does not have to be equal:

To answer this question adequately I think one would have to know the degree structures which one had in mind. Also the answer would differ from subject to subject. In the humanities and social 'sciences' I think some measure of broadening is desirable though it is important that the students are confronted with a discipline in some depth. Width often leads to superficiality and depth may produce a blinkered approach and an intellectual treadmill. I think that the old main- + subsidiary subject is a good idea. At —— we have an arrangement where students can choose flexibly any weighting from 50:50 to ⅔:⅓ in composing their degree programme and most choose the latter weighting or something like it.

(Economic and Social Studies)

Others were more sceptical about the whole idea of combining subjects:

Ambivalent. Can see advantages in terms of 'broadening horizons' in theory. But clearly can lead to loss of depth. Specially prepared joint courses can be good but have very high set up costs (hard to argue for in current times!).

(Economics)

Few students seem to be able to integrate their joint studies; instead they read two, often incomplete, halves. Frequently, the analytical courses are cut out in joint schemes, and the students gain only a superficial introduction to both subjects.

(Geography)

The third sub-type of academic course is less easy to describe, but it is broader or more general than the two-subject degree. It may involve three or more subjects studied separately but in parallel, as in the Scottish general degree or some polytechnic/college 'combined studies' degrees; or it may integrate several subjects in relation to some area, period, theme or problem, in which case it may be called interdisciplinary; or it may consist of a more open, modular system of requirements and options.

These three types of academic curriculum are distributed unevenly across the higher education system. The single-subject academic course is largely confined to the universities, reflecting their traditions of specialized scholarship and their stronger research orientation. Dual-subject degrees exist in both the universities and polytechnics, but their place in each is subtly different; in the former they are seen largely in relation to the single honours degree, which constitutes a kind of academic gold standard, whereas in the latter they come under the general rubric of 'combined studies'. Combined studies courses may involve two, three or more disciplines. Triple-subject courses are relatively rare, although some well-established ones exist [philosophy, politics and economics (PPE) and arguably classics]. They are more common in the polytechnics/colleges and Scottish universities than in the other universities.

Academic courses raise a number of important curricular issues, but there are four which merit particular attention. First, there is the question of the nature and definition of academic disciplines; secondly, and related to it, the concept of interdisciplinarity; thirdly, the issue of modularization of courses; and, finally, the relationship between 'content' and 'process' in such disciplines. Each of these will be addressed briefly in turn.

One can approach the delineation of disciplines in two ways. The first is to try to classify them in terms of the kinds of knowledge, procedures and criteria of judgement they involve. This was broadly speaking the approach adopted in Chapter 2, and it led to a model which located each discipline somewhere in a three-dimensional space, defined by its object, stance and mode, all of which may vary over time. It was noted that there may be variations and tensions within disciplines as well as between them. There is, however, a second, sociological approach to the understanding of disciplines. A discipline, it has been noted, is a body of people as well as a body of knowledge. It manifests itself in certain physical, professional and institutional forms: rooms, buildings, posts, chairs, departments, associations, journals, conferences, and so on. One must therefore ask not only what knowledge is, but how it comes into being, how it becomes accepted, who produces it, who controls it, and why it changes or does not change.

These two approaches are often, though not necessarily, associated with two different views of knowledge which can be labelled, in simple terms, knowledge as *structure* and knowledge as *construct*. The first is based on the assumption that there is a 'real' world, that that world can be known, and that the structures of knowledge should correspond to the structures of reality; thus any departure from them invites confusion. The second view is that since we are always part of the knowledge equation, we can never know if there is a 'real' world, and hence knowledge is everywhere and always a human and social construction of, or placed upon, reality, whose form will vary; the organization of knowledge is therefore artificial and relative. The first view is probably more common among natural scientists and technologists and the second among social scientists, but this is not always the case, and the debate goes on within disciplines as well as between them.

Interdisciplinarity

These two views of knowledge are rarely articulated in abstract form in undergraduate courses, although they do underlie arguments about the relationships between courses and departments. However, they do surface, often in quite sharp form, in discussions about interdisiplinarity. If the structures of knowledge that exist do reflect the structures of the real world, then any attempt to modify or erode them is likely to be unproductive. It may be that several disciplines can be brought to bear fruitfully upon an area (Europe), period (Enlightenment), problem (traffic congestion), or theme (Pastoral) while still maintaining their distinct identity; in which case the term 'multidisciplinary' (OECD 1972) becomes appropriate. But if knowledge is relative and ultimately a matter of human constructs, then such work may alter the very boundaries of our disciplines, and indeed help us to overcome the 'artificial' constraints of compartmentalized knowledge; and the appropriate label is 'interdisciplinary'.

The dual nature of disciplines, as bodies of knowledge and bodies of people, means that the difficulties of interdisciplinary work often take a concrete rather than abstract form (Squires 1975; Levin and Lind 1985). Even when academics espouse 'construct' views of knowledge, they may find it difficult, in indefinable as well as definable ways, to work together in cross-disciplinary teams. Little problems, to do with timetabling or prescribed reading or marking, can boil up into major issues. It is rather like working with people from other countries; there may be good communication at one level, but at the same time one has the sense of the difference of cultures. There may also be a deep sense of insecurity about venturing off one's own academic patch which makes people particularly sensitive. On the other hand, there may be moments of real illumination and discovery, when someone makes a comment that springs from a quite different frame of reference from one's own.

The generally pragmatic ethos of British higher education in matters of course planning means that some basic, theoretical problems may never really be faced or thrashed out, although the process of having to formulate and present an interdisciplinary case to the CNAA may mean there is some difference between the polytechnics/colleges and universities in this respect. But pragmatism also allows progress to be made where a more analytic approach might come to a halt, faced with some intractable epistemological obstacle. As part of this study, academics were asked if they had had any experience of integrated/interdisciplinary degree courses, and whether it had been positive or negative. Their responses exemplified the mixture of abstract and practical concerns described above:

> Experience has been both positive and negative: (a) negative – often students feel inadequate in that other students always have more knowledge than them, and typically they have no firm home base; (b) positive – the combination of electronics and computing, for example, is seen as highly beneficial by employers.
>
> (Computer Science)

> The experience of my current joint studies programme – which is not strictly interdisciplinary – is mixed. Students often find it difficult to move from the approach and conceptual basis of one subject to the other. Several of the subjects offered – American Studies and Sports Studies – are interdisciplinary, and generally have worked quite well. Within my CNAA experience, the success of these courses often related to the organisational structure of the degree programme as much as or rather than its academic integrity.
>
> (Course Leader BA/BSc Joint Studies)

Another writer chronicled the re-emergence of disciplinary identities within an interdisciplinary scheme:

> We began on a genuinely interdisciplinary basis with students taking, in effect, a series of one-term course units sometimes leading to joint honours but usually to a major–minor combination. These was also an attempt to devise joint one-term units, e.g. where a philosopher and a sociologist would run the course between them. As time has gone on this emphasis has diminished partly as a response to the pressures of the marketplace. The economists, for example, have insisted on more and more technical emphasis in order to (as they see it) equip 'their' graduates to compete better in the marketplace. The historians, confronted by a situation where history is spread across three schools have contrived a formula which allows students virtually to specialise in history. . . . My opinion on the basis of this experience is that interdisciplinary courses are a good idea but they do have to be worked at and the scheme defended strongly. Also the proposals have to be thought through really well and new theory and concepts have to be developed. This is all very time consuming. We do still have a few such courses and they work quite well. An additional payoff not to be sneezed at is that lecturers, forced to integrate, begin to rethink their subject! So in summary, two cheers for integration.
>
> (Sociology)

Another described some of the difficulties that can emerge in an arts course, and suggested that a core-plus-extension model might work best:

> I have experience of teaching French as part of an interdisciplinary degree course in which the study of 1 or 2 modern languages is combined with (*inter alia*) history and/or literature and/or linguistics. By and large there are few links between the French course and other components and opinion among both staff and students seems divided as to the advisability of establishing such links. There are practical difficulties due to a flexible system of options which allows students to determine the contents of their degree course relatively freely. Moreover attempts to relate language classes to other strands systematically have not always been popular, many students preferring a language course which gives them an insight into cultural trends, with texts drawn from recent magazines, broadcasts, etc.. . . . The best system in my opinion is not therefore full integration but a kind of core course with extensions varying according to the students' other studies.
>
> (French)

And, finally, the views of a physicist who also teaches in the field of environmental science:

A course many years ago in materials science, involving physics, metallurgy and chemistry was highly successful. Again, recent experience shows this kind of development to be unsaleable. In environmental science, interdisciplinarity is all. Experience here has shown it to be highly successful.

If one can hazard one generalization from the responses to this question, it is that the early enthusiasm for undergraduate interdisciplinary ventures which was evident in the 1970s has now given way to a more ambivalent attitude, perhaps because the practical institutional and professional problems have become more evident, a view found also in the OECD 'Interdisciplinarity Revisited' report (Levin and Lind 1985). On the other hand, the growth of interdisciplinary research ventures, especially in the sciences, has been striking.[10]

Modularization

If interdisciplinarity challenges the boundaries of disciplines, modularization seems to challenge their very core. Modular or unit credit courses are currently the subject of much discussion in higher education, but interest in them in this country dates back to the 1970s (much earlier in the USA) when, for example, the Nuffield team produced a report on them rather facetiously called *The Container Revolution* (Mansell 1976). But if the interest has returned, it is for different reasons this time. Whereas in the 1970s, modularity was seen variously as a means of overcoming artificial subject boundaries, promoting student choice and clarifying course objectives, the main rationales now are administrative rationalization and the promotion of credit transfer between courses, institutions, modes of study, and between the educational system and 'corporate classrooms', to use Eurich's (1985) phrase, as exemplified by the CNAA Credit Accumulation and Transfer Scheme.[11] The latter argument is based partly on the growing importance to higher education of mature students and continuing education. Modularization is not easy to define, but can be seen as one end of a spectrum of course structures which ranges from the linear to the modular, as follows:

Linear	Large core	Small core	Modular

Linear courses allow no options whatsoever, because of disciplinary logic, professional requirements, or staff shortages. However, as we saw in Chapter 2, many degree courses seem to have something between a large core (66 per cent or more, typically in the natural sciences) and a small core (20–40 per cent, typically in the arts or social sciences). It is when that figure falls below one-quarter that people begin to use the term 'modular', 'unit-credit', or its colloquial equivalents such as building-block, cafeteria, pick n'mix (or worse). Each unit or module earns its own credit, which can be aggregated or 'cashed in' for a degree when one has accumulated enough. I have explored some of the basic issues related to modular courses in two previous reports (Squires 1979, 1986) but academics were also asked as part of this study about the advantages and disadvantages of modularizing degree courses in their subject.

> Modularising is good if it allows greater choice for students, and allows them to specialise in certain parts of a rather falsely unified subject. It can deter students from seeing important links, and from studying methodological and philosophical issues that run across modules.
>
> (Geography)

> There is an advantage in modular courses, but I regard it as administrative and economic rather than academic. I am increasingly concerned that validators increasingly fail to use as an important criterion the total experience of a student. Or are we becoming more realistic in financial terms?
>
> (Combined Studies)

> I think in the light of future demographic changes, potential changes in government educational policy and the increasing problems of student finance, modular or credit based patterns of study are essential if degree courses and subjects are to survive in a much harsher higher education world. I have personally pushed through a restructuring along these lines of the degree for which I am responsible ... comprising eight subjects. I think most of the arguments against 'modular' or 'credit' based study are the product of misconception and prejudice – e.g. that they lead to cafeteria style education and do not allow progression. Any well-structured course can build in progression where necessary and if it so wishes restrict the choice of menu on offer. In other words, modular structures do not pose any major threat to subject competence or academic rigour if developed carefully. They can also create greater choice and economy of teaching across different degree courses where appropriate.
>
> (History and Politics)

> I have personal doubts on the few modular courses I know well. Obviously it is quite easy to split a subject into relatively free-standing elements, but in real life one has to use knowledge from various 'packages' to solve problems and some undergraduates do not seem to develop this ability on the modular courses.
>
> (Construction)

> The advantage would be that students could transfer between colleges. A disadvantage is that mathematics is a 'pyramid' subject which makes

modularizing particularly difficult. It could only be done with an unacceptable degree of course content imposition.

(Mathematics)

I have taught degree-level physics in both a modular and non-modular form. An advantage of the modular form is the flexibility it gives to both staff and student in organising a suitable degree course. Combined subject degrees are easy to implement under this scheme. A disadvantage is that it is not always easy to ensure that a student gains 'core' knowledge of the subject.

(Physics)

There is a dilemma in building up modular degrees, whether undergraduate or postgraduate, on a discrete unit basis where the studies should be integrative across subjects. This is especially true of some of the problem oriented components of Business Management courses. In terms of conventional undergraduate courses, I see no great pressure for a further extension of the modular pattern, but so far as universities and colleges are concerned, I foresee an explosion in the modular approach at the Continuing Education level. This particularly applies to MBA and similar types of course, which lend themselves both to credit systems and to distance learning.

(Management)

Another writer commented on the implications for staffing, recalling the importance of this contingency in course planning in Figure 1.1:

At a time of random contraction, there are considerable advantages in not being too dependent on others, who might leave or retire. The modular system helps to make adjustments to unplanned contraction easier and makes staff work-loads more even.

(Politics)

Finally, another academic justified it on motivational and cognitive grounds:

I think that given that University work is supposed to encourage intellectual activity at the highest level of which any individual is capable it is very important to increase motivation by allowing those individuals to proceed at their own pace and to establish their cognitive frames as and when they feel capable of doing so.

(Sociology)

Apart from these kinds of arguments, there is one other consideration which impinges strongly on modularization, i.e. the attitude of professional bodies. The recent study that I made (Squires 1986) attempted to get some reactions from such bodies on the subject, and while they were again mixed, a substantial number had reservations about modular schemes at the undergraduate stage, though more were in favour at the postgraduate or continuing stage. The main worry is that modular schemes might undo the progress towards an integrated approach to first degree studies which has been a feature of some professional subjects in recent years, notably in post-Finniston engineering courses. It is worth noting that in the USA, where modular structures are the norm, most professional education occurs at the postgraduate stage.[12]

Content and process

Both interdisciplinarity and modularity raise two other general questions about academic courses and the nature of disciplines. The first is about how the discipline is presented to students, both explicitly and implicitly. Is it presented as a given body of knowledge, which is somehow 'there' or as something which is the fragile and contingent outcome of human effort? Is it endowed with some kind of abstract, almost Platonic existence, or is it seen in terms of its social context? How far are students encouraged to 'stand back' from the discipline, and look at its philosophical implications? To what extent do students study the history or sociology or economics of the discipline as a discipline, and the way in which these have changed over, say, the last century?

The second question raised by the dual nature of disciplines – as bodies of knowledge and bodies of people – takes us back to the very distinction between 'academic' and 'professional' courses. It is clear that the main, though not only, point of reference for the professional course is the external profession or occupation which absorbs the majority of its graduates. By contrast, academic courses seem to be organized mainly around the intrinsic or internal demands of the discipline or disciplines. But if disciplines are bodies of people as well as bodies of knowledge, are not academic courses also 'professional' in the sense of preparing people for entry to the *academic professions*? The relatively low percentage of graduates from such courses who do eventually make their way, via postgraduate and often in the sciences post-doctoral research, into the academic professions, should not disguise the fact that academic courses do provide a preparation for such work. Indeed, the more one thinks about them, the more they conform to the conventional pattern of the apprenticeship, with their carefully graduated stages (apprentice, journeyman, master), their strict job demarcations, the emphasis on personal contact and role modelling, the gradual increase in responsibility, the mimicking of the activity of research in seminars, and library and project work. Indeed, the origins of the concept of a degree (licence) suggest just such an occupational rationale. There are few occupations which are so tightly professionalized as the academic profession (Perkin 1973, Neave 1979a); a fact which helps to explain why on the whole it seems to work fairly harmoniously with the 'external' professions. Indeed, such professions are partly inside the higher education system themselves.

But if academic courses are a *de facto* preparation for a professional occupation which few will ever actually enter, how is this rationalized and defended? It would seem on the face of it rather perverse – not to say wasteful – to induct so many people into a non-career. The typical justification for undergraduate courses involves the last of the issues related to academic courses: the distinction between 'content' and 'process'.

The provision of specialized academic courses for students, and the take-up of such courses by students, need not of course be justified in instrumental terms at all. One can argue that knowledge is good in itself, and the interest and motivation of students a sufficient justification for access to it. This may sound rather woolly, but it is in fact the instrumental arguments which tend to be woolly in failing to show the relationship between instrumental means (more business studies graduates) and desirable ends (more happiness, justice, freedom). Extrinsic arguments end up in intrinsic concepts.

But the knowledge-as-a-good-in-itself argument does not necessarily point to any particular kind of curriculum; it can be (and is in the USA) used to justify a more *general* curriculum in higher education. The instrumental rationale for the specialized academic course depends on the distinction between the process and content of a discipline, a distinction made most succinctly by Bruner (1968, p. 72):

> We teach a subject not to produce little living libraries on that subject, but rather to get a student to think mathematically for himself, to consider matters as an historian does, to take part in the process of knowledge-getting. Knowing is a process, not a product.

There are two steps in this argument. The first assumes that one can distinguish between process and content in a discipline, between methods or procedures on the one hand, and content or information on the other. This may seem plausible enough, especially where one can identify an explicit methodological element in the discipline – experimental method in science, survey methods in sociology, design in technology, diagnosis in medicine. More generally, people talk about teaching 'analysis', 'planning' or 'problem-solving' (Birch 1986). But the very idea of methodology is problematic; rather like the notion of skill, it implies something that is invariant and unaffected by the phenomenon with which one is dealing. Pushed to its limit, the argument implies that content is merely a *vehicle* for process.

In practice, however, it is often difficult to disentangle the two: the choice, use and interpretation of a method are all associated with and contingent upon the object in question. It is asking a good deal of students to abstract process from content if lecturers do not do it. The same problem arises with Bruner's injunction that the curriculum should concentrate on the essential structure of a subject. The ability to distinguish between structure and detail, essential and inessential is a function of one's knowledge of a subject. The problem is one that faces every note-taker at the beginning of a course: What is important? What do I leave out?

It is worth noting also that the 'process' argument is typically applied to academic rather than professional courses (Yudkin 1969), yet there is no logical reason for this. If historians, philosophers and mathematicians 'learn to think', then so surely do engineers, doctors and managers. Professional courses can be justified in terms of general problem-posing and problem-solving just as cogently as more academic courses, perhaps even more so; after all, they include the element of 'design' (planning, selecting, disposing) in the broad sense used by Simon (1969) and the practical problems of implementation. One suspects that the 'process' argument is sometimes deployed as a reserve justification when a mismatch between subject output and employment intake arises. Such matches and mismatches change over time, and so therefore does the use of the argument, and subjects which were previously regarded as vocational – even if only in relation to a teaching career – are now justified on general grounds.

General curricula

There is no sharp dividing-line between academic or professional courses on the one hand and general ones on the other; indeed some of the broader courses involving several disciplines which have been mentioned already may well be thought of as general – it is all a matter of degree. General courses have so far been defined in mainly negative terms, as ones which are neither geared to a specific external profession or occupation nor provide a specialized preparation for postgraduate research and, implicitly, an academic career. A general degree is sometimes seen as an alternative for students who are not up to honours standard; this is largely though not entirely the case with the Scottish ordinary degree. There, in most courses, students divide into ordinary and honours streams only at the end of the second year, although their intentions may affect their choice of first- and second-year options.

One must distinguish, however, between general degrees, which are defined by their breadth of content, and ordinary or pass degrees, which although sometimes broad, are defined by their level. The CNAA uses the category of pass degree both for courses which do not aim to achieve honours standard, and as a probationary validation category for courses which eventually acquire honours status; it should be noted that staffing and other learning resources are significant factors in such validation. In the non-Scottish universities, pass degrees are often awarded to marginal failures on an honours course, although in medicine they are common. Sometimes the difference has to do with the length and scope of the course: Open University pass degrees require six credits, while an honours degree requires eight. As usual with the UK system, Topsy-like historical growth has led to many variations and anomalies.

It should be noted in passing that the situation in the USA is very different (Squires 1976b; Gaff 1983). Whereas in the UK a general degree is a particular type of undergraduate curriculum, in the USA general education has for long been part of everyone's undergraduate degree, along with electives (options) and a major subject. The general education element is usually concentrated in the first two years ('lower division') of the four-year course, and takes the form either of distribution requirements which ensure that students cover a certain range of subjects, or else a common course organized around certain themes or topics, such as the 'Great Books' course or Boyer's (1987) suggested 'integrated core' (language, art, heritage, institutions, nature, work, identity). Much of the debate about general education in the USA concerns the pros and cons of these two approaches, although in the current vocational climate, the idea of general education itself is under considerable pressure. Nevertheless, there is a long tradition of general education in higher education there (which suggests that it is England rather than Scotland which is atypical in this respect). This may be due partly to the need consciously to establish common cultural references in a pluralistic society, whereas the historically narrow class base of British higher education meant that a lot of the cultural references could be taken for granted; the Robbins (1963, p. 7) reference to the 'transmission of a common culture and common standards of citizenship' was perhaps a sign that this cultural assumption was finally breaking down under the pressure of expansion and democratization.

We can distinguish between two kinds of rationale or emphasis in general degree courses: the *general* and the *generic*. The first provides a more general form of academic course than the specialized academic degrees described above. This may be organized and justified in various terms: as a group of cognate or faculty disciplines such as the social sciences or humanities; as a number of disciplines brought to bear on a common area (European Studies, Middle Eastern Studies) or period (Classics, The Enlightenment, Modern Studies) or problem or theme (Development Studies, Urban Studies); as a sampling of some or all of the main types of human knowledge, as provided by the foundation year at Keele University; or as a deliberate contrast between different types of knowledge (arts–science schemes). Although general courses of various kinds are found in all kinds of institution, the prime examples are the Scottish general degree, the Open University with its foundation/modular structure, and the broader courses in the arts, social sciences and natural sciences in the polytechnics and above all the English and Welsh colleges. While modular course choices may in fact be broader than many others, this is a reflection of the specialized nature of British first degrees rather than a consequence of modularity *per se*, which permits (within the limits of course requirements) either breadth or specialization.

Although the distinction between 'general' and 'generic' may seem a fine one, it is useful to have a different label for courses which are broad in *occupational* rather than academic terms. The importance of 'generic skills' has been stressed in recent years by the Manpower Services Commission (now Training Agency) as a flexible response to and preparation for a fast-changing economy. There have been attempts to classify broad 'occupational training families', and an emphasis on 'multi-skilling', particularly for those who work in the service sector. Under the heading of 'occupational generalist', Brennan and McGeevor (1988) list polytechnic/college degrees in business studies, environmental planning, hotel and catering administration, textile and fashion design and 3D design, all of which prepare the student for work in a broad occupation rather than a specific job niche.

There are three main issues related to general curricula. The first is the question of *coherence*, a worry which has already been encountered in connection with modular courses. If a student is to study a number of different subjects or courses, what guarantee is there that they will all come together and form a coherent whole? Surely there is a danger that the curriculum will simply degenerate into a rag-bag or mish-mash of different elements or soft options, with no particular logic or unity? This kind of worry is expressed more often in relation to the newer modular or semi-modular structures than the more traditional general degree which may have well-established patterns and requirements, but it nevertheless seems to be a widespread one.

At this point one has to step back and note the strength of organic metaphors in British higher education. Particularly in the universities, and even more particularly in those universities which have a strong residential and sometimes collegial tradition, the experience of higher education is regarded as a unity, a totality, an organic whole (or in more modern terms a package) which it is neither desirable nor possible to dissect. In the past, that wholeness was to be found in the college or the institution and its organic community, but in modern times it tends to be located in the subject-department, which becomes in Burke's phrase the 'little platoon' which provides the student with his or her identity, base and purpose (Mansell 1976).

All this is now being challenged by the more aggregative metaphors associated with modular courses, student choice, accessibility and flexibility, credit transfer and part-time study (Squires 1979). The 'coherence' argument about general courses is thus often an expression of a much deeper anxiety. In reality, a well-conceived general course may be just as coherent as a narrower one; after all, the study of classics traditionally involves two languages and three disciplines and who is to say that classics is not both general and coherent? There seems no reason why a broad area, problem or theme, such as Europe, third-world development or the environment, should not provide a coherent focus for study, although such courses no doubt require careful planning. And even where the student has a lot of choice, why should he or she choose incoherence? After all, logic inheres in people as well as subjects, and there may be good individual reasons for putting together what looks like an unlikely package.[13]

One must also question the assumption that single-discipline degrees are themselves immaculately unified. The inexorable growth of specialization has meant that in many cases the concept of the discipline 'as a whole' is now largely historical, and the time has long gone when one person could command a general understanding of all its facets and branches. The unity of the discipline is to some extent an external facade, a matter of appearance; from the inside, it may appear rather as a constellation of specialisms, more or less closely related. Besides, does not the practice of carving up the syllabus and letting each lecturer get on with his or her own bit not lead to overlaps, duplication, lacunae and untied threads? Of course, there may be co-ordination and team planning, but the conventions of academic autonomy, privacy and not treading on others' specialisms are strong. It would seem that the real issue is not the imputed incoherence of general curricula, but the basic metaphors of higher education.

A second criticism made of general courses is that even if they are well-planned and coherent, they must lack *depth* (Squires *et al.* 1976). It is argued that because they cover much more ground than the specialized academic or professional degree, they must inevitably be more superficial and lacking in rigour and depth; a kind of conceptual package tour. There must be some truth in this. Even if one does not believe in the principle of intellectual conservation of quantity, the same amount of study time is being poured into different shaped vessels, one tall and narrow, the other flat and wide. The second may of course have its own advantages, in terms of pluralizing and relativizing the student's perspectives on the world. But in the British system, rigour and depth are also powerful metaphors, though like many educational metaphors, difficult to unpack (Taylor 1984). Both of them imply that the process of learning involves repetition, not in the simple rote sense, but as a repeated returning to the same ground, the same problems, in the end a living with, an immersion in the subject to the point where it becomes one's world. In some cases, the process may be experienced as one of successive approximations, each one a little nearer to the mark. In others, it discloses the provisionality and contingency of all interpretations, without any sense that there is a single point of truth. Either way, the process opens up what Bernstein (1971, p. 57) has described as the 'ultimate mystery of a subject . . . not coherence but incoherence . . . not order but disorder . . . the dialectic . . . of closure and openness'. It is in this sense that higher education can be said to institutionalize not the structures of knowledge, but the experience of uncertainty.

How far can general degrees give students this kind of experience? This depends on the interpretation of another common metaphor in higher education, that of 'covering the ground' or 'field', implicitly and perhaps originally agricultural. The metaphor becomes airborne in the notions of 'survey' and 'overview'. Survey courses are much more common in the American system than in this country, where they are rather despised as the academic equivalent of *Encyclopaedia Brittanica*. Yet a judicious use of some survey courses might paradoxically allow more depth in others. Many courses in the first and second year of degrees seem to try to strike their own *balance* between breadth and depth, in terms of the amount they cover, and the detail they go into; third-year courses typically cover less ground and go into more depth. But there is no intrinsic reason why all parts of a course should try to strike that balance. A varied menu of 'survey' courses, 'normal' courses and 'in-depth' courses might meet the conflicting demands of breadth and depth.

The third and perhaps chief problem related to general degrees is their *status*, which tends to be lower in the eyes of academics, and perhaps employers, than their academic or professional counterparts. Status is a complex business, reflecting not only the content of the course, but the institution that provides it, the kinds of student it attracts, and their subsequent careers. It is also bound up with the proximity of research. The lower or uncertain status of general degrees is therefore not purely a matter of breadth of content; indeed, some relatively broad courses – classics, PPE (philosophy, politics and economics) at Oxford and the Cambridge Natural Science Tripos – have high status in the system. The lower status of general courses may be more a function of the students who take them than of their content and the association with ordinary rather than honours degrees. In Scotland, the ordinary degree has an honourable history and a recognized status, but it is still not honours; and in the rest of the country, ordinary degrees are often perceived as second-rate qualifications.

The problem of status is identified in a sharp form by Harland and Gibbs's (1986) study of the 'diversified' general curricula introduced into the English and Welsh colleges in the 1970s (see also Adelman and Gibbs 1980). College graduates with broad arts, social science and science degrees had particular employment problems in the early 1980s, when the study was carried out, and the authors advance the idea that colleges should therefore move away from such curricula towards ones that are more obviously employment-oriented; in our terms, from general to generic courses. However, the problem is to what extent the unemployment problem is a consequence of the kind of curriculum, or the kind of institution. Here, we can perhaps refer back to the discussion of graduate employment presented early in the chapter. Leaving aside for the moment differences in personal qualities and skills, which may or may not vary with the curriculum, it would seem that graduates who can offer both *expertise* and *ability* are in the strongest employment position, those who offer either one or the other may also find a job niche, but that those who offer neither are worst off. The implication is that if college graduates are relatively weak on inferred ability, they should ensure that they are strong on relevant competence.

The status of general courses is thus as much a matter of context and clientele as content, and seems likely to change only if the latter change. Altering the relative breadth, depth or pattern of courses seems likely to make only a marginal difference to their reputation inside and outside the higher education system. Three other factors could, however, lead to some change in status. The first is the trend towards broader curricula in the schools, which seems likely to have a knock-on effect on A (and AS) levels and thence higher education. The second is the need for a broader foundation for many graduate jobs, although in these again, process may be as important as content. The third is the growth of modular-credit schemes reinforced by a shift from student grants to loans, from full-time to part-time study, from young to mature entrants, all of which may have an impact – though one difficult to discern – on the breadth and structure of studies.

The hidden curriculum

The bulk of this chapter has been taken up with a discussion of the relationship between the undergraduate curriculum and just two of Lawton's eight 'cultural sub-systems' – the social and the economic – although the latter has led us into areas which are a long way from the purely economic, and seems to yield a useful typology of undergraduate courses. This emphasis could be justified on the grounds that economics – or at least a version of it – lies currently at the heart of government discourse on higher education, but it also reflects the fact that there is more to go on, in terms of information and analysis, with this aspect of the undergraduate curriculum than with the other seven. However, something must be said if only briefly about Lawton's other headings.

Higher education clearly has some impact on the 'communication' and 'technological' aspects of the culture, the latter particularly through the application of research. It may even affect current 'aesthetic' tastes and judgements, though it would be hazardous to speculate how, and the arts maintain important centres of influence outside the higher education system, in publishing, museums, galleries and the media. Indeed, the creative and performing arts never seem to have become entirely integrated into the system – they do not quite fit standard CNAA validation procedures for example – and this is perhaps no bad thing. A plurality of institutions underpins a plurality of values.

It is Lawton's three remaining headings – rationality, morality and belief – which raise some of the most interesting but elusive questions about the curriculum. All three refer to culture in the sense of the pattern of thought and behaviour; and all three involve some consideration of the effects of the 'hidden curriculum' of undergraduate education. What messages, overt or covert, does higher education transmit about how to think, how to behave and what to believe? One possible answer is none. Higher education, to many lecturers, is a matter of knowledge and skills consciously acquired and it eschews precisely those matters of thought, behaviour and belief which Lawton nominates. Not to do so would be to infringe the essential autonomy of the student and objectivity of the activity. Others would admit, indeed require, that higher education should embody rationality, and in so far as one can believe or practice that, it becomes a cultural pattern. But the relevance of the question perhaps becomes more obvious if one considers a few examples of the kind of indirect or hidden influence that higher education might have on the culture. All these examples are speculative, but all have surfaced in the recent debate on higher education.

The first has to do with one of the central themes of this chapter, namely the *professional* nature of most undergraduate education. Does this mean that the undergraduate curriculum essentially transmits professional norms and values, related to ideas such as expertise, autonomy, collegiality, service, and so on? The contrast between professional norms and bureaucratic norms is a familiar theme in the literature on professions, and is to some extent exemplified in the ambiguous relationship between academics and administrators in higher education itself. On the whole, however, professionals find ways of relating to bureaucrats; indeed, they have certain things in common, such as a belief in structure and continuity. But what of the relationship between the professional and the entrepreneur? One does come across entrepreneurial academics, but there is still something slightly suspect in the academic world about making, as distinct from earning, money which manifests itself in the grey area of consultancy. And if the Training Agency (1989) thinks it necessary to introduce an 'enterprise element' into degree courses, is that an implicit recognition that such courses tend to inculcate some other set of values?

Anti-entrepreneurial attitudes must be distinguished from anti-industrial ones; although they may go together, they need not. The charge that higher education has over a longer period contributed to an anti-industrial ethos among the educated classes in Britain has been laid by Wiener (1981) and countered in different ways by Sanderson (1972) who points to manifold examples of involvement with industry, and Shattock (1987) who tends to lay the blame elsewhere, at the door of government and industry itself. Perhaps one needs to distinguish between different parts of the higher education system in such an argument; the current system after all comprises not one (Oxbridge) tradition but several.

But there can be no doubt that higher education is largely a *mental* rather than manual occupation: in terms of the classification in the US Department of Labor's *Dictionary of Occupational Titles*, it involves work with ideas rather than work with people or work with things. There is much in Western culture which gives precedence to the first, regarding them not merely as more important but more real. Within higher education, the mental/manual dichotomy is to some extent shadowed by the pure/applied one. It would not be altogether surprising if higher education did inculcate a certain distaste for dirtying one's hands, for products and things (money, in this context, is not a thing). And the 'people professions' (such as management, social work and teaching) also seem to have a somewhat ambiguous status in the academic culture, which may lead them sometimes to de-emphasize the human aspects of their work, and emphasize the theoretical, procedural or institutional.

The case of engineering is even more complex and more interesting. Hutton and Lawrence (1981), in their comparisons of the training, careers and status of German and British engineers, argue that the relationship with pure science is different in the two countries (but see Chapter 2, note 1). They go on to suggest that the characteristic British concern with the professional status of engineers is largely compensatory, and that the status of engineers is linked to the more general status of industry in the two countries. Their data show that German engineers are more likely to be in key management positions than their British counterparts (who are relatively poorly paid even in UK terms), and they draw a general contrast between the 'profit-centred' approach which they find in Britain, and the 'product-centred' one they find in Germany:

> The corporate background for this kind of deportment by production managers is quite simply a very product-oriented one. German managers 'talk products' and manufacturing more than their British colleagues do, and this applies to German managers generally, not just those associated with design and product development. An easy way of putting this claim to the test is to ask senior German managers what, as representatives of their company, they are most proud of. The answers tend to emphasize products, product quality, design, manufacturing techniques, and after sales service, and to de-emphasise profit, turnover, market share, and acquisitions.
>
> (pp. 130–1)

Of course, concern with the product to the exclusion of everything else – customer, market, cash-flow, productivity, and so on – can lead to the kind of product fetishism which allows 'good' engineering firms to go bust. Nevertheless, one wonders to what extent higher education in the UK has played a role in creating not a military–industrial, but financial–bureaucratic complex, dominated by the City and the Treasury, which works to the long-term disadvantage of not simply manufacturing but all forms of 'producer' industries. Even the Council for Industry and Higher Education notes the 'magnetic attractions' of the financial sector (CIHE 1987). The situation may change as the nature of industry itself changes. The old pattern of capital/resource/labour-intensive manufacturing is giving way to a more knowledge-intensive one, not only in the field of information technology, but in all forms of production. One of the most interesting effects of the new technology (significantly called 'high') may be to modify the pure/applied distinction, and thereby bring higher education and industry naturally closer together.[14]

What other kinds of messages may undergraduate curricula covertly or unconsciously transmit? Another possible one has to do with time. There has been a good deal of discussion recently of time-perspectives in industrial and economic policy, with both industry and the City being accused of 'short-termism', sometimes in comparison with the Germans or Japanese. Whatever the truth of this, higher education, by contrast, embodies a kind of 'long-termism'. It thinks in years, not months or weeks: the three or four years it takes to reach a degree; the similar or longer period needed for a doctorate; the intellectual shifts that occur over decades, even centuries. To most academics, this sort of perspective seems perfectly natural, and they see nothing odd in someone working on a problem or book for years. On the whole, academics will trade time for quality, although sometimes no doubt they use quality as an excuse for not being on time. But such long-termism is out of step not only with the more immediate demands of industry, but the drum of government policy. The pressure comes most obviously in terms of the recently imposed completion rates for postgraduate research, but there also seems to be a more general irritation in policy circles with what seems to be the leisurely pace of higher education, a pace which some would link with the original meaning of the word scholar.

The hidden curriculum may transmit messages not only about the time perspective of tasks, but about identification with them, and in particular the non-identification that is implied by the idea of scepticism. This theme will be explored further in the next chapter. To some extent the notion of academic scepticism is a caricature or even downright inaccurate; the advancement of knowledge requires emotional commitment just as much as detachment, and it is the ground-rules of public research rather than the temperament of academics which sustain objective criticism. But the traditions and conventions of scepticism and proper doubt sit uneasily with the current politics of commitment and conviction, whether of the left or the right. There seems also to be a feeling not only in government but in the mass media that academics lack conviction, that they are a bit 'wet' or 'wimpish', that they produce, to use the Prime Minister's phrase, 'guffy stuff'. (This perception is if anything stronger in the popular culture in the USA, where it has bred an academic response in the form of the Extrovert Professor who can take on anybody, physically or mentally). And of course such a perception produces its own reaction, in the emphasis on common sense and experience, in people who boast of having attended the University of Life, or feel it their duty to sort out young graduates when they enter their first job, or even in anti-intellectual or irrationalist currents in higher education itself (Shils 1984).

This aspect of the culture relates very closely to the final example of the 'hidden curriculum' of higher education. Higher education is, if nothing else, analytic; it involves the inspection of assumptions, the questioning of conclusions, the detailed dissection of logical, empirical and interpretative processes. When people say that higher education teaches one to 'think', they probably have in mind this induction into the habit of analysis. The question really is what the opposite of 'analytic' is, what cultural patterns of thought and behaviour exist outside higher education with which it contrasts or even conflicts. 'Synthetic' is logical but wrong; 'normative' is possible; some might suggest 'active'. But the real contrast is surely with the tacit.

Is there an in-built tendency for continuous, unbroken cultures to become more compressed, assumptive, allusive and tacit over time? The very continuity of patterns of thought and behaviour mean that the articulation of those patterns can become ever more economical, to the point where they are increasingly condensed in symbols, codes, rituals and obliquities. (The process can also be observed in a marriage.) English, as distinct from British, culture seems to provide a good example of such a tendency; it is a culture largely undisturbed by invasion or revolution, difficult for foreigners to plumb, subtle and rich in social allusion at every level. Old, compressed cultures such as this can be notably cohesive and resilient, but they can find it increasingly difficult to adapt to radical, as distinct from incremental, changes. Such rigidities can be observed in organizations and institutions as well as whole cultures: the small, traditional engineering or textile firm which fails to adapt to the market and goes out of business; the political party caught between renewal and betrayal; the institution so deeply set in its ways that it is hardly aware of them.

It would constitute a typically academic fallacy to believe that analysis on its own – the sheer power of thought – could change or reverse such a situation, but it could well affect it. The effects of the undergraduate curriculum would in this sense always be counter-cultural, a necessary antithesis to prevailing patterns and norms. The analytic ethos of higher education, diffused through its graduates, would challenge the tacit cultures of institutions and organizations, and in so doing perhaps makes their successful evolution that bit more likely. If that were true, it would constitute a general economic as well as social rationale for higher education, and one that could be related to all of Lawton's eight headings. But the notion of the 'analytic' graduate also raises some difficult questions about the impact of the undergraduate curriculum on student develop-ment, which lead us on to the next chapter.

Notes

1 Lawton's approach may appear too mechanistic and functionalist to some, and different sociological perspectives yield different insights into the curriculum; for example Apple (1979) draws heavily on Marx, and Hargreaves (1982) on Durkheim in their work on the school curriculum. Nevertheless, Lawton's headings provide a useful point of departure here as long as one emphasizes, as he does, that they are not watertight.

2 As Williams (1984) notes, the influence of human capital theory, which partly fuelled the expansion of higher education in the 1960s, has declined, and current thinking on the relationship between education and economic growth seems much more hesitant (for a more recent discussion see Worswick 1985). The problem is partly that there are so many intervening variables, and it may

help to see these in terms of a series of tripartite regressions. There are the three classical factors of production; land (natural resources) labour and capital, although some would argue that the application of organized knowledge to the process of production (i.e. technology) constitutes a fourth. One can posit three main factors which in turn affect the labour factor; organization, skills and attitudes. Productive skills can in turn be acquired through the formal education system, non-formal education and training, or informal experiential learning (see Coombs *et al.* 1973). And one can distinguish between three sectors of formal education: compulsory, consecutive (16–22+) and continuing. Of course such a simple model takes no account of factor interaction or substitution, nor of the influence of the whole political-economic system and context on the operation of all the factors, but perhaps it can help us to identify a number of *policy* questions. For example, was Playfair (1852) right to fear that the relative advantages of the UK in natural resources and capital could lead to an underemphasis on labour as a factor of production? Has the policy emphasis in the last decade on the organization of labour (trades union reform, right to manage) and the attitudes of labour (enterprise culture) been matched by an emphasis on labour skills? At least some recent writing would suggest that the UK still has some way to go as regards the latter, particularly in terms of vocational and technical education (see NEDO/MSC 1984; Prais 1989; Cantor 1989; Squires 1989a). To what extent has the provision of formal vocational and professional education by the state been matched by nonformal provision by employers and informal learning by employees? And even if one argues for increased investment in the formal system, how do we balance the claims of higher education against those of vocational and technical further education, which is seen by some writers as being the sector where the UK compares least favourably with its competitors (see Steedman 1987; Steedman and Wagner 1987; Prais and Wagner 1988; Sanderson 1987). The main debate in the last case is between those who argue for a US/Japanese model of expanded higher education plus extensive in-company training, and those who look to continental (usually German) models of vocational/technical education. There are of course no easy answers to such questions, but they at least serve to remind us of the complexity of the relationship between higher education and the economy.

3 Two points should be made about the concept of a 'graduate labour market'. First, that market appears to be subdivided or 'segmented' in various ways. There seems to be a large general entry market which is ostensibly open to graduates of any discipline, although such apparent openness may conceal employer preferences for certain subjects or types of graduate. Then there are smaller more specialized graduate markets which may be more or less restricted to certain kinds of graduates; medicine and pharmacy are obvious examples, but there are degrees of specialization and hence closure. The segmentation of the market has implications for notions such as manpower planning and shortages. In principle, planning should be more possible in specialized than in general markets, though even in the former there are factors which make it difficult (for contrasting views see Pearson 1985 and Gordon 1986). Similarly, shortages and surpluses have to be analysed in terms of the flows between segments of the market, as well as in the context of more general graduate supply and demand. (For example, Table 3.1 shows some 'reserves' of specialized graduates who did not enter their specialist occupations in that year.) Segmentation and the flexibility of the graduate labour force may also be

increasingly affected by the growth of continuing education and 'conversion' courses of various kinds. Secondly, it should be pointed out that the notion of a graduate labour market often seems to carry with it assumptions about economic rationality and market knowledge. While the aggregate patterns of employment do seem to sustain these to some extent at least, it should be remembered that the situation in which any particular graduate or employer finds him- or herself is very far from that of a 'God's-eye view' of the market. The issue of what might be called the phenomenology of the market is of course a more general one (Shackle 1972); as regards higher education, the study by Roizen and Jepson (1985) gives some sense of the situation as perceived (or at least described) by some employers, though the methodological weaknesses of the research must cast doubt on the conclusions drawn. Perhaps we need more, ethnographic studies of the process of graduate selection to complement the aggregate, quantitative data which we already have. And as the system takes in more and more mature students, the notion of 'first destination' may itself need to be re-conceptualized in such cases.

4 One of the current debates is about the value of first destination statistics which are gathered six months after graduation, and frequently quoted in policy discussions. While the recent follow-up studies of graduates three years out (Brennan and McGeevor 1988) suggest that first destination statistics do not have much *absolute* value – for example, the average graduate unemployment rate falls sharply between six months and three years – they may still have *relative* value in discriminating between sectors and subjects, because the six-month differentials in employment appear to translate into three-year differences in the quality or level of job, with the unemployed at six months more likely to be in 'non-graduate' jobs at three years. (Teichler *et al.* 1980 question the whole idea of non-graduate jobs.) However, there is plenty of job change in the first three years among many types of graduate, and subject-related differences in the pattern of insertion into the labour market are also apparent (see, for example, Brennan and McGeevor 1988; Barnett 1989). The general analysis of graduate employment still seems geared to the young rather than mature graduate, and in the future more attention may have to be paid to the growing number of the latter, with perhaps the evolution of different employment models and concepts.

5 USR statistics allow one to calculate the percentages of graduates who go on to do university postgraduate work *in the same subject* as their first degree, and that might seem a more accurate indicator of the strength of the postgraduate link. However, I still prefer the cruder AGCAS measure, because even where graduates go on to do a postgraduate course in a related subject, sometimes with a vocational emphasis, such a pattern allows the employment frame of reference to be postponed or distanced from the first degree stage, and the 'academic' frame of reference to dominate. Detailed empirical research would be needed to establish the nature of the 'academic' frame of reference, and the extent to which it does conflict with an employment one, although the tensions between the academic and professional aspects in some professional curricula, such as engineering or law, may give some pointers. The introduction of an 'enterprise element' into degree courses seems like an attempt to reinforce the general employment frame of reference (Training Agency 1989).

6 There are obvious dangers in basing an analysis on one-year 'snapshot' statistics such as those in Tables 3.1 and 3.2. Unfortunately, although detailed USR

statistics on first destinations go back a long way, this particular tabulation is recent and hence a strict time-series is not possible. A comparison of the AGCAS figures with those for 1985 shows that although there are some differences, particularly in the polytechnics, the overall pattern is very much the same as for 1987. The point of the two tables is to establish *relativities* between different subjects; the absolute quantities are not central here.

7 The recently published statistics on Open University courses (Open University 1989) give some relevant figures for first degree courses (Table 3.2). While the titles of many of these suggest that they tend to the 'academic', 'professional' or 'general' (the latter heading seems to fit the multidisciplinary foundation courses and the broad U-courses) the final balance depends on the total configuration of a student's choice of options.

8 Reports on professional education in different fields seem to differ in this respect. Finniston (1980) does not refer to other professions but is centrally concerned with the place of engineering in British culture and its relations with science, and cites various overseas comparisons. The UKCC (1986; *Project 2000*) report on nursing, midwifery and health visiting, makes little reference outside these professions, except in the context of the general provision of medical and health care, and the preparation for it, in particular the relationship between off-the-job (education) and on-the-job (service) elements. Some recent reports on social work education do, however, draw comparisons with other professions, for example with respect to the length of training.

9 Law may be another subject which does not fit the theory–practice dichotomy neatly. Although there are recognized academic and vocational stages in the training (Twining 1987), the balance of emphasis within the undergraduate stage can also be seen in terms of a justice–law–society triangle, with the first emphasizing jurisprudence, the second what is sometimes called 'black-letter' law, and the third the socio-political aspects. The relative emphasis on these may in turn reflect the relative influence of professions and academe, which may in turn be affected by the proposals on legal education in the recent Green Paper; although as always there are differences of emphasis between departments/ faculties.

10 Interdisciplinarity may be a less salient issue now at the undergraduate level for two opposing reasons. On the one hand, some interdisciplinary courses were among the first casualties of the 1981 cuts in universities, as departments moved to protect their core subject degrees. On the other hand, some interdisciplinary courses – for example in European studies, environmental studies and business studies – have become so well established now that they attract little or only *sotto voce* comment. There may also be an institutional dimension. The course-based departments of the polytechnics and colleges may provide a happier habitat for interdisciplinary developments than the mainly subject-based university department, where the ideology of the discipline tends to be stronger. Perhaps one thing that has become clear with time is that any analysis of interdisciplinarity depends first on an analysis of the nature of the constituent disciplines, in the kinds of terms attempted in Chapter 2: core, boundaries, structure and culture. See also my fuller discussion in *The Curriculum Beyond School* (1987a, pp. 149–157.)

11 The CATS scheme operates on a 'tariff' rather than 'modular' principle. Instead of imposing a standard size or length of module on all courses (a difficult exercise), it establishes a common currency for a year's work (120

credits) which can then be sub-divided to suit the size and number of courses that make it up (e.g. 4×30, 5×24, 6×20, or any mixture of these). Courses are then accredited in terms of the number of credits and the level of work (first year, second year, etc.). This approach establishes a common currency and basis of accumulation and transfer, without forcing all courses to fit the same Procrustean modular bed. It is easier though not easy to standardize modules within institutions or faculties, but the pattern varies considerably. To my knowledge, no modular scheme in the UK even approaches the completely free-choice cafeteria stereotype (Squires 1986).

12   This raises a more general issue. UK first degree courses are relatively short and specialized by international standards, and Masters courses are likewise short at 12 months rather than the 2 years common elsewhere. The gradient of specialization is thus very steep, and affects not only the undergraduate but the secondary school curriculum. The latter is now being broadened in the National Curriculum, and this will have a knock-on effect, first on A levels, and then on undergraduate courses. One solution to the problem is a two-stage, four-year pattern, with a proportion of students terminating at the intermediate stage with a Diploma or Associate Degree. This pattern exists not only in the USA but also in France. It is difficult to design a first stage which is both transitional and self-contained, but the scope for modular structures in this country is likely to remain limited under the present system. In fact a significant proportion of first degrees are already four-year, and a head of steam is building up for the lengthening of others (see, for example, Institute of Physics 1988). A four-year pattern with a more general first stage would tend to erode the distinctions or at least tensions between academic, professional and general courses discussed in this chapter.

13   The idea that students are capable of designing their own curriculum is more familiar in adult education than higher education, and draws sustenance from the work of Tough (1971) on informal 'adult learning projects'. The co-existence in adulthood of formal with non-formal and informal types of learning perhaps helps to set the formal undergraduate curriculum in a wider perspective. The bulk of adult learning, both individual and collective, occurs outside the formal education system, and rather than seeing such learning as an 'extension' of higher education – the traditional view – one can equally see higher education as a resource for that kind of learning.

14   Despite the great differences between higher education systems in the OECD countries, it is striking how similar the pattern of post-war development has been in many of them: an initial period of reconstruction, followed in the 1960s by an emphasis on expansion and equality, displaced again by an employment/economic emphasis in the mid-1970s. The next phase is thus due, and one notes the re-emergence in the USA of neo-conservative traditionalist values (Bloom 1987) and there and elsewhere a concern with both social and environmental problems. It would be ironic if the industrially inclined UFC and PCFC were getting going just as the economic imperative had passed its zenith.

4
Curriculum and Student Development

The idea that higher education has in some way to do with the development of the student is a familiar enough one, but like other familiar ideas which have been explored in this book, proves to be more complex and elusive on closer inspection. 'Development' is currently one of those halo words which tends to disarm our critical faculties, whether in the field of economics, psychology or education. It implies that there is something to be developed; that the development of that something can be at least partly planned and influenced; and that such development is, by definition, for the better.

The notion of student development in higher education has also tended to carry an additional and accidental weight. Because until recently higher education was largely the preserve of 18- to 21-year-olds, the notion of student development became intertwined with that of the development of the young adult. Thus development was associated with ideas such as maturation, growing up, becoming a fully-fledged adult, and in practice the experience of higher education was also often the experience of leaving home, and finding one's feet in the community of one's peers. This change is interesting and important, but it is not intrinsic to the idea of student development, and with the rapid growth of mature students in the system the distinction will have to be drawn more clearly. As noted earlier, about 25 per cent of first-year, full-time degree or sub-degree students are now over 21 (with the steepest increase in the over 25s) and the proportion of mature part-timers is much higher (DES *Statistical Bulletins* 11/88, 4/89). It is not that adults do not continue to develop and change; indeed, the idea of adulthood as a kind of developmental plateau has been challenged in recent years by writers such as Riegel (1979), Cross (1982) and Mezirow (1983). However, the nature of such changes differ from those occurring on the threshold of adulthood, and their interaction with student development *per se* is therefore likely to be different.

But what do we mean by the development of the student? It is presumably the development of the student *qua* student rather than *qua* individual, person, citizen, adult, or whatever; in other words, it is development in terms of those attributes or activities which are essential to the notion of 'studenthood'. Since studenthood implies learning, and learning in higher education connotes the acquisition of organized knowledge and intellectual skills, 'development' in this particular context connotes first and foremost cognitive development, the development of the mind, or as it is sometimes put, 'learning to think'.

This can be given either a philosophical or psychological gloss. Some philosophers of education have interpreted it in terms of rationality and the development of not only a capacity for, but commitment to, reason and analysis. Such rationality, they argue, is not simply an attribute of 'mind'; it constitutes mind. The concepts of rationality and reason lie both conceptually and normatively at the heart of a good deal of philosophical writing on the curriculum (see Dearden *et al.* 1972), and in higher education are associated with names such as Barzun (1969), Nisbet (1971) and Shils (1984). Psychologists conceptualize mind in various ways (indeed, strict behaviourists tend to deny or ignore the very notion) but current cognitive theorists tend to see it in terms of a general information-processing capacity, which involves 'high-level' analytic and synthetic elements (Eysenck 1984; Richardson *et al.* 1987). To them, cognition implies a molar rather than merely molecular operation, involving general structures, strategies and processes which go a long way beyond the specific stimulus–response connections of behavioural theory.

The general powers of the mind

Perhaps the best-known statement of this cognitive view of student development comes in Robbins' declaration of the four main objectives of higher education. After the reference to 'skills suitable to play a part in the general division of labour', and before the paragraphs on the 'advancement of learning' and 'transmission of a common culture,' comes the following:

> But, secondly, while emphasising that there is no betrayal of values when institutions teach what will be of some practical use, we must postulate that what is taught should be taught in such a way as to promote the general powers of the mind. The aim should be to produce not mere specialists but rather cultivated men and women. And it is the distinguishing mark of a healthy higher education that, even where it is concerned with practical techniques, it imparts them on a plane of generality that makes possible their application to many problems – to find the one in the many, the general characteristic in the collection of particulars. It is this that the world of affairs demands of the world of learning. And it is this, and not conformity with

traditional categories, that furnishes the criterion of what institutions may properly teach.

(Robbins 1963, para. 26)

It is a highly condensed statement which the Appendices to the Report do not help us to unpack; indeed, they seem to shy away from such issues (see Robbins 1963, appendix two (B), III: 1:2). The first sentence seems to refer to both the process and the content of courses, and contains the key reference to the 'general powers of the mind'. These seem to be interpreted in terms of generalities/particulars, and implicitly theory/practice, though the term 'cultivated' adds an extra, cultural tinge. There is the assumption that these general powers can not only be applied but transferred to a range of situations and problems, particularly in the world of work, and that such transferable powers or skills are what employers essentially want of graduates. But what are these 'general powers of the mind'? Academics were asked what the phrase meant in terms of their subject. Some of the responses were as follows:

Students are consciously trained to develop logical and independent thought, communication skills, critical judgement, the ability to present reasoned argument based on sound evidence, and to exercise these skills in relation to large bodies of disparate evidence and data. While these skills are not necessarily specific to our BA Honours degree in Politics and Government, they accord with a general understanding of Robbins' 'powers of the mind'.

'General powers of the mind' as developed by History in our BA in Combined Studies would include the ability to read and extract what is significant, the ability to write and develop an argument logically and coherently, the capacity to empathise with, appreciate and understand other cultures, other peoples, other times, the recognition that developing the mind is a continual process, that learning is not to be equated with certainty, but with constant enquiry and openness to the valuation of evidence.

Being able to judge between rival explanations of a phenomenon under conditions of uncertainty.

(Sociology)

Another writer was, however, more sceptical of the whole notion:

It is not difficult to argue that an education in Statistics develops the 'general powers of the mind' far beyond any specific vocational aims. Three aspects in particular may be mentioned. (a) The subject is highly mathematical – so the student is trained in rigorous logical thinking. (b) The subject is based on the theory of probability which is extensively studied – thus the subject provides training in understanding the role of chance, in decision making in the face of uncertainty etc. (c) Both the capacity to analyse quantitative data and experience in using computers have wide applicability in the modern world. However, I suspect that the notion that degree courses develop the 'general powers of the mind' is largely a convenient argument to justify degree courses which force students to devote their time to topics which their teachers want to teach – with too little regard to the interests of the students or of the nation whose youth (the ablest part of it) is being formed.

An economist interpreted the idea in terms of appearance and reality:

Economics does keep teaching that things are not as they seem on the surface, or as they are popularly supposed – a 'weak pound' is not always a bad thing, taxes do not necessarily fall on the person who apparently pays the tax, etc. – and so encourages students to strip away the appearances, and take an analytical view of things.

Others again suggested that it had various facets in relation to their discipline:

Engineering courses tend to be fairly practical rather than philosophical. However, having said that, teaching students to design and analyse in engineering situations requires considerable development of mental faculties. In particular, students must learn to conceptualise and synthesise. There are surprising similarities as well as obvious differences between composing a piece of music or painting a picture and say designing a circuit or designing a building.

Since music combines elements of both 'art' and 'science' it serves quite well as an education in itself, requiring skills related to 'abstract' thought (analagous to mathematics) and skills in historical research and aesthetic judgement.

An emphasis is placed on the student's ability to 'think' creatively, visually and intellectually through problem-solving activities and by thorough research and evaluation into problems that are presented. This applies equally to the academic content of the course – usually by form of thesis.

(Graphic Design)

Developing the capacity to relate theory and practice. In other words, developing the ability to generalise from the particular in relation to one's own practice and to critically analyse and evaluate what one is doing and why and how one is doing it. Importantly, too, higher education in our subject should also be helping students link affect and intellect, or understanding with feeling.

(Social Work)

Sounds good, what does it mean? At the general level, the purpose of a University education is to develop intellectual abilities and personality – education in the broad. But this goes hand in hand with the acquisition of specialised knowledge and skills specific to narrower fields of study, e.g. economics – education in depth. Openness of mind and acceptiveness to new ideas, desire to learn, tolerance for the views of others, breadth of knowledge and social awareness are all part of the broader educational function of a University education.

(Economics)

Finally, one response emphasized not just the analytic but problem-solving aspect of the subject:

The course is concerned with problem solving whether about people, materials, machines or money and develops an attitude that systematically questions existing situations.

(Manufacturing Systems Engineering)

It is worth noting that some of the above statements go beyond the merely cognitive, and imply the development of skills, the inculcation of certain attitudes and values, and the emergence of a particular self-concept, for example as an academic or a professional person. But sticking for the moment to the idea of developing cognitive powers, we can identify at least 12 facets of the 'general powers of the mind', as follows:

1 *The capacity to identify assumptions.* The graduate is expected to be able to go behind or beneath the statement or method presented to him, and unearth its underlying assumptions.

2 *The capacity to evaluate statements in terms of evidence.* The graduate will typically ask what evidence or basis there is for a particular statement or approach, and will look for disconfirming as well as confirming data.

3 *The capacity to detect false logic or reasoning.* This is a capacity one associates more perhaps with medieval graduates than contemporary ones who might not know a syllogism if they met one. But at least the graduate should be aware of obvious flaws in an argument.

4 *The capacity to identify values implicit in statements or methods.* The graduate is expected to be alert to the ethical or normative implications of what is being said or done, and to be able to distinguish fact from value (even if the relationship between them is itself open to argument).

5 *The capacity to generalize appropriately.* In practice this nearly always means avoiding over-generalizing, and delighting in picking out exceptions to the rule. The specificity of much academic work may even lead graduates to under-generalize.

6 *The capacity to define terms adequately.* The graduate will often identify him- or herself and irritate others by saying 'it depends what you mean by . . .'

7 *The capacity to articulate.* Graduates are expected to be able to express themselves clearly both orally and in writing, although there is perhaps a greater premium placed on this in the arts than the sciences.

8 *The capacity to quantify data where appropriate.* This, by contrast, is associated with the sciences and technology more than the arts, but is becoming a more general skill if one includes computing.

The capacity to remain open and responsive to ideas and phenomena. The graduate is expected to have an open mind, though this takes different forms in different disciplines; where in the sciences it connotes systematic scepticism, in the arts it is associated more perhaps with sensitivity and responsiveness.

10 *The capacity to use complex causal models of problems and phenomena where appropriate.* Where commonsense thinking will often attribute an effect to a single cause (It's all the fault of . . .) the graduate will typically employ more complex causal models, and often talk in terms of 'factors' and 'variables'.

11 *The capacity to pose, formulate and solve problems.* The graduate is expected to be able to identify problems, and organize thought, resources and action to tackle them; which assumes a certain capacity for autonomy and responsibility.

12 *The capacity to apply and transfer what is known to a range of situations.* The graduate should not be 'context-bound' in the use and application of all the above, but be able to deploy them across a wide range of situations, problems and settings.

Several points should be made about such a list. First, it is difficult to find hard evidence that first degree courses do or do not develop the kinds of capacities referred to above.[1] Whereas some of the capacities (e.g. to detect false reasoning, define terms, articulate ideas and quantify data) can be assessed and measured in a fairly direct way at the end of a course, others (e.g. the evaluation of evidence or the use of complex causal models) require much more complex forms of assessment, and others again can only really be assessed some time after the course, during the graduate's first or subsequent jobs: this would apply to the capacity to remain open to ideas, to formulate and solve problems, and to apply and transfer what has been learned. One of the basic problems of higher education is that its assessments are immediate, while many of its professed aims are medium-term or long-term.

A second problem with such a list is that it may not apply evenly across all disciplines. Clearly, one will associate the arts with articulacy and the sciences with numeracy, the identification of assumptions and values with the 'pure' and problem-solving and transfer with the 'applied'. But it is difficult not to feel that the list has an underlying analytic bias which sits uneasily with the humanities. In what sense are causal models or canons of generalization relevant to the study of literature? How appropriate is the implicit fact/value distinction to the arts generally? No doubt one has to base one's statements about a piece of music or drama on *something*, but is 'evidence' quite the right word? Can one sustain the implicit distinction between cognitive and affective? And, from the perspective of the applied or active disciplines, does not the list seem concerned with knowing rather than doing? Does it not supply ammunition to those who argue that degree courses are essentially theoretical rather than practical? How far is it really concerned with 'capability' or with turning out 'reflective practitioners' in Schon's (1987) sense? The different interpretations of the 'general powers of the mind' send us back to the different facets of knowledge discussed in Chapter 2. They also send us back to the detailed data on the first destinations of graduates in various subjects given in Table 3.1. These surely provide the concrete test for assumptions about 'training the mind'. To what extent does each of the 25 subjects or courses actually develop the 12 'general powers' listed above? To what extent do the various occupations utilize such 'general powers'? And to what extent does the transfer actually occur? Such questions suggest that the transfer of learning may be rather less general, and rather more context-bound than is sometimes assumed.

Cognitive styles and multiple intelligences

An even more basic objection to the list is that the whole idea of general powers or capacities of the mind is itself fallacious. This criticism takes a 'weak' form in the concept of *cognitive style*, and a 'strong' form in the notion of *multiple intelligences*, and something must be said about each of these. Each points to difficulties in generalizing about the ways in which students think, and the kinds of thinking embodied in different disciplines.

I have reviewed some of the literature on cognitive styles elsewhere (Squires 1981a; see also Goldstein and Blackman 1978) but the main source for what follows here is Messick *et al.*, *Individuality in Learning* (1978), which seeks to 'explore the practical implications of recent research on cognitive styles and creativity for higher education' (p. v). Cognitive style research is concerned not so much with what a student knows, but 'rather with the manner in which he acquires knowledge and with his characteristic modes of processing information and experience' (p. vi). Each individual, it is argued:

has preferred ways of organizing all that he sees and remembers and thinks about. Consistent individual differences in these ways of organizing and processing information have come to be called cognitive styles. These styles represent consistencies in the manner or form of cognition, as distinct from the content of cognition or the level of skill displayed in cognitive performance. They are conceptualized as stable attitudes, preferences, or habitual strategies determining a person's typical modes of perceiving, remembering, thinking, and problem solving. As such, their influence extends to almost all human activities that implicate cognition, including social and interpersonal functioning.

(p. 5)

From this, it can be seen that cognitive styles lie at the intersection between perception, intelligence and personality, and have potential implications not only for education but for occupational choice and indeed personal and social life generally. Several points about cognitive styles can be noted right away. First, they are nearly always conceptualized in terms of a bipolar continuum. This does not of course mean that everyone is at one extreme or the other, merely that the research shows enough 'spread' to justify thinking in such terms. Secondly, there is a good deal of disagreement about how many such continua there are (Messick discusses 19). Thirdly, there is usually no implication that one end of the continuum is better than another (in contrast to intelligence scales), although some poles (e.g. reflectivity) may suit education better than others (impulsivity). Fourthly, the amount and quality of research that has been carried out on the various continua varies a good deal, and some of it is open to methodological criticisms (see Wilson 1981, pp. 135–49). Fifthly, there is some argument about how far students' thinking is a matter of fixed or at least habitual *styles*, or how far students can and do deploy an array of cognitive *strategies* in response to a particular problem or situation. It has emerged that some 'styles' were manifested in research situations not because the student habitually employed them, but because he or she thought that was what the experimenter expected. The ability to switch or vary such strategies could be an important one in both education and work, and might develop with experience.

Despite such *caveats*, the research on cognitive styles poses an interesting question for anyone concerned with student development. It is taken for granted that students differ as regards their personality and level of general ability,[2] but this research suggests they may differ in their *type* of ability – or at least style of thinking – as well. What kinds of styles? There is not room here to describe the lexicon of styles in any detail. One of the best researched is the field-dependence/field-independence continuum. Field-independent people tend to be able to abstract figures or objects from the context or field in which they are embedded more easily than their counterparts who have a stronger sense of the undifferentiated whole. Interestingly, this continuum originated in research on visual perception, but subsequent work found that it made sense in terms of cognition and even occupational differences and social relations (Witkin and Goodenough 1977). Another interesting continuum is the levelling/sharpening one:

> Persons at the levelling extreme tend to blur similar memories and to merge perceived objects or events with similar but not identical events recalled from past experience; differences in remembered objects tend to be lost or attenuated. Sharpeners, at the other extreme, are less prone to confuse similar objects and may even magnify small differences between similar memory traces, thereby exaggerating change and heightening the difference between the present and the past.
>
> (Messick and associates 1976, p. 18)

Both these style-dimensions have their roots in differences in perception, and while each is suggestive, it is difficult to see any obvious implications for the development of 'thinking' in higher education. Other styles, however, are more obviously 'cognitive'. 'Breadth of categorization', for example, has to do with the tendency towards errors of inclusion or errors of exclusion (cf. the capacity to generalize listed above) and 'conceptual differentiation' refers to the number of concepts or dimensions a person uses in categorizing phenomena. Pask and Scott (1972) initially distinguished between serialists, who tend to tackle problems step-by-step, and holists who like to get the overall picture from the very beginning, later conceptualizing the difference in terms of operation and comprehension learners. Bruner *et al.* (1967) have distinguished between problem solvers who focus or limit the amount of information they deal with at each stage, and scanners who adopt a more ambitious and inclusive strategy. Other dimensions, such as reflection/impulsivity, abstraction/concretion and strong/weak automatization may also have a bearing on 'learning to think'.

The research on cognitive styles raises interesting questions about how students 'think', and also about how they should be taught, for example by matching teaching styles and learning styles, but it is more difficult to relate it to *what* is taught, to the curriculum. For example, while some correlation between the field dependence/independence dimension and achievement in mathematics, science and engineering has been found (Witkin and Goodenough 1977), there appears to be little correlation with general academic performance. The relevance of other dimensions to the curriculum is even more tenuous. Of all the bipolar continua, it is the distinction between convergers (who look for a single, right solution) and divergers (who generate multiple possible outcomes) which has seemed the most intriguing in curricular terms. This dimension, originally posited by Guilford (1956) in his complex model of the 'structure of intellect' and later explored by Hudson (1966, 1968), seems to map on to the arts/science distinction to some extent. Convergers tend to cluster in the relatively systematic, logical and unambiguous disciplines of mathematics, the sciences and engineering, whereas divergers cluster in the more open-ended, imaginative and uncertain environments of the arts. (Parlett and King 1971 explored a somewhat similar distinction between syllabus-bound and syllabus-free students, whom they labelled 'sylbs' and 'sylfs'.) But even here the correlation is not simple. A moment's thought reveals that many disciplines have a convergent–divergent spectrum *within* them, and that a converger may well find his niche in English and a diverger within physics. Even the different branches of mathematics may involve different styles of thought.

If the notion of cognitive styles tends to nibble away at our ability to generalize about 'thinking' or the 'powers of the mind', the notion of multiple intelligence poses a direct challenge to it. Ever since the modern concept of intelligence began to emerge at the turn of the century, there have been two schools of thought about its nature. The dominant view has been that intelligence is a unitary phenomenon, and that it was therefore legitimate to conflate the measures derived from a battery of tests in a single value or quotient. This was, with individual variations, the essential view of

Binet, Spearman and other early researchers, and underlies contemporary cognitive psychologists' concern with general problem solving (see, for example, Simon, 1979a, 1979b). However, there has always been a minority view that human ability constitutes not a single process or capacity but a plurality of 'intelligences' which do not necessarily go together, and which consequently cannot all be rolled into one single measure. If one ignores the largely discredited 'faculty psychology' of the nineteenth century, this view derives from Thurstone, with his concept of a family of 'primary mental abilities', through the work of Guilford (1956) to present-day writers of whom the best known is Gardner (1983), who developed his theory in a book entitled *Frames of Mind*[3] (see also Allport 1980). Gardner's point of departure is reminiscent of Robbins:

> For well over two thousand years, at least since the rise of the Greek city-state, a certain set of ideas has dominated discussions of the human condition in our civilization. This collection of ideas stresses the existence and importance of mental powers – capacities that have been variously termed *rationality, intelligence*, or the deployment of *mind*.
>
> (p. 5)

In modern times, he goes on to argue, a divergence opened up between those who studied the mind and those who studied the brain:

> Because the history of pre-scientific psychology was entangled with philosophy rather than with medicine, and because the first psychologists themselves were eager to define their discipline as separate from physiology and neurology, there was relatively little contact between the new breed of psychologists and the individuals who were conducting experiments with the human brain. Perhaps as a result, the categories of mentation that interested psychologists proved to be remote from those that had engaged the students of the brain. Rather than thinking (like Gall) in terms of particular mental contents (like language, music or various forms of visual perception) psychologists searched (and have continued to search) for the laws of broad, 'horizontal' mental faculties – abilities like memory, perception, attention, association, and learning; these faculties were thought to operate equivalently – in fact, blindly – across diverse contents, independent of the particular sensory modality or the type of ideational content involved in the domain. In fact, such work continues to this day and makes remarkably little contact with findings emanating from the brain sciences.
>
> (p. 14)

Drawing on evidence from a variety of fields – clinical psychology, neurophysiology and anthropology – Gardner argues that we should think of the general powers of the mind in terms of seven distinguishable capacities: linguistic, logico-mathematical, spatial, musical, kinaesthetic, interpersonal and intrapersonal. He goes beyond the idea that the brain is 'lateralized' into two main types of function to assert that many of the above intelligences are relatively localized and compartmentalized, and draws on the examples of '*idiots savants*' and work with brain-damaged patients as well as more conventional experimental research to show that people who are able (and sometimes gifted) in one respect may be quite average (or even subnormal) in others.

There is not room here to examine Gardner's thesis in any detail; it is argued at some length, often convincingly, and illuminates some of the less frequently explored domains of learning, e.g. acting and athletics. There are of course problems. Whereas those who take a holistic or generic view of the mind find it hard to explain how people can be good at one thing and yet mediocre or poor at others, the 'localizers' like Gardner are always left with the 'homunculus' problem: who or what organizes or mediates between all these specific capacities and operations? In the end, do we not have to invoke some kind of general processing capacity or function, a position which Fodor (1983) in fact arrives at?

How does the concept of multiple intelligences bear on the notion of students' cognitive development? How does it relate to the curriculum? The clear implication is that the cognitive development of the student must be conceived of in a pluralistic way; we are talking not about a common set of 'powers' or capacities, but a range of types of ability which most students are unlikely to possess in equal measure. There is then the subsidiary question whether we should concentrate on developing the student's existing proclivities or strengths, or whether we should attempt to achieve a more 'balanced' development which ensures some minimum level of competence in all types. Should we concentrate on developing the existing talents of the gifted mathematician, designer or linguist, or should we attempt to ensure that each of these develops (for example) his or her interpersonal or kinaesthetic skills as well?

Even if we decide on one or the other course, however, the curricular (and occupational) implications are not straightforward. While we may associate certain disciplines with certain types of intelligence – mathematics, music and languages are perhaps the most obvious – in fact most disciplines involve a mixture of types, and a good deal depends on what aspect or sub-field of the discipline is involved.[4] As with cognitive styles, there is no simple match between type of intelligence and subject. Nevertheless, Gardner's work helps us to explicate the gut feeling that different disciplines are different not only in terms of what they are about, but in terms of the talents they require and the processes they involve. The theory of multiple intelligences challenges the undifferentiated view of 'mind' implicit in Robbins, and suggests that what is usually defined as 'intelligence' constitutes only a part of the whole. It also gives some psychological backing to curriculum theorists such as Eisner (1982) who have argued for a broader concept of 'cognition' in the curriculum.

The problem of transfer

Robbins not only posited the existence of 'general powers of the mind', he believed that such powers were applicable and transferable beyond the context in which they were initially developed – hence his reference to the 'world of affairs'. This assumption raises the thorny problem of the transfer of learning or training.

At its simplest, the concept of transfer assumes that something – some piece of information, skill, procedure or approach – which has been learned or acquired in one situation can be deployed and applied in a different one. The transfer of training involves relatively concrete and specific skills; for example, a mechanic who has learned to strip down one kind of car engine should be able to strip down a different make, because although the two models will differ the essentials of 'stripping down' will have been acquired. The 'general transfer of learning' involves broader and less concrete capabilities; for example, one might expect that someone who has been trained in legal argument would be able to argue effectively in any situation, or that a scientist or historian who had been taught to weigh evidence carefully would do so even in arguments about higher education itself. Transfer may also be negative (learning to play badminton is a bad preparation for learning to play tennis, because of the difference in wrist action), or 'zero' where there is no discernible effect, or the positive and negative effects cancel each other out.

Two sets of variables affect transfer: those related to the task and its context, and those related to the person. Some early behavioural psychologists, such as Thorndike (1924), tended to concentrate on the first, and in general concluded that unless there are strong similarities of content or process in the two tasks/contexts, transfer is unlikely to occur. This doctrine of 'identical elements' was seen at the time as discrediting the prevalent belief that particular disciplines had particular cognitive effects, e.g. that mathematics makes one precise, science makes one observant, and so on. Cognitive psychologists such as Bruner (1960, 1968), by contrast, have tended to concentrate on the person variables, and assert that if a person develops high-level, generalized approaches to learning, transfer is quite likely to occur, and that one can even speak of 'learning to learn' (Nisbet and Shucksmith 1983).[5] Indeed, the idea of transfer is so central to the notions of cognitive schemata or programmes, executive strategies and general problem solving, that is seems to be disappearing from the literature as a distinct concept. Both schools agree that learning something well in the first place, practising it in a range of situations, and being aware of the possibilities of transfer, increase the likelihood of it taking place.

The concept of general powers of the mind, and the indirect relationship between study and work implied by it, presupposes that such powers or skills are highly transferable. This has obvious consequences for the undergraduate curriculum. It means that the study of a discipline can be justified not only in terms of its intrinsic content or value, or students' interest in it, but in terms of providing, in some general and indirect fashion, a vehicle for 'training the mind' in ways which will ultimately prove useful in a wide range of occupations and situations. The argument is pushed even further: unless one specializes in that discipline, or another, and studies it properly and in depth, one will not train the mind rigorously at all (Squires 1976a). The doctrine of transfer thus provides a vocational rationale (or rationalization, depending on one's point of view) of vocationally 'irrelevant' disciplines. But is it true?

The problem is that it is difficult to design research studies which will capture the very general transfer effects that are claimed to exist.[6] Such effects would only occur over time, and over time many other variables enter and confound the problem. If a graduate applies the logical skills he acquired during his philosophy course to the analysis of his firm's marketing strategy, how far is that due to his course, his general experience of higher education, the environment of the firm, the nature of the marketing problems, or other variables altogether? The studies by Hyman and others (Hyman *et al.* 1975; Hyman and Wright 1979) of the 'enduring effects of education' are not precise enough to answer the need. Besides, there may be important individual as well as subject variables. It is conceivable that differences in cognitive style affect transfer (e.g. in terms of a tendency towards field dependence or independence) – to the extent that a person is able to abstract something from its field or context, one might expect him or her to be more able and likely to transfer it.

The research on transfer, though inconclusive, nevertheless places an important question-mark after one of the most widespread assumptions about undergraduate studies in this country, and one of the basic tenets of Robbins. It forces us to think harder about what we mean by 'learning to think', and about the extent to which the 'trained mind' is a matter of academic style rather than cognitive reality.

Beyond cognition

Thus far, it has been assumed that the development of the undergraduate is primarily a cognitive development, a change in the ways in which he or she thinks. But there is a considerable body of literature about higher education which suggests that the development of the student cannot and indeed should not be merely cognitive, even if cognitive change lies at its heart. Such literature leads us into the fields of ethical, personal, social and cultural development, and the more it does so, the more our problems become not merely empirical, as they were largely in the case of transfer, but conceptual. It becomes difficult to know what we are talking about.

Even learning psychologists concerned with cognitive development admit that cognition does not exist in a vacuum. There have been interesting studies of cross-cultural variations in cognitive styles, and

Gardner devotes a whole chapter to the 'socialization of human intelligences'. The problems of devising 'culture-fair' psychological tests are well known. If earlier generations of psychologists tended to abstract cognitive processes from their natural environment, and relied mainly on controlled experiments in laboratory settings, there is now a much wider awareness that such processes are located in an educational and social context (see Entwistle 1987; Sternberg 1987). Even apparently basic aspects of cognition such as attention cannot be understood except in terms of an individual and culturally informed sense of priorities.

The general literature on higher education has also entertained broader notions of development for a long time. Robbins' fourth aim was 'the transmission of a common culture and common standards of citizenship' (1963, para. 28). Robbins himself later backed away from assumptions of communality built into this aim (Robbins 1980) but there can be no doubt that it was meant to continue a long tradition in British higher education. And Marris's (1964) study of *The Experience of Higher Education*, published a year after Robbins, explored some of these broader aspects of the undergraduate experience:

> The ideal implies, I think, the development of a generalized rational understanding both from the courses themselves and, equally, the social environment in which a student learns. For him, university is not so much an institution, as three or four years of his life, when living away from home, making friends, falling in love or realizing his religious convictions may be as important as studying for a degree. In framing the questions, and interpreting the answers, the inquiry was especially concerned with the development, in this diffuse context, of such a general intellectual awareness.
>
> (p. 3)

Of the more recent literature, one should mention in particular the volume by Collier *et al.* (1974), *Values and Moral Development in Higher Education*, and Wilson's (1981) *Student Learning in Higher Education*, which provides a useful overview of studies of moral and intellectual development, and Lewis's (1984) *The Student Experience of Higher Education*. The great bulk of the literature is American. This may be due mainly to the vastly greater output of studies of higher education in that country, but it also reflects perhaps the desire to analyse such matters more closely. There is no doubt that individual development is part of the ethos and rhetoric of higher education here (Squires 1980) but it is often regarded as something rather private or personal, and not amenable to or a fit subject for research. It belongs largely to the domain of the tacit and the assumptive in British life, and tends to be based on rather general and commonsense ideas about 'growing up', 'finding one's feet', and so on. In the USA, both development theorists (such as Kohlberg or Loevinger) and 'humanistic' psychologists (such as Carl Rogers and Abraham Maslow) have provided a theoretical basis, however problematic, for thinking about these things.

The difference in approach and output says something about differences between the two cultures. It may be that all notions of development derive ultimately from the models of spiritual development which one finds in the major religions (the Path, the Way) and which have become secularized in modern times. Secular models also embody some idea of progression to a high, even ultimate 'level', and there are obvious spiritual parallels to concepts such as 'equilibrium', 'wholeness', 'self-actualization' or 'peak experience'. Indeed, part of the problem with the secular models is that they do not have the firm metaphysical and cultural base which the religious models enjoyed in the past; it is one thing to talk about 'knowing oneself' in a culture which is sure what it means by knowledge and the self (even if the latter is held to be illusory); it is quite another to do so in a pluralistic culture. But the main difference between the UK and the USA in this respect may be to do not with the notion of development itself, but the belief in perfectability. American culture is still characterized by a strong conviction that things can be fixed, put right or achieved by dint of thought and effort, and this applies as much to people as objects or institutions. In this country, by contrast, the idea of perfectability is more likely to evoke scepticism, irony and a certain relish in human eccentricity.

One of the best overviews of American work on models of development is provided by Cross (1982) in *Adults as Learners*. The main landmarks in an extensive field are probably Becker *et al.* (1968) *Making the Grade*, Perry's (1968) *Forms of Intellectual and Ethical Development in the College Years*, Feldman and Newcomb's (1970) massive review of studies of *The Impact of College on Students*, Astin's (1977) *Four Critical Years*, Parker's (1978) *Encouraging Development in College Students* and Chickering and Associates' (1981) *The Modern American College*. The increased proportion of mature students in American higher education has both reinforced and complicated the interest in the field, since it both detaches models of development from concern solely with the maturation of young adults, and opens them up to life-span models and perspectives.

Some idea of the potential scope of the concept of student development can be gained from the list of tables given in Vol. II of Feldman's and Newcomb's (1970) survey, which includes the following:

- Changes in Purposes of College Education Considered Important
- Changes in Attributes of Job or Career Considered Important
- Changes in Attitudes Toward Political, Economic, Social Issues
- Changes in Religious Orientation
- Changes in Intellectual Orientation and Disposition
- Changes in Authoritarianism, Dogmatism, Ethnocentrism, Prejudice
- Changes in Autonomy, Dominance, and Confidence
- Changes in Readiness to Express Impulses

- Changes in Degree of Masculinity or Femininity of Interests and Attitudes
- Changes in Need for Achievement, Persistence, and Vigour
- Changes in Sociability and Friendliness
- Changes in Psychological Well-Being

In many cases, the studies investigated possible correlations between such changes and different disciplines, although they tended not to explore differences *within* such disciplines which could well be significant. As Astin (1977) and Wilson (1981) have pointed out, there are serious methodological problems with many such studies. The typical form for such studies to take is a 'before–after' one, ideally with some non-college young people acting as a control group with which to compare the putative effects of the college experience. There are two main problems. The first is that it is much more difficult to establish an adequate control group than a student group, because the former cannot be confined to a single, convenient institution. Secondly, the measurement of 'effects' typically relies on what students say (in questionnaires and interviews), rather than what they *do*, in terms of behaviour and life-choices, and is immediate rather than delayed (though see Astin 1977, pp. 188–210). Follow-up studies are much more difficult to organize than ones which take place during or at the end of a student's course. Wilson (1981, p. 60) also comments on subsequent studies which appear to show, *inter alia*, 'increased aestheticism, greater complexity of thinking, higher religious tolerance, decreased political naiveté, increased impulse expression, decreased stereotyping of sex-typed interests, and more realistic setting of goals and aspirations'. He notes that the differences between students seem to be accentuated by study in different fields, perhaps because of a tendency to conform to, or at least appear to conform to, the culture of that field.

A more basic criticism of purely empirical studies such as the above is that they are not based on any general theory of development; they try to measure changes which seem important to the researchers at the time, but which may merely reflect the preoccupations and interpretations of the period. Studies in the 1950s and 1960s did not include attitudes to environmental issues, whereas similar studies today might well do so. The meaning of terms like 'tolerance', 'liberalism' or 'masculinity' depends on their particular socio-historical context. The alternative approach is to map out a theory of developmental phases or stages, and to see to what extent measurable changes in students conform to these or diverge from them. Such theories exist. The best-known among them are probably those of Erickson, Kohlberg and Loevinger (see Cross 1982, for an overview). Apart from their inherent conceptual problems, which were alluded to earlier, such theories suffer in this context from a more local difficulty, namely that they are not specifically related to the process of higher education. If many of the empirical studies seem contingent and atheoretical, the development theories seem too global and abstract.

There are, however, two kinds of possible changes in students which can be related both to general models of human development and to the particular aims of higher education. They are the shift from conformity to autonomy, and from belief to scepticism. The first has to do with the locus of decision-making, and the second with the process. The shift from conformity to autonomy reflects the idea that in higher education students should not merely learn to think but think for themselves. This is important not only in terms of ideas, but of values and behaviour. For example, a student from an intolerant religious or racial background might show a measurable shift towards greater tolerance during his or her course. However, this might simply be the result of conformity to the more liberal norms of higher education, and if that person then returned to the intolerant community to work, it is likely that he or she would soon revert to type. Only if the person's tolerance persisted after returning to the community could we speak of the development of autonomy.

This kind of shift can be seen in terms of Riesman's (1950) distinction between the other-directed and inner-directed person, but the more obvious reference in development theories is Kohlberg (1973), who distinguished broadly between three stages of moral development: pre-conventional or egocentric, conventional or conformist, and autonomous or principled. Thinking for oneself implies a degree of autonomy, and the development of a reasonably coherent set of personal values and stances. Autonomy is not just a matter of cognition, of thinking in the abstract; it also has moral or ethical implications (especially if thought is turned into behaviour and action), and affects a person's sense of himself or herself and relations with others – both the self-concept and roles.

Autonomy is often held to be a desirable aim of higher education, though whether it is a general outcome is open to question. But despite all the rhetoric about the value of independence and individuality, autonomous people can often be seen as troublesome, especially in occupations or organizations which require, or think they require, a good deal of conformity. Of course, nobody uses the word conformity: the demands are framed in terms of 'loyalty', 'teamwork', 'group spirit', 'pulling together', and so on. Employers sometimes criticize higher education for turning out people who are not good at working with others, and it is true that the modes of study and assessment of the undergraduate curriculum are largely though not entirely individualistic, and this may be an aspect of the process which needs to be changed. However, perhaps we should also distinguish between cooperation, which is quite compatible with ideas about autonomy, and submissiveness, which is not.

The problem may be one of scope. Employers select graduates (partly) because they value their capacity to think for themselves; but they often want to prescribe the limits within which that capacity shall be exercised, e.g. in questioning the way to carry out a task rather than the task itself. However, one of the possible messages of the hidden undergraduate curriculum is that there are no boundaries or limits to the academic task, or if there are they are artificial rather than real. Thus the conflicts which graduates may experience in their first jobs may be due less to 'arrogance' on their part and 'authoritarianism' on the employer's or supervisor's, than to the fact that the legitimate scope and limits of the work have not been explicitly thrashed out.

The second general shift has to do with the process of thinking and decision making, and the movement from belief to scepticism. 'Belief' is being used here not to refer to a rigorous system of worked-out beliefs, but in the sense of taking things on trust, of assuming them to be natural, normal or true, without personally subjecting them to a detailed, critical evaluation. In this sense, beliefs are not confined to religion or politics, but are a vast and necessary element in everyday life. We simply do not have the time, energy or information to enquire properly into most things, so we have to take them on trust. In this sense, we live very much at second-hand. The notion of belief can also be understood in terms of Husserl's 'natural attitude' or 'natural stance' (see Chapter 2) in which many aspects of the world are taken for granted or treated as unproblematic. The shift away from belief or from the natural attitude is only a matter of degree; an undergraduate education may, perhaps should, lead people to take fewer things on trust than they might otherwise do, and in particular to question and analyse the things that concern them most nearly in their work and life.

The rhetoric of learning to question, criticize and analyse is a familiar one in higher education, but in this case the human development model is more problematic. The most obvious candidate is Perry (1968, 1978). Perry's research on undergraduates in the USA over a number of years led him to elaborate a nine-stage scheme of development, which can be compressed without too much distortion into three: dualism, relativism and commitment. The student initially sees the world in fairly simple dualistic and authoritative terms; things are either right or wrong, black or white. Gradually this simplicity becomes clouded, and the student begins to recognize the validity of different points of view, and moves towards the point where everything becomes a shade of grey, and he finds it difficult if not impossible to choose between them. Then he gradually emerges from this state and finds a position to which he can commit himself, still in the knowledge that other positions are possible, and ends up by identifying himself strongly with that commitment, though not in an intolerant way. In practice, Perry's scheme is much more subtle and less schematic than this brief account might suggest, and allows for regression, marking time, and divergence from the pattern. Nevertheless, this, according to Perry, is not only a common, but desirable pattern of development.

Although Perry's work is open to methodological criticisms, mainly on account of his relatively small sample and lack of controls, it is fascinating in its verbatim, clinical detail. However, it does raise some problems. First, how contingent is it upon the particular places (Harvard and Radcliffe) and times (1950s and 1960s) in which he did it? [Allan Bloom (1987), writing nearly 20 years later, and in apparent ignorance of Perry's research, complains that relativism is now the unthinking point of departure for most students.] Secondly, how justified is Perry's assumption that relativism is an advance on dualism, and commitment an advance on relativism? It is not self-evident that relativistic views of the world are intrinsically superior to dualistic ones, nor is it self-evident that commitment is a better stance than detachment, although Perry argues that each stage incorporates previous ones, in a kind of developmental dialectic. An alternative way of thinking about the kind of development described by Perry is in terms of a shift from cognitive simplicity to cognitive complexity – for example, from monocausal to multicausal models – with a concomitant attitudinal shift in the attitude to 'evidence' and 'judgement'. However, Perry's observation that relativism can lead in some cases to a paralysis of decision which may not be overcome until after the end of the degree course, and perhaps never, will strike a chord in some.

The above shifts, from conformity to autonomy and from belief to scepticism, may represent the *minimum* model of student development which would be accepted by a majority of academics in this country, although without making an extensive empirical study one can only guess. But much of the writing on development goes much further than this 'minimum'. Hurst (1978) discusses Chickering's proposed seven 'vectors' of student development: (1) achieving competence, (2) managing emotions, (3) developing autonomy, (4) establishing identity, (5) freeing interpersonal relationships, (6) clarifying purposes and (7) developing integrity. Knefelkamp and Slepitza (1978) list nine areas of qualitative change: locus of control, analysis, synthesis, semantic structure, self-processing, openness to alternative perspectives, ability to assume responsibility, ability to take on new roles, and ability to take risks with self. Heath (1978) proposes four aspects of personality (cognitive skills, self-concept, values and interpersonal relations) and five dimensions of development: symbolization (the capacity to represent one's experience to oneself; allocentrism (the development of awareness of others and their perspectives); integration (of the various facets of our selves and lives); stabilization (of cognitive processes, self-concept and identity); and autonomy (in terms not only of thinking but self-concept and relationships). Wilson (1981), commenting on these models, notes that development along these different vectors or dimensions may itself be uneven, and reflect differences in personality.

There are three main problems with these broader models. First, some of them identify student development too closely with the development of the 18–22 age-group. That cohort has been the mainstay of higher education until recently, and may remain the largest group. But headings such as 'managing emotions', 'ability to assume responsibility' and 'stabilization' sit less easily on the mature student, who may well already be married, have a responsible job and stable life-style. Secondly, the broader the notion of development and the further it goes beyond the purely cognitive, the more contentious it seems to become. It may be good to be clear about one's purposes in many situations, but growth and development may require periods of unlearning, unclarity and uncertainty as well. Risk-taking may or may not be appropriate. Stabilization could lead to rigidity. Should emotions always be managed? And so on.

Thirdly, it is not clear how far such development can or should take place through the *curriculum*, as distinct from through student counselling, the experience of a peer-group culture or the general 'experience' of higher education, which might include living in residence, belonging to student societies or engaging in extra-curricular activities of various kinds (see Astin (1977) on the differences *between* different US institutions in this respect). In the past, the undergraduate curriculum was inextricably mixed up with all of these aspects of higher education; the implicit model was holistic rather than aggregative (Squires 1979). Now, with the growth of mature entry, part-time study and distance teaching, we may need to distinguish the curriculum more carefully from everything else around it.

Disciplines and development

The other main problem with generic models of this kind is that they do not explore differences in relation to different disciplines. One may posit that the common experience of higher education leads to certain common forms of development. But how far is it a common experience? Setting aside the very real differences between institutions, how far do students even in the same institution share a common educational experience? The writing on subject differences and 'disciplinary cultures' suggests that the variations between courses might outweigh the commonalities of the institution; that indeed the experience of higher education is primarily the experience of a particular department or course, and only secondarily a matter of institutional setting or peer-group culture.

Turning the question around: What kinds of development might we plausibly associate with particular disciplines? What messages, explicit or otherwise, do disciplines appear to carry about desirable intellectual, ethical or personal change? This issue has already been raised in Chapter 2, in the questions to do with the 'culture' of the discipline, and the extent to which it has, and possibly transmits, shared norms. In general, however, there seems to be more speculation than hard evidence about it. True, the Feldman and Newcomb survey of American studies showed differences among subjects in terms of a range of values (1969–70, Vol. II, pp. 104–10): science students valued 'theory' most and arts students least; students of business, economics and commerce rated most highly on 'economic' (materialistic!) values, while the humanities (history, music, arts, English) tended to come at the bottom, with the sciences and social sciences somewhere in between. By contrast, arts subjects came top in 'aesthetic' values, but the pattern in terms of 'social', 'political' and 'religious' values was less consistent. Another set of studies reviewed by Feldman and

Newcomb tended to associate the social sciences with 'politico-economic and social liberalism' (as defined in the USA between the 1930s and 1960s). Students in engineering and some other professional fields such as veterinary science, pharmacy, business studies (and education) scored high on tests of authoritarianism and related characteristics (such as dogmatism) in some other studies. Again, while such findings may ring some bells, their value is heavily contingent upon the concepts and perceptions of the relevant time and place. 'Liberalism' in the USA is not the same as 'liberalism' in the UK, and some of the measures of 'authoritarianism' related to attitudes to racial segregation/de-segregation at that time.

One finds a less quantitative, more qualitative approach to many of the same issues in the second and third parts of Collier *et al.* (1974) *Values and Moral Development in Higher Education*, where various writers in this country analyse the possible contribution of their own discipline to students' intellectual and moral development. Wilson, for example, argues that the study of philosophy leads the student (1) to suppress his own autistic feelings in favour of the truth, (2) to do so in a public dialogue, (3) to learn enough moral philosophy to appreciate the right sort of reasons for moral thought and action, (4) to learn a style of thought, and (5) to learn to describe the world accurately through language. Chanan explores the concept of 'character' in the study of literature; Henderson describes the sense of awe that comes with the study of history; 'awe in the face of human beings tragically committed to be always making relative choices in absolute terms' (p. 138). Edge criticizes what he sees as the 'closed' nature of much science education. Pitt characterizes the ethos of the polytechnics and applied studies generally in terms of *techne* (which is neutral, secular, amoral) rather than *sophos* (concerned with the true, beautiful or just).

Qualitative methods have been pushed even further by two writers who have adopted what may be called an 'anthropological' approach to the study of the cultures of disciplines. Becher (1989a) has provided a general analysis of *Academic Tribes and Territories* in a recent book. Elsewhere, he gives a detailed description of two disciplines in particular, physics and history. Physics, he notes:

> . . . was the only discipline among those investigated . . . whose practitioners acknowledged hierarchies of esteem, both within the discipline and outside it. Thus, even if in a half-joking way, pure theorists look down on phenomenologists. The ladder of specialism runs down from theoretical particle physics to experimental particle physics, and thence to solid state and other branches of fundamental experimental physics, and finally to areas in applied physics such as metallurgy. Taking the subject as a whole, there would seem to be some disagreement about whether mathematics and philosophy come higher or lower in the pecking order than physics, but the latter stands clearly above chemistry and biology, with chemical engineering next,

then engineering – geography and the social sciences are placed firmly beyond the pale.

(Becher forthcoming)

As to the work itself:

It seems almost an article of faith, related to the physicist's belief in the unity and simplicity of nature . . . that the right answer is always the neatest among two or more apparently valid interpretations of the same phenomenon. Complicated solutions are suspect: the ideal explanation 'can be put in one sentence'.

(Becher forthcoming)

In other disciplines, such as the social sciences, it is by contrast often the simple solution which is suspect. Becher goes on to discuss the terms of appraisal used by physicists of one another's work:

It has already been noted that elegance in a solution is a high virtue, and that economy of explanation is also seen as praiseworthy. 'Productive work' is another characteristic concept, denoting a piece of investigation which creates new possibilities for further research – that is, opens up a fresh range of issues or suggests a novel approach to existing problems. The kindred notion of 'a powerful method' acknowledges a technique which can be applied across a broad spectrum of subject-matter and which seems at the same time to have a penetrating quality. 'Sloppy' is the commonest form of condemnation, indicating a piece of work which lacks the desirable qualities of neatness and simplicity and the necessary qualities of thoroughness and reliability. 'Rigorous' is a somewhat backhanded compliment, carrying connotations of a narrowly mathematical approach which lacks imagination and misses the sense of physical reality. Perhaps because of the fast-moving quality of many areas of physics, the terms 'masterly' and 'scholarly' seem altogether inappropriate – and indeed are never used in this context.

(Becher forthcoming)

The 'culture' of history is in many ways very different. The boundaries of the discipline are, according to Becher, easily breached and readily redrawn; and despite the proliferation of specialisms, there is an underlying sense of unity, not easy to define. As regards the process:

Historians tend to be wary of the theoretical frameworks of the social sciences, though some also envy the latter their stronger grounding in theory, and regret that 'history has sources but no methods'. It is, one respondent explained, 'a matter of applying the rules of everyday life'; another took it to be 'largely a matter of common sense – it's easier to answer specific questions about methodology than to talk about historical method in general'. Arguments tend to be conducted in substantive rather than structural terms: people are quite prepared to quarrel about the evidence, but there are seldom major disputes about methodology.

(Becher 1989b)

As with physics, the terms of approbation or criticism in history are illuminating. Good work may be 'scholarly', 'original', or in rather muscular terms, 'stimulating', 'rigorous' or 'masterly'. Poor work may be 'trivializing' or 'thin', or be damned as 'jargon-ridden'. Quite unlike physicists, professional historians exist alongside 'amateurs', who can do valid work, and must be sharply distinguished from 'popularizers' who are worse than useless. Learning to become an historian involves a mixture of training and apprenticeship with a strong emphasis on the latter. The style of work tends to be solitary rather than collective. If one had to sum up the historian's view of the world in one sentence, it would be that 'everything is more complicated than it seems'.

Another study of 'disciplinary cultures', this time in Modern Languages, is provided by Colin Evans (1988, pp. 175–6), who amusingly describes the various orientations and emphases of the study of 'Emmel' in terms of tribes:

> Modern Languages is a subject with very little unity or clarity. It does not present the same sense of methodological one-ness which Becher discovered in History and Physics. The loyalty of the separate languages is stronger than loyalty to 'Modern Languages', even in institutions where languages are grouped into departments or schools. . . . But, in addition, the tribes of each language are them-selves divided, which means that other communities find dealing with them difficult. . . . First, there are the PHILITS. They are really two tribes but the older PHILOGS, fathers of all the tribes, were assimilated long ago. They still practice here and there but their main function is honorific; they give ancestral weight to the PHILIT tribe. The PHILITS, then, are a venerable tribe, respected accordingly by other communities over the hill. For many years their dominance over all the tribes of Emmel was complete. . . . Other tribes are restive and are challenging that control. For example the EFCOMS, who have always been the helots of the society, are now banding together and making war-talk. They claim that Effective Communication is Emmel's real mission. . . . The POLISOX on the other hand, are a new, young, vigorous tribe. They have no hostility towards the EFCOMS, though they too can be condescending. On the other hand, they see the PHILITS as being impossibly old-fashioned. The future lies in alliance with the SOCSCI people who are high-status tribes with granaries full of concepts and theories, some of which, they say, can even be used to understand the nature of tribes.

These descriptions of physics, history and modern languages, which are drawn from much longer studies, are quoted here simply to give some sense of what the 'culture' of a discipline may involve, and show something of the potential and interest of this kind of research for other disciplines. However, it is one thing to argue that a disciplinary culture embodies certain stances and values, but quite another to argue that students imbibe and internalize those stances and values and continue to hold and live by them in quite different contexts, such as in their first or subsequent jobs. After all, it is partly because academics *did* internalize those stances and values as undergraduates that they became academics; so they may be prone to exaggerate the influence of disciplinary cultures on students in general. We do not know how long such influences persist beyond the end of first degree courses, whether they constitute a temporary or tactical adaptation to a particular culture, or a longer-term and irreversible change in the self-concept. It is the old and thorny problem of 'transfer', and until we have firmer evidence, we should remain sceptical about the longer-term impacts of disciplinary cultures.

The price of development

It would be bad enough if some of the desirable impacts which have been explored in this chapter turned out to have no impact on students' development at all; but it would be even worse if there were impacts, and they were negative. We tend to assume a little too easily that higher education is a positive affair. But it could have effects or side-effects on its students which are unwanted and undesirable, which limit them as individuals, misfit them for society, disequip them for their jobs and undermine their development as lifelong learners. Such effects could stem from, for example, overcrowded curricula which induce 'surface' learning, methods of assessment which encourage 'strategic' learning, curricular or teaching functions which have become dysfunctions, or the transmission of closed or complacent attitudes towards continuing education.[7]

We are not talking here about the experience of learning itself, which can often be negative. To the student, undergraduate studies may involve confusion, disorientation, unlearning. The first-year student who has done A level economics or English may be told, bluntly or gently, to forget what he has learned and start again. The mature student who has already built up a tolerable system of beliefs and reasonably coherent life-style may find both challenged at a fundamental level. This can be a profoundly disturbing experience, which is sometimes compounded by insensitive teaching, but it may be a necessary one. For the point of the dark side of learning – the going backwards, or round in circles, the breaking down, the apparent regression – is that it may lead to something better in the end: more complex, sophisticated, powerful cognitive structures. It may be a case of *reculer pour mieux sauter*.

Nor are we speaking here of the inherent difficulties and pains of personal development, what Perry (1978) has called 'the costs of growth'.

Everything does not go simply onward and upward, even in the most optimistic of development theories. When we talk of the price of development, we are alluding to the possible downside of development itself: the possibility that doing one thing better may involve doing another thing worse; that development may in some respects be a zero-sum game. Even if it is not, it may lead to what Veblen once called 'trained incapacity': limitations, incompetences, or blind spots which are actually the product of education.

Two 'costs' of this kind have already been discussed in relation to the simple typology of development presented earlier. The development of student autonomy, and the capacity to think for oneself, may make it more difficult for students to work with others, in teams or groups. This may be more of a problem in the arts and social sciences than sciences and technology, and is probably being modified by the steady increase in group work of various kinds – small group discussion and seminars, team projects, even peer assessment. It is not, however, only a matter of group work *vs* individual work, but rather a question of the range of *types* of working experience and environments to which undergraduates are exposed. For example, although group work is common, few students emerge from the first degree courses with much experience of organizing others and leading a project team or, conversely, being led; a point sometimes made in armed services advertisements comparing the relative value of a degree and a short-service commission for subsequent employment. And one wonders how systematically the pace and length of projects are varied. It is important for a group to learn how to work fast to an immediate deadline as well as on a longer-term cycle or rhythm.

The second potential cost of development has already been discussed; it is the increasing inability to commit oneself and take decisions as a consequence of the inculcation of sceptical, questioning habits of thought. Everyday life and work necessitate commitment, and the culture of higher education may to some extent run counter to this. This balance may of course change when the graduate leaves the culture of higher education and enters the world of work, but the tension may lie behind the complaints of employers that higher education and its graduates are too theoretical and not applied or practical enough. The problem may be less one of knowledge or cognition *per se* than of attitudes and stance.

There are other possible costs or incapacities. The milieu of higher education is decidedly more middle-class and professional than the population as a whole, and this may restrict the linguistic register and social range of graduates, and make them unused to or even incapable of communicating and getting on with people who are not 'educated'. Again, this may change with the first job, but it may also lie behind the charge that some new graduates are stand-offish or even arrogant. Universities, polytechnics or colleges can hardly be described as social microcosms of the world at large. Another possibility already mentioned is that students imitate the professional role models provided by academic staff, and hence find it more difficult after their higher education to adopt either bureaucratic or entrepreneurial attitudes than they would have before. However, this assumes that academics do provide such models (some academic researchers behave much more like entrepreneurs), that students do identify with them and that the effects persist beyond the academic environment. None of these assumptions can be taken for granted.

Another possibility is that higher education develops not moral but immoral or amoral types of attitudes and behaviour (Wilson 1981): the capacity to deceive, to bluff one's way out of problems, to give the impression of knowing about something when one really doesn't, to engage in cut-throat competition, to rationalize dubious motives, to do just enough to get by. The research of both Becker *et al.* (1968) and Snyder (1971) in the USA highlighted the extent to which undergraduate studies could be treated as a 'game', with students learning to play the system and bend the rules to their advantage, and there is no reason to think that things are much different here.

But the most profound 'cost' of development may be an inescapable consequence of the very nature of the academic enterprise. Although the concept of student development may be more or less broadly interpreted, there is little doubt that it is rational, cognitive development which lies at its heart. However, such an emphasis may lead students to believe that knowledge is all that is needed to bring about change in the world, where it is not. It may lead to an uncritical attitude to rationality itself, as if its bases were self-evident; although the very notions of rationality and reason can be examined in terms of their historical and social provenance, particularly in the rise of Western science and in the Enlightenment. And, finally, it may make it difficult for them to comprehend the power of metaphors other than those of rational cognition: sight, clarity, transparency.

Notes

1 Brennan and McGeevor (1988) asked polytechnic and college graduates whether they thought their higher education had helped them to improve any of a number of abilities. The rank order of the positive responses was as follows, beginning with the highest: critical thinking, independence, organizing their own work, application of knowledge and skills, written communication, self-confidence, understanding of other people, logical thinking, spoken communication, cooperation with other people, sense of responsibility, use of numbers, political consciousness, and leadership. There were, however, noticeable differences between subjects in the rankings and over 22% of all the graduates felt that they had had insufficient opportunities to develop oral communication and numerical and computing skills, with figures rising to over 40% and 50% in some subjects (pp. 121–5). See also the American research on transferable intellectual and personal skills reported by Bradshaw (1985) and the interesting autobiographical approach of Powell (1985) which attempts to identify the 'residues of learning'.

2 The economist's notion of 'screening' depends ultimately on some such concept of general ability. In its simplest form, the screening hypothesis holds that many employers are looking primarily for bright young people and rely on the education system to sort out the bright from the less bright. However, since most bright 18-year-olds now go on to higher education, employers have to wait to get hold of them as graduates, although they may still rely on A levels (which are thought to be a standard, national measure) rather than degree classifications (which are not) in selecting applicants. This hypothesis encounters several difficulties. First, it assumes that there is such a thing as general ability, which as we have seen is open to question. Secondly, it assumes that educational assessments are a good measure of the kinds of ability employers want, which may be more or less true depending on the job. Thirdly, it ignores the fact that the correlation between A level grades and degree classes is very low in some subjects (Choppin *et al.* 1973; Goacher 1984). And, finally, it assumes that young people's ability is completely unaffected by the experience and environment of undergraduate studies, a view that is difficult to sustain because it abstracts the notion of ability from any manifestation or test of it. (It also ignores Riegel's 1979, contention that adult intelligence is characteristically dialectical rather than formal operational.) One further point is worth adding: a Japanese colleague has pointed out that in the Japanese educational system there is relatively less emphasis on ability *per se* and more on 'effortism' – the idea that native wit counts for less than motivation, hard work and perseverance (Iwaki 1988). Perhaps as employers and researchers we are too obsessed with the notion of some intrinsic, unitary and stable ability which can be measured and screened.

3 For a current view of the state of research into human intelligence, see the sally by Howe (1988) and the reply by Sternberg (1988). Although both writers refer respectfully to Gardner, his work is tangential to the main stream of such research, much of which is currently concerned either with the validity of inspection time and reaction time as measures of 'g' (general intelligence) or with the implications of broad, information-processing and componential models for the understanding of intelligence. However, the difference between generic and multiple models of intelligence should not be over-polarized (for an interesting intermediate model, see Gustafsson 1984).

4 As Gardner has pointed out, even disciplines such as mathematics, music and languages may utilize not one but several types of intelligence, or facets thereof. Some mathematicians have suggested to me that at an advanced level, the different branches of mathematics require quite different types of 'mind'. Musical ability involves not only a sense of pitch, but of rhythm and timbre, and involves aural, visual and manipulative skills in varying mixtures; and language learning involves both analytic and mimetic skills as well as oral and written modes.

5 The experimental psychological literature on 'learning to learn' can be distinguished from the more practical and often atheoretical study manuals which have been around in great numbers for a long time. The former is concerned with the possibility of general-purpose learning strategies (see, for example, Baron 1978), the latter with concrete study skills. However, some of the more applied literature has now moved from viewing learning merely as a matter of tricks and skills to a more thoughtful and strategic approach (see Gibbs 1981; Smith 1982; Squires 1982).

6 The recent volume edited by Cormier and Hagman (1987) gives a useful

retrospective view of research on transfer in both the Foreword and Introduction. The chapter on the transfer of cognitive skills by Gray and Orasanu displays some of the fruits of the 'cognitive revolution' in psychology, using concepts such as problem-space and productions (see Simon above) to reconceptualize transfer, and drawing an important distinction between declarative (i.e. informational) knowledge and *procedural* knowledge, which they see as lying at the heart of the process. The general direction of such research seems to be towards a reformulation of transfer in terms of processes rather than contents. But it also raises the interesting question of how far the very concept of transfer, with its assumptions about discrete tasks and situations, is essentially a behavioural one. It may be more fruitful to think of the whole process in terms of the development of general learning strategies and procedures, and ultimately the *relativizing* of learning so that it is less stimulus-bound or context-bound. That notion would tie up with the emphasis on relativity of perspective in Chapter 5.

7 Recent research by Entwistle and Waterston (1988) on student approaches to learning in higher education has elaborated an earlier deep/surface dichotomy into four dimensions: deep/elaborative, surface, organized and strategic/competitive. The first is, broadly speaking, learning for understanding or meaning, the others responses of varying authenticity and adequacy to academic tasks. Entwistle and Waterston do, however, caution against a decontextualized view of student learning, and note that the 'learning environment has profound effects on studying'. This view seems compatible with the contingent model presented in Fig. 1.1 of this book. It may also be that these different approaches to learning have implications for the transferability of learning, and that the deep/elaborative approach helps to generate the high-level transferable strategies implied by the idea of 'learning to think'.

5

Curriculum Policy

Some of the current policy issues related to the undergraduate curriculum have already been touched on in previous chapters, in either the text or the notes at the end of each chapter. There was some discussion of the size of the higher education system in Chapter 1. Chapter 2 raised questions about subject balance, the arts/science dichotomy and the relationship between science and technology. In Chapter 3, the analysis touched on issues to do with graduate employment, subject specialization, the development of modular schemes and the general relationship between higher education and the economy. The analysis in Chapter 4 was less directly concerned with policy, but nevertheless raised questions about the concept of screening, transferable skills and non-cognitive aspects of the curriculum. However, the main thrust of the book has been analytic rather than prescriptive, and it has therefore seemed right to confine such points mainly to the notes at the ends of chapters since, important as they are, they do not flow logically from the main analysis.

In this final chapter, too, the comments on curriculum policy will be of a general nature, and confined to those issues which seem to flow fairly directly from the ideas, models and arguments presented already. Of course, even the analytic approach adopted so far has involved certain kinds of assumptions, and any discussion of policy is bound to be even more deeply implicated in presuppositions and preferences. However, I hope that even where a position is taken in the following pages, it will be stated clearly enough for readers to see why they disagree with it when they do. The main policy implications of the three middle chapters will be discussed in turn, with a final section on one of the issues with which the book began, namely the control of the curriculum.

Knowledge

Much of the analysis in Chapter 2 was shot through with the duality of the curriculum as constituting both bodies of knowledge and bodies of people.

This duality points back to some basic epistemological issues, but it also has implications for policy. To put it at its simplest, higher education institutions cannot live without curriculum structures, but neither can they live entirely within them. Figure 2.1 offered a general, three-dimensional model of the curriculum as knowledge, but as pointed out at the time, such a model only provides a limited purchase on the complexities of organized knowledge; the movements of information and influence within it are extremely subtle and difficult to foresee.

The complexity of knowledge is such that perhaps our minds, daunted by it, seek refuge in the comparative simplicity of professional and institutional structures. Whatever the balance of a particular epistemological argument, it seems likely to be tipped slightly in favour of the existing structure of faculties, schools, departments, courses or options, simply because they are there and make life if not comprehensible then at least manageable. We need structures, but we are aware that they are not the whole story. Time and again, in this study, I was warned by academics not to take labels too seriously, to look beyond the official explicit curriculum to what 'really goes on', to be aware that appearance and reality were not always quite the same. This was more than the usual *caveat* in social research; it revealed something important about the way the British system works. Or rather, did work. For the means of coping with the necessity but limitations of curricular structures in the past was often to use the informal system to get round the formal one. Academics would often deal directly with one another, by-passing or cross-cutting the existing structures and channels, if they felt that a certain development should take place.

Certainly, this is easier to do in a period of expansion, where there is some margin in the system, and development is not a zero-sum game, than in the current conditions of stasis or contraction. But the main threat to the informal structures comes not simply from the dynamics of the system, but from the adoption of rational models of management. In clearing the dead wood and undergrowth of the system, managers risk scything new plants and saplings as well. The emphasis on rational management tilts the balance between formal and informal structures in favour of the former, and risks upsetting the subtle interaction between the two. There are two possible solutions to the problem. The first, rational one, is to set in place countervailing structures which allow the existing ones to be overridden in certain circumstances (special innovation funds, academic 'enterprise zones'). The second is to accept that the system should not be 'managed' too well.

But given the inherent duality and ambiguity of curricular structures, does the analysis suggest any guiding principles for the undergraduate curriculum? The diversity of curricular objectives and types of knowledge makes it impossible to lay down general rules in terms of numbers of subjects, core requirements, or progression from one year to the next. If anything, a bit more diversity in the system might be welcome in this respect. However, one conclusion that could be drawn from the analysis in

Chapter 2 is that all courses should be planned in the light of three basic criteria: depth, relativity and reflexivity.

Behind the need for depth lies the uncomfortable fact that in order to reach a high level of knowledge or competence in anything one has to specialize: that the very concept of *higher* education implies a degree of specialization relative to lower levels of education. There seems to be no way round this. One cannot simply abstract the 'structure' of a subject from its 'content', because one has to know the subject in order to make the very distinction. Nor can one abstract the 'content' of a subject from its 'culture'; one has to experience it to comprehend it. But the idea of depth goes beyond the idea of specialization in its suggestion of immersion, and in the connotations of mystery and uncertainty. Knowing involves not knowing; depth involves living with the difficulty of the world, whether of theory or of practice.

However, the need for depth has to be reconciled with two other necessities. The first is in some ways the opposite of depth: not breadth *per se*, but a sense of the relativity of different types of knowledge and different frames of reference, the realization that however powerful and inclusive one's own discipline seems to be, there are others; that the outside of one discipline is the inside of another. This suggests that students should come into substantial contact with more than one kind of knowledge during their undergraduate studies. This would normally involve several 'subjects' as conventionally defined, but it could perhaps be done in other ways as well, by emphasizing differences of perspective within the same 'subject', or by organizing mixed-discipline seminars in which students explicate the nature of their discipline to those in other fields. No doubt the staff of various departments could feed usefully into such an exercise, but it might be more meaningful for students to use their own experience of the curriculum as the point of departure. Such an exercise might help to guard against the common danger of specialization, which is that graduates emerge as intellectual pre-Copernicans believing that their subject is at the centre of the known universe. After all, in our working and social lives, being able to communicate with others who have and hold different frames of reference is an important asset.

The other curricular requirement is for reflexivity; for turning the mind back on itself, and turning the discipline back on itself, asking questions about what is usually taken for granted or for normal in the discipline or profession. Such activities were described in Figure 2.1 in terms of a continuum ranging from the normal through the reflexive to the philosophical. To some extent reflexivity can be and is achieved within a particular subject or field, but there might also be a generic role for philosophers in this which does not of course deny their specific roles as disciplinary specialists.

The emphasis on depth, relativity and reflexivity, as well as the means of realizing them, may no doubt vary from course to course. But it is also affected by the general pattern of undergraduate studies. The British system is relatively specialized compared to those in other countries, though some parts of it are more specialized than others. The main organizational (as distinct from professional) obstacle to meeting the three criteria outlined above is time; it would be much easier to achieve depth/competence and a relative and reflexive understanding if degree courses were longer. The pressure of specialization means that any time devoted to something other than the main subject or field is seen as time away from it, and there is a constant pressure from specialist departments, academics and sometimes students to cut down on anything that is regarded as marginal to the main thrust of the course.

A substantial number of degree courses already last four rather than three years, and there is pressure in others, such as physics, to extend the length. This pressure may intensify as the effects of a broader school curriculum feed through into the higher education system. The example of four-year patterns in other countries, not only in North America but in other parts of Europe, may become more telling. The financial *quid pro quo* for such an extension would probably be the adoption of a two-stage system, such as exists both in the USA and some European countries, with substantial numbers of students obtaining a two-year diploma or associate degree (in my view, a two-year bachelor's degree would not be recognized internationally). There are many aspects of such a change which would need to be discussed and cannot be here; suffice to say that in curricular terms it might have a good deal to recommend it in terms of moving towards a broader, more flexible and perhaps less age-specific pattern of undergraduate studies. Such a change would also allow the broadening of A levels which seems to me highly desirable for reasons which I have spelled out elsewhere (Squires 1989a), perhaps to something closer to the pattern of Scottish 'highers'.

An undergraduate curriculum which embodied the ideas of depth, relativity and reflexivity would not only provide students with a coherent and balanced course leading to their first degree, it would bring a new unity to institutions. There is a certain nostalgia in higher education for unifying ideas or models, such the medieval trivium and quadrivium, or the original notions of a liberal or polytechnical education. The nostalgia is more interesting than the ideas, because it points to a sense of loss of institutional and communal coherence. Never mind that such a sense is based partly on a myth: Clark Kerr's (1963) term 'multi-versity' seems all too apt, and institutions are held together only by the appearances of ritual and the realities of administration. Apart from a few, small specialized colleges, modern British higher education institutions are essentially aggregates of units which combine and compete on more or less amicable terms. Such disaggregation also facilitates division and rule. Institutional identity, such as it is, is not underpinned by any strong sense of academic unity; indeed, the very idea has become so remote as to sound either abstract or foreign and probably both. Whatever its shortcomings, Figure 2.1 suggests a way of defining the limits of the undergraduate curriculum. Within those limits, parties would no doubt continue to compete for space; but at least they would share the same universe.

Culture

In Chapter 3 the frame of reference shifted from an epistemological one to a socio-cultural one: how did the undergraduate curriculum appear in terms of its social, economic and cultural context? Much of the analysis stemmed from a discussion of the employment of graduates, and it was suggested that in this four factors may be particularly relevant: specific expertise, general ability, personal qualities and the acquisition of basic employment skills.

The simplest and most concrete issue related to graduate employment has to do with the basic skills that graduates do or do not possess: skills of oral and written communication in one or more languages, and of numeracy and computing. The lack of such skills has long been a grumble of employers, although an unquantified one; but Brennan and McGeevor's (1988) follow-up study found that substantial numbers of polytechnic and college graduates themselves thought that they had not been given sufficient opportunities to develop such skills during their undergraduate courses.

There is now a good deal of activity in this field; many institutions offer short courses, sometimes under the aegis of their careers service, in oral and written communication, computing, numeracy and sometimes foreign languages. The question is whether it would be useful to standardize such courses, so that they lead to nationally validated skills certificates which undergraduates could obtain. Standardization might lead to rigidity; on the other hand it would provide a marketable certificate which employers could demand and graduates offer. If there proved to be little demand for it, it would show that employers' complaints should be taken at less than face value. It was argued in Chapter 2 that undergraduate studies are typically thought of as *transcending* skills, but this is not to say that skills cannot be taught as an adjunct to the main curriculum. However, it might be best to keep the design of such courses or tests out of the hands of subject specialists, in case they made them too ambitious.

Beyond such basic and concrete skills, the economic and employment issues become much more complex. In some ways, the top policy priorities seem to lie outside higher education altogether: the need to create a broad and effective school curriculum; the need to develop a system of vocational and technical education which will stand comparison with our neighbours'; and the need to encourage not simply a system but a culture of continuing education and learning both in and outside the workplace.

Each of these, however, has a bearing on higher education. Plans to change the subject mix of the graduate output – for example, to increase the numbers of scientists or engineers – are pie in the sky unless there is an adequate intake in such subjects from the schools. A well-developed system of vocational and technical education provides a second route into higher education, and continuing education can lead to a second chance.

But what of higher education itself? There are some reasons for thinking that the current size and mix of graduate output is about right in economic and employment terms. Although there are larger higher education systems, the British system is not small in international terms. The subject mix also seems comparable to that in some other countries. Lindley (1981) found little evidence of manpower shortages in the 1960s and 1970s, and although one cannot rule out future ones in rapidly growing specialized fields, most 'shortages' may only be shortages at a particular level of salary. As Table 3.1 showed, there are reserves of specialized labour in most fields which currently go into the general graduate labour market; and continuing education can be used to facilitate conversion and substitution. It was suggested that the lower the inferred 'ability' of a graduate, the more he or she may have to stress relevant 'expertise' in order to improve employment prospects; but that is a relative matter. The general analysis seems to point to a steady rather than massive increase in the number of graduates, and to stress breadth and flexibility rather than quantity.

And yet there are worries, which can perhaps best be expressed by saying that higher education may provide the right supply for the wrong demand. Such worries relate to macro-economic policies and changes rather than to higher education itself. We have already noted Playfair's belief than even in the 1850s the UK under-emphasized labour because of its relative advantages in land (i.e. natural resources) and capital. To the extent that we are moving away not simply from specific-skilled, well-demarcated modes of production to more fluid and multi-skilled ones, but to a *knowledge-led* economy in which the value added is mainly the result of the application of knowledge and skills, any under-emphasis on such knowledge and skills – and the opportunity to use them productively – becomes not merely undesirable but critical.

There is also the issue of the shift from manufacturing to services, evident both in the current trade figures and the employment statistics cited in Chapter 3. This shift has occurred in all OECD countries; the question is why. The analysis suggests that over and above the purely economic factors bringing about such a change – factors which affect all advanced industrialized countries – there have been cultural factors in the UK which may have given an extra impetus to the shift. Such factors are difficult to pin down, but they have to do with the low social status of industry (as compared with the City, for example) and the wider disparagement of making things as distinct from making money.

Higher education would seem, if anything, to pass on and perpetuate such cultural traits rather than originate them, and one can see the dubious status of traditional engineering as one example of such transmission. The new technology may fare better: significantly it is dubbed 'high', is less obviously material, and is associated not only with work but with play (which as Grignon 1971, noted can be characteristic of a dominant culture). However, the problem may go deeper, and be connected with the strength in higher education of the 'trained mind' doctrine which emphasizes process rather than content, general transferable skills rather than specialized knowledge. One effect of this notion may be subtly to dissociate mind from matter, knowledge from things. The key distinction in curriculum terms may therefore not be between 'arts' and 'science' but between the mental and the material. One of the features of British higher education, and especially of the universities, is the prevalence of a disembodied concept of mind.

The economic frame of reference is currently the dominant one in higher education policy, but of course this may not last. As was pointed out in Chapter 3, policy themes seem to come in waves, and the next wave is due, at a time when other concerns are working their way up the agenda. Societies are judged, explicitly or implicitly, not only in terms of their economies, but by the nature of their activities (or lack of them), their institutions, their human relations, and increasingly their environments. A European government has just fallen over an environmental issue; the first but probably not the last. It would be ironic if the ruling bodies of British higher education were to be weighted towards employment and the economy just when the movement away from that frame of reference was gathering momentum.

But the possible changes in the dominant frame of reference suggest a more general point about the relationship between curriculum and culture. We have talked as if culture were an all-inclusive category; yet cultures exclude and preclude as well as include. Just as we learn to make only a proportion of the total possible speech sounds when we acquire our first language, so we grow up within a certain pattern of cultural possibilities, unaware of or discounting others. However, the frame of reference of the undergraduate curriculum can never be wholly that of the current culture; not only does it have a historical and comparative frame of reference, but the habit of questioning that is institutionalized in higher education and especially in research must mean that the curriculum can never quite take the culture for granted. Certainly, in many ways it will transmit (to use Robbins' word) and sustain it, not least in meeting current employment needs, but at the same time it will use the alternative frames of reference of 'knowledge' and 'student development' to challenge and transcend it.

The relationship between the undergraduate curriculum and the dominant culture is thus bound to be somewhat ambiguous, because while the curriculum is in that culture, it is not wholly of it. This is why higher education institutions need a measure of protection from their societies, and why academics need a measure of protection from their institutions and from one another. More perhaps than any other sector of education, undergraduate education has multiple frames of reference, based on the notions of knowledge, culture and student development outlined in the three previous chapters. It serves three masters, not one, and hence exists in a constant state of tension; but any attempt to simplify its allegiances risks betraying its purposes.

Development

The implications for policy of the discussion in Chapter 4 of student development are neither clear nor direct. The chapter analysed the notion of cognitive development and also discussed some ways in which the concept of student development goes beyond the cognitive. However, the implications of that discussion are more likely to be of interest to those who actually plan and teach courses than those who are concerned with the broad sweep of higher education policy.

Two general observations should, however, be made. The first comes back to the notion of general, transferable cognitive skills which was referred to above. As noted already, the belief in the generality and transferability of such skills is a feature of the British system, to the point where content almost becomes a vehicle for process. Such a belief has policy consequences. The stronger that belief, the more one can justify an indirect relationship between the content of a degree course and subsequent employment; the weaker the belief, the more 'relevant' such courses have to be.

One can see arguments for the indirect approach. Many academics, students and employers believe in it. The main employment growth has been in service sector jobs, many of which may require just those general, cognitive skills which academics say their courses develop. The indirect approach also seems to be characteristic of the USA and Japan, although in the first, student demand has led to a major swing towards vocational courses especially in the two-year colleges in recent years, and in both countries the rather general pattern of undergraduate studies is comple-mented by the existence of large numbers of applied postgraduate courses or a widespread commitment to on-the-job education and training, neither of which is as common in the UK. The research on general transfer of learning does not yield a clear answer, partly because there are competing models, and partly because it is extremely difficult to devise research studies which will capture the hypothesized general transfer effects.

On the other hand, one can see how the general transfer argument can be used simply as a rationalization for courses which might not be justified on other grounds. As noted, the 'trained mind' argument tends to be used in subjects which have a 'weak' employment link, whereas one can just as well argue that subjects such as medicine and engineering also develop generic, transferable skills, although the particular pattern of skills will vary from subject to subject. In addition, it was suggested in Chapter 4 that many 'academic' courses are *de facto* professional courses preparing people implicitly for work in the academic professions, in which case the contrast is not between the academic and the professional but between two kinds of profession, external and internal.

This is perhaps the nub or rub of the 'trained mind' argument, at least in its present form. If an 'academic' course – in any subject – does in fact develop the general, transferable skills that it claims to, then such a course is as economically 'relevant' as an overtly professional one, perhaps even more so in a fast-changing economy (a point made by Becker in *Human Capital* as long ago as 1964). However, if such a course is actually an academic-professional course, which concentrates on developing those skills which will equip people who will never enter the academic profession to enter it, then we have reason to question it at least on employment grounds. All this adds up to saying that if people use the 'trained mind' argument, they should take it seriously.

One way forward may lie in identifying 'foundation skills' which are neither as specific (and limited) as subject skills, nor as general (and indirect) as process skills: a kind of half-way-house between the 'vocational relevance' and 'trained mind' arguments. For example, work in many service sector jobs seems to require four kinds of foundation skill: financial, organizational, informational and interpersonal (Squires 1989a). Such skills need to be brought to bear on the core tasks and skills of each particular occupation (which might be better learned on the job) and also illuminated by an understanding of the wider social context. For undergraduates in more clearly defined professional fields, such skills could be seen as useful adjuncts to their primary expertise, as to some extent they already are in engineering.

The second point that arises out of Chapter 4 is a very general one. It is that we should think of first degree courses not simply in terms of their content, but in terms of their methods and environments. Teaching methods are not simply a means to an end; they encourage or discourage certain approaches to and styles of learning, which may be crucial not only on the course itself, but subsequently. It is important that students develop 'deep' rather than more superficial or tactical approaches to learning (Entwistle 1987) first, because such 'depth' is consistent with the aims and rhetoric of higher education and, secondly, because it relates to generic concepts such as 'problem solving'.

But the matter of teaching goes beyond this. There is a contrast between the stimulating content of many courses and the rather routine and humdrum procedures and methods associated with them. The concept of the curriculum implicit in Figure 1.1 goes well beyond syllabus content, and draws our attention to the methods, materials, environments and assessments that are used. In planning a course, it is important to take all these things into account, because together they constitute the totality that is the course. One way to put this is to say that methods too are a kind of content, as are teachers and even assessments. And it may also be that there is room to diversify the environments of learning during the undergraduate course, for example by including more off-campus experience, or different study formats.

Control

Finally, we come to the question of control, and the question raised in Chapter 1: who should decide what is taught? This issue can be tackled at two levels, that of broad policy and that of detailed management.

Clark (1983) has proposed a triangular model of policy making in higher education which comprises state authority, academic oligarchy and market forces. He locates various countries somewhere within this triangle in terms of the relative importance of these three influences, although he also sub-divides each category and points out that the balance of power can vary from level to level, and change over time. Roughly speaking, the three influences embody bureaucratic, professional and consumer models of higher education, although again as Clark points out there are nuances and variants within each model.

One can see how each principle, unchecked by the others, can develop its own pathology. Unbridled academic power can lead to an introverted, arrogant and self-serving system, a point which academics are more likely to recognize in professions other than their own. But there have been plenty of examples of this in the past, and such examples or fears seem to have animated some aspects of government policy in the last decade. Unlimited state power, on the other hand, can lead in its mild form to creaking and sometimes absurd bureaucracy and, at the extreme, to totalitarian control. Academics who participated in some of the planning exercises of the mid-1980s may feel that they have experienced the former. The classic argument against centralized planning advanced by Hayek (1944) – that planners can never *know* enough to plan – applies with particular force in higher education, since it of all systems is 'information-rich'.

Although it is difficult to assess current policy trends, government policy at the time of writing seems to be moving away from centralized planning towards a market model, implicit in the proposed increase in the proportion of institutions' income coming from student fees and the decrease in direct grants. It is important, therefore, to stress that the market model too has its potential pathologies. Potential students, graduate employees and graduate employers often do not have the information on which to base rational decisions, and getting it itself costs time and money. It is often more difficult for the consumer to select services than goods, especially ones with long-term returns such as higher education. And there is the whole impact of cultural patterns and preferences on economic decisions; a particular educational choice might be culturally rational without being economically rational.

It is difficult to avoid the conclusion that some balance must be struck between Clark's three principles, and indeed this is the position he leans towards, while recognizing the importance of other contingent factors. Common sense [*sic*] would suggest that the undergraduate curriculum should be the combined product of government strategy, professional judgement and consumer demand, the latter expressed not only by students but also by alumni and indirect consumers such as employers and professional bodies. The problem is that such a compromise suggests more than a whiff of corporatism, an odour as little liked by the current government as it is common in some of our continental neighbours, and perhaps the tacit ideology of the European Community, although the historical associations of the term preclude its explicit use on mainland Europe.

Perhaps we should distinguish not only between liberal corporatism and its totalitarian or centralist version, but between it and its peculiarly British manifestation in 'tripartism' in the 1960s and 1970s, and in the famous *Butskellite* consensus. There were two main problems with this. First, the consensus was premature or false, in that it left unresolved profound problems of economic productivity and social relations, problems which led ultimately to its collapse. And, secondly, tripartism is a merely sectional approach to corporatism, in which each party is out only for its own interests, without any sense of an underlying consensus. The kind of pluralistic approach to policy making envisaged here would only work if the various parties to it recognized the legitimacy of the three principles (if not always the positions) embodied in each: in government, the principle of planning; in the profession, the principle of (informed) participation; and in the consumer, the principle of the market. The problem of curriculum policy making is not simply one of establishing the right institutions or mechanisms, but of acknowledging the validity of the different perspectives.

But all this still leaves the detailed planning and management of courses unresolved. Who is to do this, on what basis, and who is to validate or approve the results? Such questions raise issues about the general management of higher education institutions which we cannot go into here, but two final points can be made. First, it is difficult not to feel that the styles of management currently being introduced into higher education may be the very styles which are now beginning to disappear from industry. This is no doubt to overstate the point, but perhaps one critical example can be given. In the mid-1980s, the Committee of Vice-Chancellors and Principals set up a steering committee to look at the efficiency of universities. This committee posed seven basic questions about the efficiency of universities, and the key word in each question was as follows: planning, allocation, allocation, information, allocation, control and accountability (Jarratt 1985). This kind of centralized financial control model of management sits uneasily with the talk of flattened hierarchies, semi-autonomous work units, loose-tight properties, staff motivation and customer orientation which one finds in some of the recent management literature (Peters and Waterman 1982; Williams and Williams 1987).

There is a second, more academic, point. The Jarratt report assumed a basic management process, and went on to state that 'Universities exhibit a number of features which complicate the managerial and administrative process', features such as a diversity of activities, professional loyalties, traditions of participation and self-government, and academic tenure (para. 2.7). Such an approach assumes a disjunction between a basic, invariant management process and its content and context.

Figure 1.1 in this book implies that, at least as regards the curriculum, the reality is more contingent. Instead of regarding the basic characteristics of academic institutions as complications, we would surely do better to analyse carefully those characteristics and decide on the optimum management process in the light of them. That means exploring the inputs, environment and outputs of institutions, and basic features such as their scale, time-scale, structure and culture. Above all, it means exploring the undergraduate curriculum, since along with postgraduate work, research and continuing education, it is one of the main outputs of the system. Unless we understand what it is we are producing, for whom and in what context, we are unlikely to be able to manage it effectively.

Glossary

A Level: Normal entrance qualification for higher education in England and Wales, usually taken at the age of 18 at the end of secondary schooling; minimum requirement of two A levels (university entry usually requires three) except for adult students for whom the requirements may be wholly or partly waived.

AGCAS: Association of Graduate Careers Advisory Services.

AS Level: Qualification of the same level as A level but half the content.

BTEC: Business and Technician Education Council. Body overseeing intermediate technician or equivalent level courses mainly in colleges of further education in England and Wales; higher body exists in Scotland.

CNAA: Council for National Academic Awards. Body founded in 1964 to validate degree courses in polytechnics and colleges, some of which have now become self-validating.

CRAC: Careers Research and Advisory Council. Independent non-profit-making body concerned with development of all aspects of career guidance and education.

GCSE: General Certificate of Secondary Education. Qualification replacing O levels and Certificate of Secondary Education usually obtained at the age of 16 at the end of compulsory education in England and Wales.

Highers: Normal entrance qualification for higher education in Scotland, taken about one year earlier than A levels and in up to five subjects.

NAB: National Advisory Body for Public Sector Education. Body charged with oversight of polytechnics and colleges in England and Wales until its replacement by PCFC in April 1989.

NCVQ: National Council for Vocational Qualifications. Body established in 1987 to rationalize system of vocational and technical qualifications in England and Wales.

OECD: Organization for Economic Cooperation and Development. International organization concerned with economic and social development of non-communist industrialized countries.

PCFC: Polytechnics and Colleges Funding Council. Body responsible for general funding and development of polytechnics and colleges in England and Wales from April 1989.

Training Agency: Agency of the Department of Employment responsible for youth and adult employment training, temporarily Training Commission and previously Manpower Services Commission (MSC).

TVEI: Technical and Vocational Education Initiative. Programme to develop these forms of education in secondary schools.

UFC: Universities Funding Council. Body responsible for general funding and development of universities from April 1989.

UGC: University Grants Committee. Body responsible for general funding and development of UK universities until replacement by UFC.

UK: United Kingdom, comprising England, Wales, Scotland and Northern Ireland; Great Britain (GB) comprises the first three. The respective education departments are the Department of Education and Science, Welsh Education Department, Scottish Education Department, and Department of Education for Northern Ireland.

USR: Universities Statistical Record.

Bibliography

Abbs, P. (1989). 'Tactful approach to life', *Times Higher Education Supplement*, 13 January.

Adelman, C. and Gibbs, I. (1980). 'Curriculum development and the changing constituency of students: The case of the Colleges of Higher Education', *Journal of Curriculum Studies*, 12(2), 167–71.

Ahlstrom, G. (1982). *Engineers and Industrial Growth*. London, Croom Helm.

Albrow, M. (1986). 'The undergraduate curriculum in sociology – A core for humane education', *Sociology*, 20(3), 335–46.

Alexander, K. (1988). 'Higher education – A personal view', *Scottish Educational Review*, 20(2), 76–82.

Allport, D. A. (1980). 'Patterns and actions: Cognitive mechanisms are content specific', in Claxton, G. L. (ed.), *Cognitive Psychology: New Directions*. London, Routledge and Kegan Paul.

Apple, M. (1979). *Ideology and Curriculum*. London, Routledge and Kegan Paul.

Apple, M. (1981). 'Social structure, ideology and curriculum', in Lawn, M. and Barton, L. (eds), *Rethinking Curriculum Studies*. London, Croom Helm.

Argles, M. (1964). *South Kensington to Robbins*. London, Longmans.

Argyris, C. (1982). *Reasoning, Learning and Action*. San Francisco, Jossey-Bass.

Association of Commonwealth Universities (1988). *Higher Education in the United Kingdom 1989–90*. London, Longman.

Association of Graduate Careers Advisory Services (annual). *What Do Graduates Do?* Cambridge, AGCAS/Hobsons Press.

Astin, A. W. (1977). *Four Critical Years: Effects of College on Beliefs, Attitudes and Knowledge*. San Francisco, Jossey-Bass.

Bandura, A. (1971). *Social Learning Theory*. New York, General Learning Press.

Barnes, B. (1974). *Scientific Knowledge and Sociological Theory*. London, Routledge and Kegan Paul.

Barnett, R. A. (1985). 'Higher education: Legitimation crisis', *Studies in Higher Education*, 10(3), 241–55.

Barnett, R. A. (1989). *Art and Design Graduates: Degree Results and Employment Destinations*. London, CNAA.

Barnett, R. A., Becher, R. A. and Cork, M. M. (1987). 'Models of professional preparation: Pharmacy, nursing and teacher education', *Studies in Higher Education*, 12(1), 51–64.

Baron, J. (1978). 'Intelligence and general strategies', in Underwood, G. (ed.), *Strategies of Information Processing*. London and San Diego, Academic Press.

Barzun, J. (1969). *The American University*. Oxford, Oxford University Press.

Beard, R. M. (1976). *Teaching and Learning in Higher Education*, 3rd edn. Harmondsworth, Penguin.

Becher, T. (1981). 'Towards a definition of disciplinary cultures', *Studies in Higher Education*, 6(2), 109–22.

Becher, T. (1987). 'Disciplinary discourse', *Studies in Higher Education*, 12(3), 261–74.

Becher, T. (1989a). *Academic Tribes and Territories*. Milton Keynes, SRHE/Open University Press.

Becher, T. (1989b). 'Scholars and gentlemen: Historians on history', *Studies in Higher Education*, 14(3).

Becher, T. (forthcoming). 'The aristocracy of the intellect: Physicists on physics', *Studies in Higher Education*.

Becher, T. and Kogan, M. (1980). *Process and Structure in Higher Education*. London, Heinemann.

Becker, G. (1964). *Human Capital*. New York, National Bureau of Economic Research.

Becker, H. S., Gear, B. and Hughes, E. C. (1968). *Making the Grade*. New York, John Wiley.

Bell, R. (1971). 'The growth of the modern university', in Hooper, R. (ed.), *The Curriculum: Context, Design and Development*. Edinburgh, Oliver and Boyd.

Bell, R. (1987). Review of 'The Crisis of the Democratic Intellect', *Scottish Educational Review*, 19(1), 55–8.

Bergendahl, G. (ed.) (1984). *Knowledge Policies and the Traditions of Higher Education*. Stockholm, Almqvist and Wiksell.

Berger, P. and Luckmann, T. (1971). *The Social Construction of Reality*. Harmondsworth, Penguin.

Bernstein, B. (1971). 'On the classification and framing of educational knowledge', in Young, M. F. D. (ed.), *Knowledge and Control*. London, Collier-Macmillan.

Biglan, A. (1973). 'The characteristics of subject matter in different scientific areas', *Journal of Applied Psychology*, 57(3), 195–203.

Billing, D. (ed.) (1978). *Course Design and Student Learning*. Guildford, SRHE.

Birch, W. (1986). 'Towards a model for problem-based learning', *Studies in Higher Education*, 11(1), 73–82.

Blackstone, T. (1981). 'The entrenched generalists', *New Universities Quarterly*, 35(3), 280–92.

Blaug, M. (1983). *Where are We Now in the Economics of Education?* London, University of London Institute of Education.

Bloom, A. (1987). *The Closing of the American Mind*. Harmondsworth, Penguin.

Bloom, B. (ed.). (1956). *Taxonomy of Educational Objectives, Handbook I: Cognitive Domain*. London, Longman.

Bobbitt, F. (1918). *The Curriculum*. Boston, Houghton Mifflin.

Boreham, N. C. (1988). 'Models of diagnosis and their implications for adult professional education', *Studies in the Education of Adults*, 20(2), 95–108.

Bourner, T. (1984). *Handbook for the Graduates First Destinations Transbinary Database*. London, CNAA.

Boyer, E. (1987). *College: The Undergraduate Experience in America*. New York, Harper and Row.

Boys, C. J. and Kirkland, J. (1988). *Degrees of Success*. London, Jessica Kingsley.

Boys, C. J., Brennan, J., Henkel, M., Kirkland, J., Kogan, M. and Youll, P. J., (1988). *Higher Education and the Preparation for Work*. London, Jessica Kingsley.

Bradshaw, D. (1985). 'Transferable intellectual and personal skills', *Oxford Review of Education*, 11(2), 201–16.

Brennan, J. and McGeevor, P. (1988). *Graduates at Work: Degree Courses and the Labour Market*. London, Jessica Kingsley.

Broady, M. (1978–9). 'Down with academic standards', *New Universities Quarterly*, 33(1), 3–19.

Brock, W. H. and Meadows, A. J. (1977). 'Physics, chemistry and higher education in the UK', *Studies in Higher Education*, 2(2), 109–23.

Bruner, J. S. (1960). *The Process of Education*. Cambridge, Mass., Harvard University Press.

Bruner, J. S. (1968). *Toward a Theory of Instruction*. New York, Norton.

Bruner, J. S., Goodnow, J. T. and Austin, G. A. (1967). *A Study of Thinking*. New York, John Wiley.

Burgess, T. (1977). *Education after School*. Harmondsworth, Penguin.

Burgoyne, J. (1984). 'Curricula and teaching methods in management education', in Goodlad, S. (ed.), *Education for the Professions*. Guildford, SRHE.

Burnhill, P, and McPherson, A. (1983). 'The Scottish universities and undergraduate expectations, 1971–81', *Universities Quarterly*, 37(3), 253–70.

Cantor, L. (1989). *Vocational Education and Training in the Developed World*. London, Routledge.

Chickering, A. W. and associates (1981). *The Modern American College*. San Francisco, Jossey-Bass.

Choppin, B., Orr, L., Korle, S. D. M., Fara, P. and James, G., (1973). *The Prediction of Academic Success*. Windsor, National Foundation for Educational Research.

Church, C. (1978). 'Constraints on the historian', *Studies in Higher Education*, 3(2), 127–38.

Clark, B. R. (1983). *The Higher Education System*. Berkeley, University of California Press.

Clark, B. R. (ed.) (1984). *Perspectives on Higher Education*. Berkeley, University of California Press.

Cobban, A. B. (1975). *The Medieval Universities*. London, Methuen.

Collier, G., Tomlinson, P. and Wilson, J. (1974). *Values and Moral Development in Higher Education*. London, Croom Helm.

Cook, T. G. (ed.) (1973). *Education and the Professions*. London, Methuen.

Coombs, P. H., Prosser, R. and Ahmed, M. (1973). *New Paths to Learning*. New York, International Council for Educational Development.

Cormier, S. M. and Hagman, J. D. (eds) (1987). *Transfer of Learning: Contemporary Research and Applications*. London, Academic Press.

Cornbleth, C. (1984). 'Beyond hidden curriculum', *Journal of Curriculum Studies*, 16(1), 29–36.

Cotterrell, R. B. M. (1979). 'Interdisciplinarity: The expansion of knowledge and the design of research', *Higher Education Review*, 11(3), 47–57.

168   *First Degree*

Council for Industry and Higher Education (1987). *Towards a Partnership*. London, CIHE.
Council for National Academic Awards (1986). *Handbook 1986*. London, CNAA.
CRE-information (1984). 'Which curricula?', No. 66, 6–56.
Cross, K. P. (1982). *Adults as Learners*. San Francisco, Jossey-Bass.
Davie, G. (1961). *The Democratic Intellect*. Edinburgh, Edinburgh University Press.
Davie, G. (1986). *The Crisis of the Democratic Intellect*. Edinburgh, Polygon.
Dearden, R. F., Hirst, P. H. and Peters, R. S. (eds) (1972). *Education and the Development of Reason*. London, Routledge and Kegan Paul.
De Francesco, C. and Jarousse, J.-P. (1983). 'Under-utilisation and market value of university degrees', *European Journal of Education*, 18(1), 65–79.
Department of Education and Science (annual). *Education Statistics for the United Kingdom*. London, DES.
Department of Education and Science (irregular). *Statistical Bulletins*. London, DES.
Department of Education and Science (1985a). *An Assessment of the Costs and Benefits of Sandwich Education*. London, DES.
Department of Education and Science (1985b). *The Development of Higher Education into the 1990s*. Cmnd. 9524. London, HMSO.
Department of Education and Science (1987). *Higher Education: Meeting the Challenge*. London, HMSO.
DeVille, H. G. (Chr.) (1986). *Review of Vocational Qualifications in England and Wales*. London, DES/DoE/MSC.
Dohn, H. and Wagner, K. D. (1987). Learning problems – when arts students encounter computer science', *Higher Education*, 16, 231–5.
Donald, J. (1986). 'Knowledge and the university curriculum', *Higher Education*, 15, 267–82.
Donaldson, L. (1975). *Policy and the Polytechnics*. Farnborough, Saxon House.
Doyal, L. (1974). 'Interdisciplinary studies in higher education', *Universities Quarterly*, 28(4), 470–87.
Eisner, E. (1982). *Cognition and Curriculum*. New York, Longman.
Entwistle, N. (1987). 'A model of the teaching learning process' in Richardson, J. J., Eysenck, M. W. and Warren Piper, D. (eds), *Student Learning*. Milton Keynes, SRHE/Open University Press.
Entwistle, N. and Waterston, S. (1988). 'Approaches to studying and levels of processing in university students', *British Journal of Educational Psychology*, 58, 258–65.
Eraut, M. (1985). 'Knowledge creation and knowledge use in professional contexts', *Studies in Higher Education*, 10(2), 117–33.
Etzioni, A. (ed.) (1969). *The Semi-Professions and their Organization*. New York, Free Press.
Eurich, N. (1985). *Corporate Classrooms*. Princeton, Carnegie Foundation for the Advancement of Teaching.
Evans, C. (1988). *Language People*. Milton Keynes, SRHE/Open University Press.
Evans, N. (1988). *The Assessment of Prior Experiential Learning*. London, CNAA.
Evans, R. N. (1971). *Foundations of Vocational Education*. Columbus, Ohio, Charles E. Merrill.
Eysenck, M. (1984). *A Handbook of Cognitive Psychology*. London, Lawrence Erlbaum Associates Ltd.
Feldman, K. A. and Newcomb, T. M. (1969–70). *The Impact of College on Students*, 2 vols. San Francisco, Jossey-Bass.

Finniston, Sir M. (Chr.) (1980). *Engineering Our Future (Report of the Committee of Enquiry into the Engineering Professions)*. Cmnd. 7794. London, HMSO.

Fitts, P. M. and Posner, M. I. (1973). *Human Performance*. London, Prentice-Hall.

Fodor, J. (1983). *The Modularity of Mind*. Cambridge, Mass., MIT Press.

Fores, M. and Pratt, J. (1980). 'Engineering: Our last chance', *Higher Education Review*, 12(3), 5–26.

Fores, M. and Rey, L. (1979). 'Technik: The relevance of a missing concept', *Higher Education Review*, 11(2), 43–57.

Fulton, O. (ed.) (1981). *Access to Higher Education*. Guildford, SRHE.

Fulton, O., Gordon, A. and Williams, G. (1982). *Higher Education and Manpower Planning*. Geneva, International Labour Organization.

Furth, D. (1982). 'New hierarchies in higher education', *European Journal of Education*, 17(2), 145–51.

Gaff, J. G. (1983). *General Education Today*. San Francisco, Jossey-Bass.

Gaff, J. G. and Wilson, R. C. (1971). 'Faculty cultures and interdisciplinary studies', *Journal of Higher Education*, 43(3), 186–201.

Gagne, R. (1969). *The Conditions of Learning*. London, Holt, Rinehart and Winston.

Gagne, R. (1975). *Essentials of Learning for Instruction*. Hinsdale, Ill., Dryden Press.

Gardner, H. (1983). *Frames of Mind*. London, Heinemann.

Garfinkel, H. (1967). *Studies in Ethnomethodology*. London, Prentice-Hall.

Gibbs, G. (1981). *Teaching Students to Learn*. Milton Keynes, Open University Press.

Gleeson, D. and Mardle, C. (1980). *Further Education or Training?* London, Routledge and Kegan Paul.

Glover, I. (1980). 'Social science, engineering and society', *Higher Education Review*, 12(3), 27–41.

Goacher, B. (1984). *Selection Post-16: The Role of Examination Results*. Schools Council Examination Bulletin 48. London, Methuen.

Goldstein, K. M. and Blackman, J. (1978). *Cognitive Style: Five Approaches and Relevant Research*. New York, John Wiley.

Goodlad, S. (1976). *Conflict and Consensus in Higher Education*. London, Hodder and Stoughton.

Goodlad, S. (ed.) (1984). *Education for the Professions*. Guildford, SRHE.

Gordon, A. (1983). 'Attitudes of employers to the recruitment of graduates', *Educational Studies*, 9(1), 45–64.

Gordon, A. (1986). 'Education and training for information technology', *Studies in Higher Education*, 11(2), 189–98.

Green, J. M., Shearn, D. and Bolton, N. (1983). 'A numeracy course for arts undergraduates', *Studies in Higher Education*, 8(1), 57–65.

Griffiths, D. and Moseley, R. (1978). 'Science, technology and society: Some courses and student reactions to them', *Studies in Higher Education*, 3(1), 97–103.

Griffiths, R. (1982). 'Generalist v specialist: A non-issue?', *Universities Quarterly*, 37(1), 25–30.

Grignon, C. (1971). *L'Ordre des Choses*. Paris, Minuit.

Guilford, J. P. (1956). 'The structure of intellect', *Psychological Bulletin*, 53(4), 267–93.

Gustafsson, J.-E. (1984). 'A unifying model for the structure of intellectual abilities', *Intelligence*, 8, 179–203.

Habermas, J. (1974). *Theory and Practice* (trans. J. Viertel). London, Heinemann.

Hajnal, J. (1972). *The Student Trap*. Harmondsworth, Penguin.

Halsey, A. H. and Trow, M. (1971). *The British Academics*. London, Faber.

Hargreaves, D. (1982). *The Challenge for the Comprehensive School*. London, Routledge and Kegan Paul.

Harland, J. and Gibbs, I. (1986). *Beyond Graduation*. Guildford, SRHE.

Harrisberger, L. (1984). 'Curricula and teaching methods in engineering education', in Goodlad, S. (ed.), *Education for the Professions*. Guildford, SRHE.

Hayek, F. (1944). *The Road to Serfdom*. London, George Routledge.

Heath, D. (1978). 'A model of becoming a liberally educated and mature student', in Parker, C. A. (ed.), *Encouraging Development in College Students*. Minneapolis, University of Minnesota Press.

Hepburn, R. W. (1980). 'The education of feeling and emotion', *New Universities Quarterly*, 35(1), 110–29.

Heron, E. (1989). 'Decline of the classics empire', *Times Higher Education Supplement*, 3 March.

Heyman, R. (1981). 'Analyzing the curriculum', *International Review of Education*, XXVII(4), 449–70.

Hirst, P. H. (1969). 'The logic of the curriculum', *Journal of Curriculum Studies*, 1(2), 142–58.

Hirst, P. H. (1974). *Knowledge and the Curriculum*. London, Routledge and Kegan Paul.

Hirst, P. H. (ed.) (1983). *Educational Theory and its Foundation Disciplines*. London, Routledge and Kegan Paul.

Hodgson, P. (1985). 'Layers of matter', in Peacocke, A. (ed.), *Reductionism in Academic Disciplines*. Guildford, SRHE.

Hoggart, R. (1957). *The Uses of Literacy*. London, Chatto and Windus.

Holbrook, D. (1980). 'The arts and the need for meaning', *New Universities Quarterly*, 35(1), 89–109.

Horner, W. (1985). ' "Technik" and "Technology": Some consequences of terminological differences for educational policy-making', *Oxford Review of Education*, 11(3), 317–24.

Howe, M. (1987). 'Using cognitive psychology to help students learn how to learn', in Richardson, J. J., Eysenck, M. W. and Warren Piper, D. (eds), *Student Learning*. Milton Keynes, SRHE/Open University Press.

Howe, M. (1988) 'Intelligence as an explanation', *British Journal of Psychology*, 79, 349–60.

Hudson, L. (1966). *Contrary Imaginations*. London, Methuen.

Hudson, L. (1968). *Frames of Mind*. London, Methuen.

Hurst, J. C. (1978). 'Chickering's vectors of development and student affairs programming', in Parker, C. A. (ed.), *Encouraging Development in College Students*. Minneapolis, University of Minnesota Press.

Husserl, E. (1931). *Ideas* (trans. W. R. Boyce Gibson). London, George Allen and Unwin.

Hutton, S. and Lawrence, P. (1981). *German Engineers: The Anatomy of a Profession*. Oxford, Clarendon Press.

Hyman, H. H. and Wright, C. R. (1979). *Education's Lasting Influence on Values*. Chicago, University of Chicago Press.

Hyman, H. H., Wright, C. R. and Reed, J. S. (1975). *The Enduring Effects of Education*. Chicago, University of Chicago Press.

Illich, I. (1977). *Disabling Professions*. London, Marion Boyars.

Iliffe, A. H. (1968). 'The foundation year at the University of Keele', *Sociological Review Monograph*, No. 12.

Institute of Physics (1988). *Physics in Higher Education: Analysis and Recommendations*. London, Institute of Physics.

Iwaki, H. (1988). *The Organisation and Content of Studies at the Post-compulsory Level: Country Study: Japan*. OECD Educational Monographs. Paris, Organization for Economic Cooperation and Development.

Jackson, J. (ed.) (1970). *Professions and Professionalisation*. Cambridge, Cambridge University Press.

Jarratt, Sir. A. (Chr.) (1985). *Report of the Steering Committee for Efficiency Studies in Universities*. London, Committee of Vice-Chancellors and Principals.

Jarvis, P. (1983). *Professional Education*. London, Croom Helm.

Jenkinson, S. and Neave, G. (1980). 'The Finniston Report: An enquiry into a profession in transition', *Higher Education Review*, 12(3), 42–53.

Kaim-Caudle, P. (Chr.) (1977). *Teaching Social Policy and Administration in Britain and Ireland*. London, Joint University Council for Social and Public Administration.

Kan, A. R. (1988). 'The search for optimal curriculum', *CRE-action*, 84, 13–22.

Keller, A. (1984). 'Has science created technology?', *Minerva*, XXII(2), 160–82.

Kelsall, R. K., Poole, A. and Kuhn, A., (1972). *Graduates: The Sociology of an Elite*. London, Methuen.

Kerr, C. (1963). *The Uses of the University*. Cambridge, Mass., Harvard University Press.

Kerr, J. F. (ed.) (1968). *Changing the Curriculum*. London, University of London Press.

Knefelkamp, L. L. and Slepitza, R. (1978). 'A cognitive–developmental model of career development: An adaptation of the Perry scheme', in Parker, C. A. (ed.), *Encouraging Development in College Students*. Minneapolis, University of Minnesota Press.

Kohlberg, L. (1973). 'Continuities in childhood and adult moral development revisited', in Baltes, P. and Schaie, K. W. (eds), *Life-span Developmental Psychology: Personality and Socialization*. London and San Diego, Academic Press.

Kolb, D. (1981). 'Learning styles and disciplinary differences', in Chickering, A. W. and associates (eds), *The Modern American College*. San Francisco, Jossey-Bass.

Krathwohl, D. R., Bloom, B. S. and Masia, B. (1964). *Taxonomy of Educational Objectives, Handbook II: Affective Domain*. London, Longman.

Kuhn, T. S. (1962). *The Structure of Scientific Revolutions*. Chicago, University of Chicago Press.

Lakatos, I. and Musgrave, A. (eds) (1970). *Criticism and the Growth of Knowledge*. Cambridge, Cambridge University Press.

Lane, J. E. (1985). 'Academic profession in academic organisation', *Higher Education*, 14, 241–68.

Lane, J. E. (1987). 'Against administration', *Studies in Higher Education*, 12(3), 249–60.

Lane, M. (1975). *Design for Degrees*. London, MacMillan.

Lawn, M. and Barton, L. (eds) (1981). *Rethinking Curriculum Studies*. London, Croom Helm.

Lawton, D. (1983). *Curriculum Studies and Educational Planning*. London, Hodder and Stoughton.

Leavis, F. R. (1952). 'Literary criticism and philosophy', in *The Common Pursuit*. London, Chatto and Windus.

Leavis, F. R. and Yudkin, M. (1962). *Two Cultures? The Significance of C. P. Snow.* London, Chatto and Windus.

Lee, H. D. P. (1955). *Plato: the Republic* (translated by H. D. P. Lee) Harmondsworth, Penguin.

Levin, L. and Lind, I. (eds) (1985). *Interdisciplinarity Revisited.* Stockholm, Liber Forlag/Paris, OECD.

Levine, A. (1978). *Handbook on Undergraduate Curriculum.* San Francisco, Jossey-Bass.

Levine, A. and Weingart, J. (1973). *Reform of Undergraduate Education.* San Francisco, Jossey-Bass.

Lewis, I. (1984). *The Student Experience of Higher Education.* London, Croom Helm.

Lindblom, C. (1959). 'The science of "muddling through" ', *Public Administration Review*, 19(2), 79–88.

Lindblom, C. (1979). 'Still muddling, not yet through', *Public Administration Review*, 39(6), 517–26.

Lindley, R. (ed.) (1981). 'The challenge of market imperatives', in *Higher Education and the Labour Market.* Guildford, SRHE.

Lobkowicz, N. (1967). *Theory and Practice.* Notre Dame, Ind., University of Notre Dame Press.

Lobkowicz, N. (1984). 'The academic ethic: Politics and academic citizenship', *Minerva*, XXII(2), 236–44.

MacCabe, C. (1982). *Towards a Modern Trivium – English Studies Today* (Inaugural lecture). University of Strathclyde.

Mansell, T. (1984). 'Some aspects of the history of biological education over the last two hundred years', *Studies in Higher Education*, 9(2), 97–111.

Mansell, T. *et al.* (1976). *The Container Revolution.* London, The Nuffield Foundation.

Marris, P. (1964). *The Experience of Higher Education.* London, Routledge and Kegan Paul.

Martineau, H., (1853). *The Positive Philosophy of Auguste Comte*, 2 vols. London, John Chapman.

Marton, F., Hounsell, D. and Entwistle, N. (1984). *The Experience of Learning.* Edinburgh, Scottish Academic Press.

Mellers, W. (1980). 'Music and musical education', *New Universities Quarterly*, 35(1), 73–88.

Merleau-Ponty, M. (1964). *L'Oeil et L'Esprit.* Paris, Gallimard.

Merton, R. K. (1973). *The Sociology of Science.* Chicago, University of Chicago Press.

Messick, S. and associates. (1978). *Individuality in Learning.* San Francisco, Jossey-Bass.

Mezirow, J. (1983). 'A critical theory of adult learning and education', in Tight, M. (ed.), *Adult Learning and Education.* London, Croom Helm.

Miller, A. H. (1987). *Course Design for University Lecturers.* London, Kogan Page.

Mingat, A. and Eicher, J. C. (1982). 'Higher education and employment markets in France', *Higher Education*, 11, 211–20.

National Committee for Philosophy (1988). *NCP Submission to the UGC Philosophy Working Party.* Leeds, Mimeo.

National Council for Vocational Qualifications (1988). *The NCVQ Criteria and Related Guidance.* London, NCVQ.

National Economic Development Office/Manpower Services Commission (1984). *Competence and Competition.* London, NEDO/MSC.

Neave, G. (1978). 'Polytechnics: A policy drift?', *Studies in Higher Education*, 3(1), 105–11.

Neave, G. (1979a). 'The professionalization of higher education', *Higher Education Review*, 12(1), 70–6.

Neave, G. (1979b). 'Academic drift: Some views from Europe', *Studies in Higher Education*, 4(2), 143–59.

Needham, J. (1969). *The Grand Titration*. London, George Allen and Unwin.

Newman, J. H. (1982). *The Idea of a University*. Notre Dame, Ind., University of Notre Dame Press.

Nisbet, J. and Shucksmith, J. (1983). *Learning to Learn*. Paper presented to the British Psychological Society Education Section, Glasgow.

Nisbet, R. (1971). *The Degradation of the Academic Dogma*. London, Heinemann.

Oakeshott, M. (1962). *Rationalism in Politics*. London, Methuen.

Open University (1989). *Open University Statistics 1987: Students, Staff and Finance*. Milton Keynes, Open University Press.

Organization for Economic Cooperation and Development (1972). *Interdisciplinarity*. Paris, OECD.

Organization for Economic Cooperation and Development (1983). *Policies for Higher Education in the 1980s*. Paris, OECD.

Organization for Economic Cooperation and Development (1988). *Education in OECD Countries 1985–86: Comparative Statistics*. Paris, OECD.

Pantin, C. F. (1968). *The Relations between the Sciences*. Cambridge, Cambridge University Press.

Parker, C. A. (ed.) (1978). *Encouraging Development in College Students*. Minneapolis, University of Minnesota Press.

Parlett, M. and King, J. G. (1971). *Concentrated Study*. London, SRHE.

Pask, G. and Scott, B. C. E. (1972). 'Learning strategies and individual competence', *International Journal of Man–Machine Studies*, 4, 217–53.

Peacocke, A. (ed.) (1985). *Reductionism in Academic Disciplines*. Guildford, SRHE.

Pearson, R. (1985). 'The demands of the labour market', in Jacques, D. and Richardson, J. (eds), *The Future for Higher Education*. Guildford, SRHE/NFER-Nelson.

Perkin, H. (1973). 'The professionalization of university teaching', in Cook, T. G. (ed.), *Education and the Professions*. London, Methuen.

Perry, W. G. (1968). *Forms of Intellectual and Ethical Development in the College Years: A Scheme*. New York, Holt Rinehart and Winston.

Perry, W. G. (1978). 'Sharing in the costs of growth,' in Parker, C. A. (ed.), *Encouraging Development in College Students*. Minneapolis, University of Minnesota Press.

Peters, T. J. and Waterman, R. H. (1982). *In Search of Excellence: Lessons from America's Best-run Companies*. New York, Harper and Row.

Phenix, P. H. (1964). *Realms of Meaning*. New York, McGraw-Hill.

Playfair, L. (1852). *Industrial Instruction on the Continent*. London, HMSO.

Plumb, J. H. (ed.) (1964). *Crisis in the Humanities*. Harmondsworth, Penguin.

Powell, J. P. (1966, 1971). *Universities and University Education: A Select Bibliography*. Slough, National Foundation for Educational Research.

Powell, J. (1985). 'The residues of learning: Autobiographical accounts by graduates of the impact of higher education', *Higher Education*, 14(2), 127–47.

Prais, S. J. (1989). 'Qualified manpower in engineering', *National Institute Economic Review*, February, 76–83.

Prais, S. J. and Wagner, K. (1988). 'Productivity and management: The training of foremen in Britain and Germany', *National Institute Economic Review*, February 34–47.

Pratt, J. and Burgess, T. (1974). *Polytechnics: A Report*. London, Pitman.

Pring, R. (1971). 'Bloom's taxonomy: A philosophical critique (2)', *Cambridge Journal of Education*, 1(2), 83–91.

Reid, W. (1978). *Thinking about the Curriculum*. London, Routledge and Kegan Paul.

Revans, R. W. (1982). *The Origins and Growth of Action Learning*. Bromley, Chatwell-Pratt.

Richards, C. (1984). *Curriculum Studies: An Introductory Annotated Bibliography*, 2nd edn. London, Falmer Press.

Richardson, J. J., Eysenck, M. W. and Warren Piper, D. (eds) (1987). *Student Learning*. Milton Keynes, Open University Press/SRHE.

Riegel, K. P. (1979). *Foundations of Dialectical Psychology*. London and San Diego, Academic Press.

Riesman, D. (1950). *The Lonely Crowd*. New Haven, Yale University Press.

Robbins, Lord (Chr.) (1963). *Higher Education*. (Report of the Committee under the Chairmanship of Lord Robbins.) Cmnd. 2154. London, HMSO.

Robbins, Lord (1980). *Higher Education Revisited*. London, Macmillan.

Robinson, K. (ed.) (1982). *The Arts and Higher Education*. Guildford, SRHE.

Roizen, J. and Jepson, M. (1985). *Degrees for Jobs*. Guildford, SRHE/NFER-Nelson.

Ross, W. D. (1928). *The Works of Aristotle, Vol VIII: Metaphysica*. Oxford, Clarendon Press.

Rothblatt, S. (1976). *Tradition and Change in English Liberal Education*. London, Faber and Faber.

Rowntree, D. (1974). *Educational Technology in Curriculum Development*. London, Harper and Row.

Rudd, D. (1984). 'The intimidating bastion of scientific knowledge: A way to breach the ramparts', *Studies in Higher Education*, 9(2), 113–21.

Ruegg, W. (1986). 'The academic ethos', *Minerva*, XXIV(4), 393–412.

Ryan, D. (1984). 'The professional and the personal – are they compatible?', in Goodlad, S. (ed.), *Accountable Autonomy*. Guildford, SRHE.

Sanderson, M. (1972). *The Universities and British Industry 1850–1970*. London, Routledge and Kegan Paul.

Sanderson, M. (1987). *Educational Opportunity and Social Change*. London, Faber and Faber.

Schein, E. H. (1972). *Professional Education: Some New Directions*. New York, McGraw-Hill.

Schilling, M. (1986). 'Knowledge and liberal education: A critique of Paul Hirst', *Journal of Curriculum Studies*, 18(1), 1–16.

Schon, D. A. (1987). *Educating the Reflective Practitioner*. San Francisco, Jossey-Bass.

Schutz, A. (1970). *Collected Papers III: Studies in Phenomenological Philosophy*. The Hague, Martinus Nijhoff.

Schwab, J. J. (1964). 'Problems, topics and issues', in Elam, S. (ed.), *Education and the Structure of Knowledge*. Chicago, Rand McNally.

Scott, P. (1984a). *The Crisis of the University*. London, Croom Helm.

Scott, P. (1984b). 'Ideologies of the university', in Bergendahl, G. (ed.), *Knowledge Policies and the Traditions of Higher Education*. Stockholm, Almqvist and Wiksell.

Scott, P. (1987). 'The knowledge business', *Times Higher Education Supplement*, 7, 14, 21, 28 August.

Seager, P. (1984). 'Curricula and teaching methods in medical education,' in Goodlad, S. (ed.), *Education for the Professions*. Guildford, SRHE.

Shackle, G. L. S. (1972). *Epistemics and Economics: a Critique of Economic Doctrines*. Cambridge, Cambridge University Press.

Shannon, C. E. and Weaver, W. (1949). *The Mathematical Theory of Communication*. Urbana, University of Illinois Press.

Shattock, M. (1987). 'False images but a new promise in universities, contribution to industrial and technological advance', *Studies in Higher Education*, 12(1), 23–7.

Shils, E. (1984). *The Academic Ethic*. London, University of Chicago Press.

Silverman, R. (1984). 'Knowlege types in higher education', in Bergendahl, G. (ed.), *Knowledge Policies and the Traditions of Higher Education*. Stockholm, Almqvist and Wiksell.

Simon, H. A. (1969). *The Sciences of the Artificial*. Cambridge, Mass., MIT Press.

Simon, H. A. (1979a). 'Information processing models of cognition', *Annual Review of Psychology*, 30, 363–96.

Simon, H. A. (1979b). *Models of Thought*. New Haven, Yale University Press.

Skilbeck, M. (1984). *School-based Curriculum Development*. London, Harper and Row.

Slee, P. R. H. (1986). *Learning and a Liberal Education*. Manchester, Manchester University Press.

Smith, R. M. (1982). *Learning How to Learn*. Milton Keynes, Open University Press.

Smithers, A. (1970). 'Open-mindedness and the university curriculum', *Journal of Curriculum Studies*, 2(1), 73–7.

Smithers, A. (1976). *Sandwich Courses: An Integrated Education?* Slough, National Foundation for Educational Research.

Snow, C. P. (1964). *The Two Cultures: And a Second Look*. Cambridge, Cambridge University Press.

Snyder, B. (1971). *The Hidden Curriculum*. New York, Knopf.

Society for Research into Higher Education (1983). *Excellence in Diversity: Towards a New Strategy for Higher Education*. Guildford, SRHE.

Sockett, H. (1971). 'Bloom's taxonomy – a philosophical critique', *Cambridge Journal of Education*, 1(1), 16–25.

Squires, G. (1975). *Interdisciplinarity*. London, Nuffield Foundation.

Squires, G. (1976a). *Breadth and Depth*. London, Nuffield Foundation.

Squires, G. (1976b). 'The resuscitation of general education', *Studies in Higher Education*, 1(1), 83–9.

Squires, G. (1979). 'Innovations in British higher education and their implications for adult education', in OECD, *Learning Opportunities for Adults, Vol II*. Paris, OECD.

Squires, G. (1980). 'Individuality in higher education', *Studies in Higher Education*, 5(2), 217–26.

Squires, G. (1981a). *Cognitive Styles and Adult Learning*. Nottingham, University of Nottingham Department of Adult Education.

Squires, G. (1981b). 'Mature entry', in Fulton, O. (ed.), *Access to Higher Education*. Guildford, SRHE.

Squires, G. (1982). *Learning to Learn* (Newland Paper No. 6). Hull, University of Hull School of Adult and Continuing Education.

Squires, G. (ed.) (1983a). *Innovation Through Recession*. Guildford, SRHE.

Squires, G. (1983b). 'New groups in higher education', in OECD, *Policies for Higher Education in the 1980s*. Paris, OECD.

Squires, G. (1985). 'Organisation and content of studies', in OECD, *Education and Training after Basic Schooling*. Paris, OECD.

Squires, G. (1986). *Modularisation*. Manchester, Consortium for Advanced Continuing Education and Training of the Universities of Manchester and Salford, UMIST and Manchester Polytechnic.

Squires, G. (1987a). *The Curriculum Beyond School*. London, Hodder and Stoughton.

Squires, G. (1987b). 'The curriculum', in Becher, T. (ed.), *British Higher Education*. London, Allen and Unwin.

Squires, G. (1988). *Teaching and Training: A contingent Approach* (Newland Paper No. 15). Hull, University of Hull School of Adult and Continuing Education.

Squires, G. (1989a). *Pathways for Learning: Education and Training from Sixteen to Nineteen*. Paris, OECD.

Squires, G. (1989b). 'Review of "Education for the Professions" ', *Studies in Higher Education*, 14(1), 112–15.

Stacey, N., Alsalam, N., Gilmore, J. and To, D.-L. (1988). *Education and Training of 16–19 Year Olds after Compulsory Schooling in the United States*. Paris, OECD (mimeo).

Stark, J. S. and Lowther, M. A. (1986). *Designing the Learning Plan: A Review of Research and Theory Related to College Curricula*. Ann Arbor, National Center for Research to Improve Post-Secondary Teaching and Learning, University of Michigan.

Startup, R. (1979). *The University Teacher and his World*. Farnborough, Saxon House.

Steedman, H. (1987). Vocational training in France and Britain: office work', *National Institute Economic Review*, May, 58–70.

Steedman, H. and Wagner, K. (1987). 'A second look at productivity, machinery and skills in Britain and Germany', *National Institute Economic Review*, November 84–95.

Sternberg, R. J. (1987). 'The triarchic theory of human intelligence', in Richardson, J. J., Eysenck, M. W. and Warren Piper, D. (eds), *Student Learning*. Milton Keynes, Open University Press/SRHE.

Sternberg, R. J. (1988). 'Explaining away intelligence: A reply to Howe', *British Journal of Psychology*, 79, 527–33.

Tarsh, J. (1988). 'The Graduate labour market in the United Kingdom' in *Higher Education and the Labour Market – Flexible Responses to Change*. London, Higher Education International/Council for National Academic Awards.

Taylor, P. H. and Richards, C. M. (1985). *An Introduction to Curriculum Studies*, 2nd edn. Windsor, NFER-Nelson.

Taylor, W. (ed.) (1984). *Metaphors of Education*. London, Heinemann.

Taylor, W. (1987). *Universities Under Scrutiny*. Paris, OECD.

Teichler, U., Hartung, D. and Nuthmann, R. (1980). *Higher Education and the Needs of Society*. Slough, National Foundation for Educational Research.

Thorndike, E. L. (1924). 'Mental discipline in high school studies', *Journal of Educational Psychology*, 1(2), 1–22, 83–98.

Tight, M. (1986). 'The provision of part-time first degree courses in the United Kingdom', *Studies in Higher Education*, 11(2), 173–88.

Tight, M. (1987). *Part-time Degrees, Diplomas and Certificates*. Cambridge, CRAC/Hobsons Press.

Tough, A. (1971). *The Adult's Learning Projects*. Toronto, Ontario Institute for Studies in Education.

Training Agency (1989). *Enterprise in Higher Education: Key Features of the Enterprise in Higher Education Proposals*. Sheffield, Training Agency.

Trow, M. (1974). 'Problems in the transition from elite to mass higher education', in OECD, *Policies for Higher Education*. Paris, OECD.

Trow, M. (1975). 'The public and private lives of higher education', *Daedalus*, 104, 113–27.

Trow, M. (1976). 'The American academic department as a context for learning', *Studies in Higher Education*, 1(1), 11–22.

Turner, J. D. and Rushton, J. (eds) (1976). *Education for the Professions*. Manchester, Manchester University Press.

Turney, J. (1989). 'New models for matrix management', *Times Higher Education Supplement*, 23 March.

Twining, W. (1987). 'A law unto itself', *Times Higher Education Supplement*, 9 January.

Tyler, R. (1949). *Basic Principles of Curriculum and Instruction*. Chicago, University of Chicago Press.

UKCC (1986). *Project 2000: A New Preparation for Practice*. London, United Kingdom Central Council for Nursing, Midwifery and Health Visiting.

Usher, R. (1985). 'Beyond the anecdotal – adult learning and the use of experience', *Studies in the Education of Adults*, 17(1), 59–74.

Usher, R. S. and Bryant, I. (1987). 'Re-examining the theory–practice relationship in continuing professional education', *Studies in Higher Education*, 12(2), 201–12.

Vales, C. P. (1988). 'Curricula reform and new degrees in Spanish universities', *CRE-action*, 81, 53–8.

Veblen, T. (1957). *The Higher Learning in America*. New York, Sagamore.

Wagner, D. L. (1983). *The Seven Liberal Arts in the Middle Ages*. Bloomington, Indiana University Press.

Wasser, H. (1985). 'Instrumental versus disciplinary curricula', *European Journal of Education*, 20(1), 67–72.

Welch, R. (1987). 'Arnold's Sofa and Derrida's Gymnasium', *Times Higher Education Supplement*, 23 January.

Whitburn, J., Mealing, M. and Cox, C. (1976). *People in Polytechnics*. Guildford, SRHE.

Wiener, M. (1981). *English Culture and the Decline of the Industrial Spirit 1850–1980*. Cambridge, Cambridge University Press.

Wiener, N. (1948). *Cybernetics*. New York, John Wiley.

Williams, G. (1984). 'The economic approach' in Clark, B. R. (ed.) *Perspectives on Higher Education*. Berkeley, University of California Press.

Williams, G. (1985). 'Graduate employment and vocationalism in higher education', *European Journal of Education*, 20(2–3), 181–92.

Williams, G. and Blackstone, T. (1983). *Response to Adversity*. Guildford, SRHE.

Williams, K. and Williams, J. (1987). 'M-way crash', *Times Higher Education Supplement*, 16 October.

Williams, R. (1988). *Social Science Graduates: Degree Results and First Employment Destinations*. London, CNAA.

Willis, P. (1977). *Learning to Labour*. London, Saxon House.

Wilson, J. D. (1981). *Student Learning in Higher Education*. London, Croom Helm.

Witkin, H. and Goodenough, D. R. (1977). *Field Dependence Revisited*. Princeton, N.J., Educational Testing Service.

Worswick, G. D. N. (ed.) (1985). *Education and Economic Performance*. Aldershot, Gower.

Wright, P. (1988). 'Rethinking the aims of higher education,' in Eggins, H. (ed.), *Restructuring Higher Education*. Milton Keynes, SRHE/Open University Press.

Young, M. F. D. (ed.) (1971). *Knowledge and Control*. London, Collier-Macmillan.

Yudkin, M. (ed.) (1969). *General Education*. Harmondsworth, Penguin.

Index

mathematics, 38, 46–8, 55, 58, 79,
105, 125, 131, 144
medicine, 24, 54, 56, 58, 59, 60, 63, 66,
79, 88, 90, 95, 97
methodology, 57, 72
modularization, 24, 28, 32, 104–7,
110, 111, 114, 122

NCVQ, 34
'normal science', 55
Northern Ireland, 9, 11, 12, 28

Open University, 4, 8, 11, 14, 26, 28,
34, 86, 109, 121

part-time degrees, 12, 13
PCFC, 122
phenomenology, 54, 55
  of the curriculum, 7
  of the market, 120
  in physics, 58
philosophy (as a subject), 46, 47, 56–9,
60, 66, 71, 72, 99, 143, 153
physics, 62, 63, 66, 81, 106, 144–5
planning (of the curriculum), 4–8,
33–4, 152, 160–2
polytechnical education, 30, 154
polytechnics, 9, 10, 11, 14, 24, 36, 86,
121, 143, 148
positivism, 42, 47, 48
post-experience courses, 89
post-graduate studies, 33, 84, 85, 120,
121
problem-solving, 105, 108, 126–9,
135, 159
process and content, 29, 46, 49, 50, 77,
107–9
professional curricula, 2, 24, 44, 50,
68, 83, 84, 86–92, 109, 121
  and autonomy, 91
  and continuing education, 90
  control of, 91, 92
  innovation in, 96, 97
  issues in, 90–2
  modularization of, 106–7
  patterns of, 88–9
  and the professions, 88, 90, 91, 96,
  97
  theory and practice in, 92–6
pure knowledge, 47, 59, 70

rationality, 10, 42, 114, 124, 148
reductionism, 48
reflexivity, 56, 57
relativism, 70, 71, 140, 141, 153
research, 10, 47, 52, 68, 70, 85, 96,
104, 113
role modelling, 50, 97, 147, 148

sandwich courses, 28, 89
scepticism, 140, 147
schools, 29–31, 32, 34, 46, 155
sciences, 24, 27, 36–9, 44, 54, 56, 57,
62, 63, 66, 67, 70, 78, 92, 99, 104,
106, 131, 143
Scotland, 9, 11–13, 28, 34, 35, 51, 71,
72, 86, 109, 110
single subject degrees, 2, 12, 14, 24
16–19 education, 31, 32, 36, 76, 119,
155
  see also A levels; vocational/technical
  education
skills, 42, 43, 148, 155, 159
social sciences, 24, 36, 44, 52, 58, 60,
61, 63–7, 72, 78, 80, 92, 93, 99,
100, 103, 105, 106, 125, 127, 142,
144
socialization, 75, 97, 114, 115, 136, 147
sociology (of the curriculum), 74, 75
specialization, 33, 121–2, 153, 154
student development, 123–50
  and cognitive development, 124–34
  concepts of, 123, 124
  and disciplines, 142–6
  ethical, 30, 139–41, 148
  price of, 146–8
students
  enrolments, 12–14, 24, 25
  influence on curriculum, 92
  subject distribution by sex, 27
  see also adult students
survey courses, 112, 113

teaching and learning, 4, 5, 50, 147,
150, 159
  see also learning, transfer of learning
Technik, 69
technology, *see* engineering/
technology
theory and practice, 43, 46, 47, 54, 58,
88–90, 92–6, 126, 128

The Society for Research into Higher Education

The Society exists both to encourage and coordinate research and development into all aspects of higher education, including academic, organizational and policy issues; and also to provide a forum for debate – verbal and printed.

The Society's income derives from subscriptions, book sales, conference fees, and grants. It receives no subsidies and is wholly independent. Its corporate members are institutions of higher education, research institutions and professional, industrial, and governmental bodies. Its individual members include teachers and researchers, administrators and students. Members are found in all parts of the world and the Society regards its international work as amongst its most important activities.

The Society discusses and comments on policy, organizes conferences, and encourages research. Under the imprint SRHE & OPEN UNIVERSITY PRESS, it is a specialist publisher of research, having some 40 titles in print. It also publishes *Studies in Higher Education* (three times a year) which is mainly concerned with academic issues; *Higher Education Quarterly* (formerly *Universities Quarterly*) mainly concerned with policy issues; *Abstracts* (three times a year); an *International Newsletter* (twice a year) and *SRHE News* (four times a year).

The Society's committees, study groups and branches are run by members (with help from a small secretariat at Guildford), and aim to provide a forum for discussion. The groups at present include a Teacher Education Study Group, a Staff Development Group, and a Continuing Education Group, each of which may have their own organization, subscriptions, or publications (e.g. the *Staff Development Newsletter*). A further *Questions of Quality* Group has organized a series of Anglo-American seminars in the USA and the UK.

The Governing Council, elected by members, comments on current issues; and discusses policies with leading figures, notably at its evening forums. The Society organizes seminars on current research, and is in touch with bodies in the UK such as the UFC, CVCP, PCFC, CNAA and with sister-bodies overseas. It cooperates with the British Council on courses run in conjunction with its conferences.

The Society's conferences are often held jointly; and have considered 'Standards and Criteria' (1986, with Bulmershe College); 'Restructuring' (1987, with the City of Birmingham Polytechnic); 'Academic Freedom' (1988, with the University of Surrey). In 1989, 'Access and Institutional Change' (with the Polytechnic of North

London). In 1990, the topic will be 'Industry and Higher Education' (with the University of Surrey). In 1991, the topic will be 'Research in HE'. Other conferences have considered the DES 'Green Paper' (1985); 'HE After the Election' (1987) and 'After the Reform Act' (July 1988). An annual series on 'The First Year Experience' with the University of South Carolina and Teesside Polytechnic held two meetings in 1988 in Cambridge, and another in St Andrew's in July 1989. For some of the Society's conferences, special studies are commissioned in advance, as *Precedings*.

Members receive free of charge the Society's *Abstracts*, annual conference Proceedings (or *Precedings*), *SRHE News* and *International Newsletter*. They may buy SRHE & Open University Press books at discount, and *Higher Education Quarterly* on special terms. Corporate members also receive the Society's journal *Studies in Higher Education* free (individuals on special terms). Members may also obtain certain other journals at a discount, including the NFER *Register of Educational Research*. There is a substantial discount to members, and to staff of corporate members, on annual and some other conference fees.

Further Information: SRHE at the University, Guildford GU2 5XH, UK (0483) 39003.